Christmas Evans

of Wild \

His country, his times, and his contemporaries

Edwin Paxton Hood

Alpha Editions

This edition published in 2024

ISBN : 9789367244388

Design and Setting By
Alpha Editions
www.alphaedis.com
Email - info@alphaedis.com

As per information held with us this book is in Public Domain.
This book is a reproduction of an important historical work. Alpha Editions uses the best technology to reproduce historical work in the same manner it was first published to preserve its original nature. Any marks or number seen are left intentionally to preserve its true form.

Contents

CHAPTER I. SOME GENERAL CHARACTERISTICS OF WELSH PREACHING. .... - 1 -

CHAPTER II. EARLY LIFE UNTIL HIS ENTRANCE INTO THE MINISTRY. .... - 23 -

CHAPTER III. THE MINISTRY IN THE ISLAND OF ANGLESEA. .... - 36 -

CHAPTER IV. THE MINISTRY IN ANGLESEA (CONTINUED). .... - 66 -

CHAPTER V. CONTEMPORARIES IN THE WELSH PULPIT—WILLIAMS OF WERN. .... - 108 -

CHAPTER VI. CONTEMPORARIES—JOHN ELIAS. .... - 119 -

CHAPTER VII. CONTEMPORARIES—DAVIES OF SWANSEA. .... - 129 -

CHAPTER VIII. THE PREACHERS OF WILD WALES. ... - 138 -

CHAPTER IX. CHRISTMAS EVANS CONTINUED— HIS MINISTRY AT CAERPHILLY. .... - 164 -

CHAPTER X. CAERNARVON AND LAST DAYS. .... - 182 -

CHAPTER XI. SUMMARY OF GENERAL CHARACTERISTICS OF CHRISTMAS EVANS, AS A MAN AND A PREACHER. .... - 194 -

CHAPTER XII. SUMMARY OF GENERAL CHARACTERISTICS OF CHRISTMAS EVANS AS A PREACHER. .... - 205 -

APPENDATORY. SELECTION OF ILLUSTRATIVE SERMONS. .... - 231 -

Footnotes. .... - 268 -

CHAPTER I.
SOME GENERAL CHARACTERISTICS OF WELSH PREACHING.

Wales, the Country and the People—Individuality of the Welsh Pulpit—St. David—The Religious Sense of the People—Association Meetings—Gryffyth of Caernarvon—Bardic Character of the Sermons—A Repetition of Sermons—Peculiarities of the Welsh Language—Its Singular Effects as Spoken—Its Vowels—Its Pictorial Character—The *Hwyl*—Welsh Scenery—Isolated Character of the Old Chapels—Plain Living and High Thinking—Ludicrous Incidents of Uncertain Service—Superstitions of Heathenism—Fondness of the People for Allegory—Haunted Wales—The Rev. John Jones and the Mysterious Horseman—Old Wild Wales—St. David's—Kilgerran—Welsh Nomenclature—John Dyer—Old Customs.

WE propose, in the following pages, to give some account of Christmas Evans, the great Welsh preacher; believing that he had a style and manner of preaching which, to English minds and readers, will seem altogether his own, perhaps more admirable than imitable. But before we enter upon the delineation of his life, or attempt to unfold his style, or to represent his method as displayed in his sermons, it may be well to present some concise view of Welsh preaching and Welsh preachers in general, especially those of the last age; for as an order of preaching it has possessed its own very distinctive peculiarities. Some readers may at first indeed inquire, Is not preaching very much the same everywhere, in all counties and in all countries? And Wales, which seems itself in its nearness now only like a district of England, and that district for the most part wild and but scantily peopled,—can there be anything so remarkable about its pulpit work as to make it either capable or worthy of any separate account of its singularities and idiosyncrasies? To most English people Welsh preaching is a phase of religious life entirely unknown: thousands of tourists visit the more conspicuous highways of Wales from year to year, its few places of public resort or more manifest beauty; but Wales is still, for the most part, unknown; its isolation is indeed somewhat disturbed now, its villages are no longer so insulated as of old, and the sounds of advancing life are breaking in upon its solitudes, yet, perhaps, its fairest scenes are still uninvaded. But if the country be unknown, still more unknown are the people, and of its singular preaching phenomena scarcely anything is known, or ever can be known by English people; yet it is not too much to say that, in that little land, during the last hundred years, amidst its wild glens and sombre mountain shadows, its villages retreating into desolate moorlands and winding vales, where seldom a traveller passes by, there have appeared such a succession and race of remarkable preachers as could be rivalled—in their own peculiar popular power over the hearts and minds of many thousands, for their eminence and variety—in no other country. Among these, Christmas Evans seems to us singularly representative; eminently Welsh, his attributes of power seem to be especially indicative of the characteristics of the Welsh mind, an order of mind as remarkably singular and individual, and worthy of study, as any national character in the great human family. But even before we mention these, it may be well to notice what were some of the reasons for the eminent influence and usefulness of Christmas Evans, and some of his extraordinary preaching comrades and contemporaries to whom we shall have occasion to refer.

Preaching is, in Wales, the great national characteristic; the Derby Day is not more truly a characteristic of England than the great gatherings and meetings of the Associations all grouped around some popular favourites. The dwellers among those mountains and upon those hill-sides have no concerts, no theatres, no means of stimulating or satisfying their curiosity. For we, who care little for preaching, to whom the whole sermon system is perhaps becoming more tedious, can form but little idea, and have but little sympathy with that form of religious society where the pulpit is the orchestra, the stage, and the platform, and where the charms of music, painting, and acting are looked for, and found in the preacher. We very likely would be disposed even to look with complacent pity upon such a state of society,—it has not yet expired,—where the Bulwers, the Dickenses, the Thackerays, and Scotts are altogether unknown,—but where the peculiar forms of their genius— certainly without their peculiar education—display themselves in the pulpit. If our readers suppose, therefore, a large amount of ignorance,— well, upon such a subject, certainly, it is possible to enter easily upon the illimitable. Yet it is such an ignorance as that which developed itself in Job, and in his companions, and in his age—an ignorance like that which we may conceive in Æschylus. In fact, in Wales, the gates of every man's being have been opened. It is possible to know much of the grammar, and the history, and the lexicography of things, and yet to be so utterly ignorant of *things* as never to have felt the sentiment of strangeness and of terror; and without having been informed about the names of things, it is possible to have been brought into the presence and power of *things* themselves. Thus, the ignorance of one man may be higher than the intelligence of another. There may be a large memory and a very narrow consciousness. On the contrary, there may be a large consciousness, while the forms it embraces may be uncertain and undefined in the misty twilight of the soul. This is much the state of many minds in Wales. It is the state of feeling, and of poetry, of subtle questionings, high religious musings, and raptures. This state has been aided by the secludedness of the country, and the exclusiveness of the language,—not less than by the rugged force and masculine majesty and strength of the language;—a language full of angles and sharp goads, admirably fitted for the masters of assemblies, admirably fitted to move like a wind over the soul, rousing and soothing, stirring into storm, and lulling into rest. Something in it makes an orator almost ludicrous when he attempts to convey himself in another language, but very powerful and impressive in that. It is a speaking and living language, a language without any shallows, a language which seems to compel the necessity of thought before using it. Our language is fast becoming serviceable for all that large part of the human family who speak without thinking. To this state the Welsh can never come. That unaccommodating tongue only moves with a soul behind it.

Thus, it is not the first reason, but it is not unimportant to remember, that, until very recently, the pulpit in Wales has been the only means of popular excitement, instruction, or even of entertainment; until very recently the Welsh, like the ancient Hebrew lady, have dwelt among their own people, they have possessed no popular fictions, no published poems, no published emanations either of metaphysics or natural science; immured in their own language, as they were, less than a century since, among their own mountains, their language proved a barrier to the importation of many works accessible to almost all the other languages of Europe. It may be said that religion, as represented through the men of the pulpit, has made Wales what she is. When the first men of the pulpit, Howell Harris, Daniel Rowlands, and others, arose, they found their country lying under a night of spiritual darkness, and they effected an amazing reformation; but then they had no competitive influences to interfere with their progress, or none beyond that rough, rude sensuality, that barbarism of character, which everywhere sets itself in an attitude of hostility to spiritual truth and to elevated holiness; there were no theatres or race courses, there was no possibility that the minds of the multitudes should be occupied by the intellectual casuistries of a later day; Wales possessed no Universities or Colleges, and very few Schools; on the other hand, there were some characteristics of the national mind very favourable to the impulse these men gave, and the impressions they produced. So it has happened that the Welsh preacher has been elevated into an importance, reminding us of the Welsh tradition concerning St. David, the patron saint of Wales, regarding whom it is said, that, while preaching in the year 520, in Cardigan, against the Pelagian heresy, such was the force of his argument, and the eloquence of his oratory, that the very ground on which he stood rose beneath his feet and elevated itself into a hillock; and there, in after ages, a church was erected upon the spot to which awful tradition pointed as the marvellous pulpit of the patron saint.

Three-fourths of any amount of power which either or any of these first preachers, or their successors, have obtained over their countrymen, and countrywomen, arises from the fact that the Welsh possess, in an eminent degree, what we call a Religious Nature; they are very open to Wonder; they have a most keen and curious propensity to inquire into the hidden causes of things, not mere material causes, but Spiritual causes, what we call Metaphysics; the Unseen Universe is to them as to all of us a mystery, but it is a mystery over which they cannot but brood; when education is lacking, this realizing of the unseen is apt to give rise to superstitious feelings, and superstitions still loiter and linger among the glens, the churchyards, and old castles and ruins of Wales, although the spread of Christian truth has divested them of much of their ancient extravagance; when, therefore, the earnest voice of their native speech became the vehicle for unfolding the higher doctrines of the Christian life, the sufferings of the Redeemer and their relation to eternal laws and human conditions, probably a people was never found whose ears were more open, or whose hearts were more ready to receive, and to be stirred to their utmost depths. Thus Religion—Evangelical Religion—became the very life of the land of Wales.

"There is not a heathen man, woman, or child in all the Principality," said a very eminent Welshman to us once, probably with some measure of exaggeration; "there are wicked men, and women," he continued, "unconverted men, and women, but there is not a man, woman, or child throughout Wales who does not know all about Jesus Christ, and why He came into the world, and what He came to do." Thus, within the memory of the writer of this volume, Religion was the one topic upon which you might talk intelligently anywhere in Wales: with the pitman in the coalmine, with the iron-smelter at the forge, with the farmer by his ingleside, with the labourer in his mountain shieling; and not merely on the first more elementary lessons of the catechism, but on the great bearings and infinite relations of religious things. Jonathan Edwards, and Williams of Rotherham, and Owen, and Bunyan, and Flavel,—these men and their works, and a few others like them, were well known; and, especially, the new aspects which the modified opinions of Andrew Fuller had introduced into religious thought; thus, you might often feel surprised when, sitting down in some lowly cottage, you found yourself suddenly caught, and carried along by its owner in a coil of metaphysical argument. This was the soil on which the Welsh preachers had to work, and cast abroad their seed.

No person can have heard anything of the Welsh religious life without having heard also of the immense annual gatherings, the Association meetings, a sort of great movable festival, annually held in Wales, to which everything had to give place, and to which all the various tribes of the various Houses of the Lord came up. Their ordinary Sunday services were crowded, but, upon these great occasions, twenty or twenty-five thousand people would come together; and, to such congregations, their great men, their great preachers, such as those we are about to mention, addressed themselves—

addressed themselves not to a mass ignorant and unintelligent, but all thoroughly informed in religious matters, and prepared to follow their preacher whithersoever his imagination or thought might lead him. The reader must not smile when we remind him that Wales was,—had been for ages,—the land of Bards; a love of poetry, poetry chanted or recited, had always been the Welshman's passion, and those great writers of our literature who best know what poetry is, have taught us that we are not to look upon those productions with contempt. For ages there had been held in Wales what has been called, and is still called the *Eisteddfod*, or *Cymreigyddion*, or the meeting of the Bards and Minstrels; they were, as Pennant has called them, British Olympics, where none but Bards of merit were suffered to rehearse their pieces, or Minstrels of skill to perform. These Association meetings were a kind of religious Eisteddfodd, where the great Welsh preacher was a kind of sacred Bard; he knew nothing of written sermons; he carried no notes nor writings with him to his pulpit or platform, but he made the law and doctrine of religious metaphysics march to the minstrelsy and music of speech; on the other hand, he did not indulge himself in casting about wildfire, all had been thoroughly prepared and rooted in his understanding; and then he went with his sermon, which was a kind of high song, to chant it over the hearts of the multitude. We shall have occasion to show, by many instances, from the lives of their greatest men, how their own hearts had been marvellously prepared.

There is a pleasant anecdote told of one of them, Gryffyth of Caernarvon, how he had to preach one night. Before preaching, staying at a farmhouse on the spot, he desired permission to retire before the service began; he remained in his room a considerable time; the congregation had assembled, still he did not come; there was no sign of his making his appearance. The good man of the house sent the servant to request him to come, as the people had been for some time assembled and waiting. Approaching the room she heard, what seemed to her to be a conversation, going on between two persons, in a subdued tone of voice, and she caught from Mr. Gryffyth the expression, "*I* will not go unless *you* come with me." She went back to her master, and said, "I do not think Mr. Gryffyth will come to-night; there is some one with him, and he is telling him that he will not come unless the other will come too; but I did not hear the other reply, so I think Mr. Gryffyth will not come to-night."

"Yes, yes," said the farmer, "*he* will come, and I warrant the *other* will come too, if matters are as you say between them; but we had better begin singing and reading until the *two* do come." And the story goes on to say that Mr. Gryffyth did come, and the other One with him, for they had a very extraordinary meeting that night, and the whole neighbourhood was stirred by it and numbers were changed and converted. It was Williams of Wern who used to tell this pleasing anecdote; it is an anecdote of one man, but, so far as we have been able to see, it illustrates the way in which they all prepared themselves before they began to speak.

It must not be supposed from this that they imagined that prayer was to dispense with preparation; their great preachers studied hard and deeply, and Williams of Wern, one of the greatest of them all, says, "In order to be a good preacher, usefulness must be the grand aim, usefulness must choose the text and divide it, usefulness must compose the sermon and sit at the helm during the delivery; if the introduction be not clear and pertinent it is evident the preacher does not know whither he is going, and if the inferences are of the same character, it is obvious he does not know where he has been. Unstudied sermons are not worth hearing or having; who would trust his life in the hands of a physician who had never thought of his profession?" But these men never permitted the understanding to supersede emotion, and, when they met the people face to face, the greatest of them went prepared, warmed and kindled, and ready to warm and kindle.

Thus their sermons became a sort of inspired song, full of imagination— imagination very often, and usually, deriving its imagery from no far-off and recondite allusions, never losing itself in a flowery wilderness of expressions, but homely illustrations, ministered to by the things and affairs of ordinary life, and, therefore, instantly preacher and people in emotion were one.

It is indeed true that many of their great preachers repeated the same sermon many times. Why not? So did Whitfield, so did Wesley, so have most eminent preachers done; but this need in no way interfere with—it did not interfere with—the felt necessity for unction on the part of the minister; and as to the people they liked to hear an old favourite again, or a sermon, which they had never heard although they had heard much about it. We believe it was to Christmas Evans a pert young preacher said, "Well, you have given us an old sermon again to-day."

"What then, my boy?" said the Master of Assemblies; "had you a new one?"

"Certainly," was the answer.

"Well, but look you," said the unblushing old culprit, "I would not take a dozen new sermons like yours for this one old sermon of mine."

"No, nor I," chimed in a gruff old deacon. "Oh yes, and look you, I should like to hear it again; but as for *yours*, I never heard it before, and I do not want to hear it again."

But then the *Language*! Of course the language had a great deal to do with this preaching power, we do not mean generally, but particularly; on all hands the Welsh is acknowledged to be a wonderful language. A Welshman will tell you that there is no language like it on the face of the earth, but that is a testimony borne by many scholars who are not Welshmen; perhaps there is no other language which so instantly conveys a meaning and at the same time touches emotion to the quick. True, like the Welshman himself, it is bony, and strangers to its power laugh somewhat ignorantly at its never-ending succession of consonants. Somebody has said that the whole language is as if it were made up of such words as our word "*strength*," and if the reader will compare in his mind the effect of the word *power* as contrasted with the word *strength*, he will feel something of the force of the language, and its fitness for the purposes of impression; but still this conveys but a poor idea of its great attributes.

It is so *literal* that the competent hearer, or reader, instantly realizes, from its words, things. Well do we remember sitting in Wales with a group of Welsh ministers and Welshmen round a pleasant tea-table; we were talking of the Welsh language, and one of our company, who had perhaps done more than any one of his own country for popular Welsh literature, and was one of the order of eminent Welsh preachers of whom we are speaking, broke forth: "Oh!" he said, "you English people cannot see all the things in your Bible that a Welshman can see; now your word '*blessed*,' it seems a very dear sweet thing to an Englishman and to a Welshman, but a Welshman sees the *thing* in the word, '*Gwyn ei fyd*,' that is, '*a white world*—white,' literally, white their world; so a Welshman would see there is a '*white world*' for the pure in heart, a '*white world*' for the poor in spirit, a '*white world*' for them who are reviled and persecuted for righteousness' sake; and when you read, '*B*lessed is the man unto whom the Lord imputeth not iniquity,' the Welshman reads his Bible and sees there is a '*white world*' for such a one, that is, all sin wiped out, the place quite clean, to begin again."

This is not all. We are not intending to devote any considerable space to a vindication of the Welsh language, but, when we speak of it with reference to the effects it produces as the vehicle of Oratory, it is necessary to remark that, so far from being,—as many have supposed who have only looked at it in its strange combination of letters on a page, perhaps unable to read it, and never having heard it spoken,—so far from being harsh and rugged, coarse or guttural, it probably yields to no language in delicious softness, in melting sweetness; in this it has been likened to the Italian language by those who have been best able to judge. Lord Lyttleton, in his "Letters from Wales," says, that when he first passed some of the Welsh hills, and heard the harp and the beautiful female peasants accompanying it with their melodious voices, he could not help indulging in the idea that he had descended the Alps, and was enjoying the harmonious pleasures of the Italian Paradise. And as we have already said, there has long prevailed an idea that the Welsh language is a multitude of consonants; but indeed the reverse is the case; the learned Eliezer Williams says, in his "Historical Anecdotes of the Welsh Language," "The alphabet itself demonstrates that the charge of a multiplicity of consonants is fallacious, since, whether the number of letters be reckoned twenty-two or twenty-four, seven are vowels; there remain therefore a more inconsiderable number than most of the European languages are obliged to admit . . . . Y and *w* are considered as vowels, and sounded as such; *w* is pronounced like *o u* in French in the word *oui*." To persons ignorant of the language, how strange is the appearance, and how erroneous the idea of the sound to be conveyed by *dd, ll, ch*, but indeed all these are indications of the softening of the letter; in a word, the impressions entertained of the harshness of the language are altogether erroneous.

The supposition that the Welsh language is made up of consonants is more especially singular from the fact that it possesses, says a writer in the *Quarterly Review*, what perhaps no other nation has,—a poem of eight lines in which there is not a single consonant. These verses are very old, dating from the seventeenth century;—of course the reader will remember that the Welsh language has seven vowels, both *w* and *y* being considered and sounded as such. This epigram or poem is on the Spider, and originally stood thus,—

> "O'i wiw ŵy i weu e â;—o'i iau Ei wyau a wea,
> E wywa ei wê aua, A'i weau yw ieuau ia."

To this, the great Gronwy Owen added a kind of counter change of vowels, and the translation has been given as follows:—

> "From out its womb it weaves with care
>   Its web beneath the roof;
> Its wintry web it spreadeth there—
>   Wires of ice its woof.
>
> "And doth it weave against the wall
>   Thin ropes of ice on high?
> And must its little liver all
>   The wondrous stuff supply?"

A singular illustration of the vowel power in a language ignorantly supposed to possess no vowels.

And these remarks are not at all unnecessary, for they illustrate to the reader, unacquainted with the language, the way in which it becomes such a means of immediate emotion; its words start before the eye like pictures, but are conveyed to the mind like music; and yet the bony character of the language, to which we have referred before, adds to the picture dramatic action and living strength. What a language, then, is this for a competent orator to play upon,—a man with an imaginative mind, and a fervid and fiery soul! Then is brought into play that element of Welsh preaching, without knowing and apprehending which there would be no possibility of understanding the secret of its great power; it is the "*hwyl.*" When the Welsh preacher speaks in his best mood, and with great unction, the highest compliment that can be paid him, the loftiest commendation that can be given, is, that he had the "*hwyl.*" "*Hwyl*" is the Welsh word for the canvas of a ship; and probably the derivation of the meaning is, from the canvas or sails of a ship filled with a breeze: the word for breeze, *awel,* is like it, and is used to denote a similar effect. Some years since, when the most eminent Welsh preacher we have recently seen in England, at an ordination service, was addressing his nephew in a crowded church in the neighbourhood of London, he said, "And, my dear boy, remember you are a Welshman; don't try to speak English, and don't try to speak like the English." A great many of his hearers wondered what the good man could mean; but both he and his nephew, and several others of the initiated, very well knew. He meant, speak your words with an *accent*, and an accent formed from a soul giving life and meaning to an expression. This, we know, is what the singer does,—this is what the musician tries to do. All words are not the same words in their meaning; the Welsh preacher seeks to play upon them as keys; the words themselves help him to do so. Literally, they are full of meaning; verbally, he attempts to pronounce that meaning; hence, as he rises in feeling he rises in variety of intonation, and his words sway to and fro, up and down,—bass, minor, and soprano all play their part, a series of intonings. In English, this very frequently sounds monotonous, sometimes even affected; in Welsh, the soul of the man is said to have caught the *hwyl*,—that is, he is in full sail, he has feeling and fire: the people catch it too. A Welsh writer, describing this, quotes the words of Jean Paul Richter: "Pictures during music are seen into more deeply and warmly by spectators; nay, many masters have in creating them acknowledged help from music." Great Welsh preaching, is very often a kind of wild, irregular chant, a jubilant refrain, recurring again and again. The people catch the power of it; shouts rise—prayers! "*Bendigedig*" ("blessed," or synonymous with our "Bless the Lord!") Amen! "*Diolch byth!*" and other expressions, rise, and roll over the multitude; they, too, have caught the *hwyl*. It is singular that, with us, the only circumstances and scenes in which such manifestations can take place, are purely secular, or on the occasions of great public meetings. The Welshman very much estimates the greatness of a preacher by his power to move men; but it does not follow, that this power shall be associated with great apparent bodily action. The words of John Elias and Williams of Wern consumed like flames, and divided like swords; but they were men of immense self-possession, and apparently very quiet. It has always been the aim of the greater Welsh preachers to find out such "acceptable"—that is, fitting and piercing—words, so that the words alone shall have the effect of action.

But, in any account of Welsh preaching, the place ought never to be forgotten—the scenery. We have said, the country is losing, now, many of its old characteristics of solitude and isolation; the railways are running along at the foot of the tall mountains, and spots, which we knew thirty years since as hamlets and villages, have now grown into large towns. It has often been the case, that populations born and reared amidst remote mountain solitudes, have possessed strong religious susceptibilities. The Welshman's chapel was very frequently reared in the midst of an unpeopled district, likely to provoke wonder in the mind of the passing stranger, as to whence it could derive its congregation. The building was erected there because it was favourable to a confluence of neighbourhoods. Take a region near to the spot where Christmas Evans was born,—a wild, mountainous tract of country, lying between the counties Brecon and Cardigan; for long miles, in every direction, there are no human habitations,—only, perhaps, here and there, in a deep dingle, some lone house, the residence of a sheep farmer, with three or four cultivated fields in its immediate neighbourhood; and at some distance, on the slopes of the mountain, an occasional shepherd's hut. It is a scene of the wildest magnificence. The traveller, as he passes along, discerns nothing but a sea of mountains,—rugged and precipitous bluffs, and precipices innumerable; here the grand and sportive streams, the Irvon, the Towy, and the Dothia, spring from their rocky channels, and tumble along, rushing and gurgling with deafening roar; here, as you pass along, you encounter more than one or two "wolves' leaps;"—dark caverns are there, from whence these brotherly rivers rush into each other's embrace. These regions, when we were in the habit of crossing them, many years since,—and we often crossed them,—we very naturally regarded as the Highlands, the sequestered mountain retreats, of Wales; this was Twm Shon Catty's, the Welsh Rob Roy's, country; for let Scotland boast as she will—

> "Wales has had a thief as good,
> She has her own Rob Roy."

And wonderfully romantic is the story of this same Welsh gentleman, and predatory chieftain. Here you find, to this day, his cave, from whence the bold and humorous outlaw was wont to spring forth, to spread terror and rapine over the whole region. It is thirty years since we passed through these desolations; they are probably much the same now as they were then; let the traveller shout as he will as he passes along, it is not from any human being, it is only from the wild rock, or screaming bird, he will have a reply.

Now, what do our readers think of a large and commodious chapel in the midst of a wild region like this? But one there is, in the very heart of the wilderness. Up to this place the worshippers come, on Sabbath mornings, from distances varying from two to eight miles. It is a Calvinistic-Methodist chapel; and the Rev. William Williams, in his interesting little historical sketch of Welsh Calvinistic-Methodism, tells how he preached in this building, several years since, when the chapel was crowded with worshippers; and in the yard adjoining, between fifty and sixty ponies, which had borne the worshippers to the place, with or without vehicles, were waiting the time for the return journey. This building had its birth from a congregation gathered first in one of the farm houses in these inaccessible wilds, in 1847. It seems strange to think how far people will travel to Divine Service when they have no such service near their own doors. We were struck with this, a short time since, in Norway; we found our way to a little village church, and there, on a spot where was next to no population, we found the Lutheran church crowded; and outside, a large square space thronged with carioles, ancient old shandydan landaus, carts, and every kind of conveyance,—horses and ponies stabled in the sheds all round; and we learned that many of the congregation had travelled in this way, beside the numbers who had walked, twelve, sixteen, eighteen miles to the service.

And thus, also, in Wales, many were the long and weary miles usually traversed, and through every variety of weather; and it seemed to be usually thought that the service, or services, repaid all the toil. And there was very little, externally, to aid the imagination, or to charm the taste, either in the building itself, or in the ritual adopted;—all was of the plainest and most severe order. The building, no doubt, was little more than a shelter from the weather; generally, perhaps, huge and capacious,—that was necessary,—but it was quite unadorned; the minister had nothing in the way of robes or attire to aid the impressions of reverence; there was no organ,—usually no instrument of any description,—although if an entire stranger to the language had entered, and heard the long, low, plaintive wail of almost any of their hymns,—most of them seeming to express a kind of dirge-like feeling of an exiled, conquered, and trampled people, a tone with its often-renewed refrain, its long-drawn minor, now sobbing into grief, occasionally swelling into triumph,—he might have found the notes of an organ were not needed to compel the unexpected tear. An exiled, conquered, and trampled people,—that expresses a great deal of truth. Wales has wrongs quite as bitter as any which Ireland ever knew;—the very cause of the existence of most of her chapels arose from the fact that, in many of her parish churches, not a word of Welsh was spoken; and perhaps frequently their ministers could not speak the native language;—the very judges who dispensed justice from the Bench were usually English, and needed an interpreter, that they might be able to understand the case upon which they were to give a judgment. Wales has had very little for which to thank England, but her people have never been seditious. Pious, industrious people, with their simple amusements and weird superstitions, and blossoming out into their great religious revivals and reformations, they have had to thank themselves, chiefly, for all the good which has unfolded itself upon their soil. These circumstances, however, have no doubt aided their peculiar and isolated religious life.

But, in those great assemblies, the Association meetings to which we have referred, many of the great preachers stood, with their vast congregations round them, in Nature's open Cathedral. Christmas Evans preached many of his noblest sermons amidst the imposing ruins of Caerphilly, Pembroke, and Manobear Castles; or the preacher found himself with his audience on the slope of some sweet, gorse-covered hill, in the neighbourhood of tumbling torrents, which did not sing so loudly in their melody as to interfere with the sweet restfulness of the surrounding scene. Preachers and hearers were accustomed to plain living,—one of the most essential conditions of high thinking; neither of them knew anything of luxury; and when most of them spoke, the age of luxury, even with us, had not yet set in. Bread and milk, or oatmeal and milk, were the favourite diet of all, in those days; even tea was all but unknown, and the potato almost their nearest approach to a dainty dish. They lived on good terms with Nature, with whom we have been quarrelling now for some years past; and thus they were prepared to receive such lessons as Nature might give, to aid and illustrate the deeper lessons of Divine Grace.

Of course, there was considerable uncertainty about the services,—excepting those more imposing and important occasions; and this gave, very frequently, a tone of the ludicrous to their announcement of the services. Thus, if a stranger asked what time the service would commence, it would often have been quite impossible to get any information; and failures, says Mr. D. M. Evans, were so frequent, that the announcement was often made with perfect gravity, "— will be here next Sunday, if he comes." Mr. Evans continues, that he well knew a deacon who claimed the prerogative to make announcements to the congregation, but who every week was guilty of such blunders, that he was implored to resign the honour to some other brother; to which he indignantly replied, that it was his crown, and was he not told in Scripture, "Hold fast that which thou hast, that no man take thy crown"? Often, when the preacher appeared, he showed himself in the pulpit almost out of breath, sometimes in sad disarray, sometimes apparently as if smothered with wrappers and top-coats; and by his panting and puffing, as someone said, "seeming to show that God Almighty had asked him to preach the Gospel, but had given him no time for it."

In a word, it is impossible, knowing Wales as we know it in our own day, to form any very distinct idea of the country as it was when these great preachers arose; and, when the tides of a new spiritual life rolled over the Principality, the singular relics of even heathenish superstition were loitering still among the secluded valleys and mountains of the land. No doubt, the proclamation of the Gospel, and the elevated faith which its great truths bring in its train, broke the fascination, the charm, and power of many of these; but they lingered even until within the last forty or fifty years,—indeed, the superstition of the Sin-Eater is said to [23] linger even now in the secluded vale of Cwm-Aman, in Caermarthenshire. The meaning of this most singular institution of superstition was, that when a person died, the friends sent for the Sin-Eater of the district, who, on his arrival, placed a plate of salt and bread on the breast of the deceased person; he then uttered an incantation over the bread, after which, he proceeded to eat it,—thereby eating the sins of the dead person; this done, he received a fee of two-and-sixpence,—which, we suppose, was much more than many a preacher received for a long and painful service. Having received this, he vanished as swiftly as possible, all the friends and relatives of the departed aiding his exit with blows and kicks, and other indications of their faith in the service he had rendered. A hundred years since, and through the ages beyond that time, we suppose this curious superstition was everywhere prevalent.

Another odd custom was the manner in which public opinion expressed itself on account of any domestic or social delinquency. A large crowd assembled before the house of the delinquent, one of whom was dressed up in what seemed to be a horse's head; the crowd then burst forth into strong vituperative abuse, accompanying the execrations with the rough music of old kettles, marrow-bones, and cleavers; finally, the effigy of the sinner was burnt before the house, and the sacred wrath of the multitude appeased. The majesty of outraged opinion being vindicated, they dispersed.

Some superstitions were of a more gentle character; the fairies, or "little men in green," as they were popularly called, continued to hold their tenantry of Wales long after they had departed from England; and even Glamorganshire, one of the counties nearest to England,—its roads forming the most considerable highway through Wales,—was, perhaps, the county where they lingered last; certainly not many years have passed by since, in the Vale of Neath, in the same county, there would have been a fear in taking some secluded pathway in the night, lest the "little people" should be offended by the intrusion upon their haunts.

With all these singular observances and superstitions, there was yet a kind of Christian faith prevalent among the people, but buried beneath dark ignorance and social folly. At Christmas time, at night, it was usual to illuminate all the churches in the villages. And upon the New Year's morning, children came waking the dawning, knocking at the doors,—usually obtaining admittance,—when they proceeded to sprinkle the furniture with water, singing as they did so the following words, which we quote on account of their quaint, sweet, old-world simplicity:—

> "Here we bring new water from the well so clear,
> For to worship God with this happy new year.
> Sing levy dew, sing levy dew, the water and the wine,
> With seven bright gold wires and bugles that do shine.
> Sing reign of fair maid, with gold upon her toe,
> Open you the west door, and turn the old year go.
> Sing reign of fair maid, with gold upon her chin,
> Open you the east door, and let the new year in."

It is admitted on all hands that the dissolution of the mists of darkness and superstition is owing to the people usually called Dissenters; the Church of the Establishment—and this is said in no spirit of unkindness—did very little to humanise or soften the rugged character, or to put to flight the debasing habits of the people. Of course, there are high and honourable exceptions; but while many clergymen devoted themselves, with great enthusiasm, to the perpetuation of the singular lore, the wild bardic songs, the triads, or the strange fables and mythic histories of the country, we can call to mind the names of but very few who attempted to improve, or to ameliorate, the social condition. So that the preachers, and the vast gatherings of the people by whom the preachers were surrounded, when the rays of knowledge were shed abroad, and devotion fired, were not so much the result of any antagonism to the Established Church,—*that* came afterwards; they were a necessity created by the painful exigencies of the country.

The remarks on the superstitions of Wales are not at all irrelevant to the more general observations on Welsh preaching; they are so essentially inwoven with the type of character, and nationality. The Welsh appears to be intimately related to the Breton; the languages assimilate,—so also do the folk-lores of the people; and the traditions and fanciful fables which have been woven from the grasses of the field, the leaves of the forest, and the clouds of the heavens, would have furnished Christmas Evans with allegoric texts which he might have expanded into sermons. It is not possible to doubt that these form one branch, from the great Celtic stem, of the human family. And not only are they alike in language and tradition, but also in the melancholy religiousness, in the metaphysical brooding over natural causes, and in the absence of any genuine humour, except in some grim or gloomy and grotesque utterance. The stories, the heroes, and the heroines, are very much the same; historic memory in both looks back to a fantastic fairyland, and presents those fantastic pictures of cities and castles strangely submerged beneath the sea, and romantic shadows and spectral forms of wonderful kings and queens, such as we meet in the Mabinogi of Taliesin, in the Fairy Queen of Spenser, and in the Idylls of our Laureate. Thus, all that could stir wonder, excite the imagination and the fancy, and describe the nearness of the supernatural to the natural, would become very charming to a

Welshman's ears; and we instantly have suggested to us one of the sources of the power and popularity of Christmas Evans with his countrymen.

Even the spread and prevalence of Christian knowledge have scarcely disenchanted Wales of its superstitions. Few persons who know anything at all of the country, however slight such knowledge may be, are unaware of this characteristic of the people. This remark was, no doubt, far more applicable even twenty-five years since than now. The writer of this volume has listened to the stories of many who believed that they had seen the *Canwyll-y-corph*—corpse-candles—wending their way from houses, more or less remote, to the churchyard. Mr. Borrow, also, in his "Wild Wales," tells us how he conversed with people in his travels who believed that they had seen the corpse-candles. But a hundred years ago, this was a universal object of faith; as was also the belief in coffins and burial trains seen wending their way, in the dead of night, to the churchyard. Omens and predictions abounded everywhere, while singular legends and traditions in many districts hung also round church bells. And yet with all this the same writer, remarking on Welsh character, says, "What a difference between a Welshman and an Englishman of the lower class!" He had just been conversing with a miller's man,—a working labourer in the lowliest walk of life; and found him conversant with the old poets, and the old traditions of the country, and quite interested in them; and he says, "What would a Suffolk miller's man have said, if I had repeated to him verses out of Beowulf or even Chaucer, and had asked him about the residence of Skelton?" We must bear this in mind as we attempt to estimate the character with which the preacher had to deal. Haunted houses were numerous. A lonely old place, very distinct to the writer's knowledge, had hung round it some wild traditions not unlike "Blind Willie's Story" in "Redgauntlet." No doubt, now, all these things have, to a considerable extent, disappeared,—although there are wild nooks, far wilder than any we have in England, where the faith in the old superstitions lingers. In the great preaching days, those men who shook the hearts of the thousands of their listeners, as they dealt with unseen terrors, believed themselves to be—as it was believed of them that they were—covered with the shadow of an Unseen Hand, and surrounded by the guardianship of the old Hebrew prophet—"chariots of fire, and horses of fire;" they believed themselves to be the care of a special Providence; and some of the stories then current would only move the contempt of that modern intelligence which has, at any rate, laid all the ghosts.

It is not within the province of this volume to recapitulate and classify Welsh superstitions; they were, and probably, in many neighbourhoods, are still, very various: we must satisfy our readers with a slight illustration. Perhaps some may object to the retailing such stories, for instance, as the following. The apology for its insertion, then, must be, that it is one of a number tending to illustrate that sense which the old Welsh mind had, of its residence upon the borders of, and relation to, the Invisible World. The Rev. John Jones, of Holywell, in Flintshire, was one of the most renowned ministers in the Principality; he was a man of extraordinary zeal and fervour as a preacher, and his life and character were, in unblemished reputation, equal to his gifts and zeal. He used to recite, with peculiar solemnity, a story of a mysterious horseman, by whom he believed he had been delivered from a position of extreme danger, when he was travelling, alone, from Bala, in Merionethshire, to Machynlleth, in the county of Montgomery. He travelled on horseback through a wild, desolate country, at that time almost uninhabited; he had performed nearly half his journey, when, as he was emerging from a wood, he says, "I observed coming towards me a man on foot. By his appearance, judging from the sickle which he carried sheathed in straw over his shoulder, he was doubtless a reaper in search of employment. As he drew near, I recognized a man whom I had seen at the door of the village inn at Llanwhellyn, where I had stopped to bait my horse. On our meeting, he touched his hat, and asked if I could tell him the time of day. I pulled out my watch for the purpose,—noticing, at the same time, the peculiar look which the man cast at its heavy silver case. Nothing else, however, occurred to excite any suspicion on my part; so, wishing him a good afternoon, I continued my journey." We must condense Mr. Jones's narration, feeling that the story loses much of its graphic strength in so doing. He pursued his way down a hill, and, at some distance farther on, noticed something moving on the other side of a large hedge; he soon discovered it to be a man, running in a stooping position. He watched the figure with curiosity, which grew into something like fear as he recognized the reaper with whom he had spoken a short time before, and that, as he moved on, he was engaged in tearing the straw band from his sickle. The man hurried on, and Mr. Jones saw him conceal himself behind a thicker part of the hedge, within a few yards of the road, and near where a gate crossed the park. Mr. Jones says he did not doubt, then, that he intended to attack and, perhaps, murder him for the sake of the watch, and whatever money he might have about him. He looked round: no other person was in sight,—no house near; he was hemmed in by rocky banks and high hedges on either side.

"I could not turn back," he says; "my business was of the utmost importance to the cause for which I was journeying." He could not urge his horse with speed, for the gate was not open through which he had to pass; he felt that he was weak and unarmed, and had no chance against a powerful man with a dangerous weapon in his hand. "In despair," he says, "rather than in a spirit of humble trust and confidence, I bowed my head, and offered up a silent prayer. At this juncture, my horse, growing impatient of delay, started off. I clutched the reins, which I had let fall on his neck,—when, happening to turn my eyes, I saw, to my utter astonishment, that I was no longer alone: there, by my side, I beheld a horseman, in a dark dress, mounted on a white steed. In intense amazement, I gazed upon him. Where could he have come from? He appeared as suddenly as if he had sprung from the earth; he must have been riding behind, and have overtaken me,—and yet I had not heard the slightest sound. It was mysterious, inexplicable; but joy overcame my feelings of wonder, and I began at once to address my companion. I asked him if he had seen any one; and then described to him what had taken place, and how relieved I felt by his sudden appearance. He made no reply, and, on looking at his face, he seemed paying but slight attention to my words, but continued intently gazing in the direction of the gate,—now about a quarter of a mile ahead. I followed his gaze, and saw the reaper emerge from his concealment, and run across a field to our left, resheathing his sickle as he hurried along. He had evidently seen that I was no longer alone, and had relinquished his intended attempt."

Mr. Jones sought to enter into conversation with his mysterious companion, but he gave him no word in reply. He says he "was hurt at his companion's mysterious silence;" only once did he hear his voice. Having watched the figure of the reaper disappear over the brow of a neighbouring hill, he turned to the stranger, and said, "'Can it for a moment be doubted that my prayer was heard, and that you were sent for my deliverance by the Lord?' Then it was that I thought I heard the horseman speak, and that he uttered the single word, 'Amen!' Not another word did he give utterance to, though I spoke to him both in English and Welsh. We were now approaching the gate, which I hastened to open; and having done so, I waited at the side of the road for him to pass through,—but he came not. I turned my head to look; the mysterious horseman was gone; he was not to be seen; he had disappeared as mysteriously as he had come. What could have become of him? He could not have gone through the gate, nor have made his horse leap the high hedges, which on both sides shut in the road. Where was he? had I been dreaming? was it an apparition, a spectre, which had been riding by my side for the last ten minutes?—was it but a creature of my imagination? I tried hard to convince myself that this was the case; but why had the reaper resheathed his murderous-looking sickle and fled? And then, a feeling of profound awe began to creep over my soul. I remembered the singular way of his first appearance,—his long silence, and the single word to which he had given utterance after I had mentioned the name of the Lord; the single occasion on which I had done so. What could I, then, believe, but that my prayer had been heard, and that help had been given me at a time of great danger? I dismounted, and throwing myself on my knees, I offered up my thankfulness to Him who had heard my cry. I then mounted my horse, and continued my journey; but through the long years that have elapsed since that memorable summer's day, I have never for a moment wavered in my belief, that in the mysterious horseman I had a special interference of Providence, by which I was delivered from a position of extreme danger."

Now, however our readers may account for such incidents, the only purpose in introducing such a story here, is to say that it gives a fair illustration of that peculiar cast of ideal imagination which pervaded the Welsh mind, and influenced at once the impressions both of preachers and hearers.

There is, perhaps, no other spot on our British soil where "the old order" has so suddenly "changed" as in Wales: the breaking open the mountains for mining purposes has led to the thronging of dense populations on spots which were, only a few years since, unbroken solitudes. Ruins, which the sentimental idler never visited, wrecks of castles and abbeys crumbling into dust, isolated places through which we passed thirty years since, which seemed as though they never could be invaded by the railway whistle, or scarcely reached by the penny postman, now lie on the great highway of the train. It is not saying too much to affirm that there is no spot in Europe where the traveller is so constantly brought into the neighbourhood of old magnificence, the relics of vanished cities.

The wonder grows as to what was the state of ancient society in Wales. An eminent traveller says: "In England our ancestors have left us, dispersed in various places, splendid remains of their greatness; but in Wales you cannot travel ten miles without coming upon some vestige of antiquity which in another country you would go fifty to trace out." It is of such spots that a Welsh poet, Dyer, says:—

> "The pilgrim oft,
> At dead of night, 'mid his orisons hears,
> Aghast, the voice of Time disparting towers,
> Tumbling all precipitate, all down-dashed,
> Rattling around, loud thundering to the moon."

What an illustration of this is St. David's!—a little miserable village, with the magnificent remains of its great palace, and the indications of its once splendid cathedral; itself now a kind of suffragan, it once numbered seven suffragans within its metropolitan pale—Worcester, Hereford, Llandaff, Bangor, St. Asaph, Llanbadarn, and Margam. The mitre now dimly beaming at almost the lowest step of the ecclesiastical ladder, once shone with so proud a lustre as to attract the loftiest ecclesiastics. St. David's numbers one saint, three lord-treasurers, one lord privy-seal, one chancellor of Oxford, one chancellor of England, and, in Farrar, one illustrious martyr.

Travel through the country, and similar reflections will meet you in every direction. You step a little off the high-road, and—as, for instance, in

Kilgerran—you come to the traditional King Arthur's castle, the far-famed Welsh Tintagel, of which Warton sings,—

> "Stately the feast, and high the cheer,
> Girt with many an armèd peer,
> And canopied with golden pall,
> Amid Kilgerran's castle hall;
> Illumining the vaulted roof,
> A thousand torches flamed aloof;
> The storied tapestry was hung,
> With minstrelsy the arches rung,
> Of harps that with reflected light
> From the proud gallery glittered bright."

Or, in the neighbourhood of the magnificent coast of Pembrokeshire, the wondrous little chapel of St. Govan's, the hermitage of the hundred steps; and those splendid wrecks of castles, Manopear, the home of Giraldus Cambrensis, and the graceful and almost interminable recesses of Carew. A traveller may plunge about among innumerable villages bearing the names of saints for whom he will look in vain in the Romish calendar,—St. Athan's, St. Siebald's, St. Dubric's, St. Dogmael's, St. Ishmael's, and crowds besides. All such places are girdled round with traditions and legends known to Welsh archæologists—the very nomenclature of Wales involving poetry and historical romance, and often deep tragedy. The names of the villages have a whisper of fabulous and traditional times, and are like the half-effaced hieroglyphs upon an old Egyptian tomb. There is the *Fynnon Waedog* (Bloody Well), *the Pald of Gwaye* (the Hollow of Woe), the *Maen Achwynfan*, (the Stone of Lamentation and Weeping), the *Leysan Gwaed Gwyr* (the Plant of the Blood of Man), *Merthyr Tydvil* is the Martyred Tydvil. Villages and fields with names like these, remind us of the Hebrew names of places, really significant of some buried tragedy, long holding its place in the heart, and terror of the neighbourhood.

In a land-locked solitude like that of Nevern, Cardiganshire,—where, by-the-bye, we might loiter some time to recite some anecdotes of its admirable clergyman and great preacher, one of the Griffiths,—the wanderer, after a piece of agreeable wildness, comes to a village, enchanting for its beauty, lying on the brink of a charming river, with indications of a decayed importance; the venerable yew-trees of its churchyard shadowing over a singular—we may venture to speak of it as a piece of inexplicable—Runic antiquity, in a stone of a quadrangular form, about two feet broad, eighteen inches thick, and thirteen feet high, with a cross at the top. Few countries can boast, like Wales, the charm of places in wildest and most delicious scenery, with all that can stir an artist's, poet's, or antiquarian's sensibility. What a neighbourhood is Llandilo!—the home of the really great poet, John Dyer, the author of "Grongar Hill," a delicious spot in this neighbourhood. Here, too, is Golden Grove, the retreat of our own Jeremy Taylor; and here, in his days of exile, many of the matchless sermons of him who has been called, by some, "the English Chrysostom," and, by others, the "Milton of the English pulpit," were preached. We made a pilgrimage there ourselves some few years since, urged by love to the memory of Jeremy Taylor. We found the old church gone, and in its place a new one,—the taste of which did not particularly impress us; and we inquired for Taylor's pulpit, and were told it had been chopped up for fire-wood! Then we inquired for a path through the fields, which for a hundred and fifty years had been called "Taylor's Walk," where the great bishop was wont to meditate,—and found it had been delivered over to the plough. We hope we may be forgiven if we say, that we hurried in disgust from a village which, in spite of its new noble mansion, had lost to us its chief charm. But this neighbourhood, with its Dynevor Castle and its charming river, the Towey, and all the scenery described by the exquisite Welsh poet, in whose verse beauty and sublimity equally reign, compels us to feel that if he somewhat pardonably over-coloured, by his own associations, the lovely shrine of his birth, he only naturally described the country through which these preachers wandered, when he says,—

> "Ever charming, ever new,
> When will the landscape tire the view!
> The fountain's fall, the river's flow,
> The woody valleys, warm and low:
> The windy summit, wild and high,
> Roughly rushing on the sky!
> The pleasant seat, the ruin'd tow'r,
> The naked rock, the shady bow'r;
> The town and village, dome and farm,
> Each give to each a double charm,
> As pearls upon an Ethiop's arm."

The manners of the people, a few years since, were as singular and primeval as their country; in all the villages there were singular usages. The "biddings" to their weddings,—which have, perhaps, yielded to advanced good taste,—had a sweeter relief in other customs, at weddings and funerals, tending to civilize, and refine. Throughout Glamorganshire, especially, and not many years since, it was the universal custom, when young unmarried persons died, to strew the way to the grave with sweet flowers and evergreens. Mr. Malkin, in his interesting work on South Wales, published now seventy years since, says: "There is in the world an unfeeling kind of false philosophy, which will treat such customs as I mention with ridicule; but what can be more affecting than to see all the youth of both sexes in a village, and in every village through which the corpse passes, dressed in their best apparel, and strewing with sweet-scented flowers the ways along which one of their beloved neighbours was carried to his, or her last home?" No doubt such customs are very much changed, but they were prevalent during that period to which most of those preachers whose manners we have mentioned belonged.

Such pathetic usages, indicating a simple state of society, are commonly associated, as we have seen, with others of a rougher kind and character. The Welsh preachers were the pioneers of civilization,—although advanced society might still think much had to be done in the amelioration of the national manners. They probably touched a few practices which were really in themselves simple and affecting, but they swept away many superstitions, quite destroyed many rude and degrading practices, and introduced many usages, which, while they were in conformity with the national instincts of the people (such as preaching and singing, and assembling themselves together in large companies), tended to refine and elevate the mind and heart.

Such were the circumstances, and such the scenery, in which the great Welsh preachers arose.

We have not thought of those Welsh preachers who have made themselves especially known in England. Many have, from time to time, settled as pastors with us, who have deserved a large amount of our esteem and honour, blending in their minds high reverence, the tender sensitiveness of a poetic imagination, with the instinct of philosophic inquisitiveness—even shading off into an order of scepticism,—but all united to a strong and impressive eloquence. These attributes seem all essentially to adhere in the character of the cultured Welsh preacher. Caleb Morris finely illustrates all this; perhaps he was no whit inferior, in the build and architecture of his mind, to Horace Bushnell, whom he greatly resembled; but, unlike Bushnell, he never committed any of his soliloquies of thought, or feeling to the press. The present writer possesses volumes of his reported sermons which have never seen the light.

And what a Welshman was Rowland Williams! Who can read his life without feeling the spirit of devotion, however languid, inflamed and fired? And how, in spite of all the heresies attributed to him, and, growing up in the midst of the sacred ardours of his character, we find illustrated the wonder of the curious and searching eye, united to the warmth of the tender and revering heart!—attributes, we repeat, which seemed to mingle in very inferior types of Welsh preachers, as well as in the more eminent, and which, as they kindle into a passion in the man's nature who desires to instruct his fellow-men, combine to make preaching, if they be absent, an infamy, a pastime, a day labour, or a handicraft, an art or a science; or, by their presence, constitute it a virtue and a mighty power over human souls. Eminently these men seem to hear a voice saying, "*The prophet that hath a dream, let him tell a dream! What is the chaff to the wheat? saith the Lord.*"

Note to "Cwm-Aman," *page* 23.

Dr. Thos. Rees, in a letter to the Editor of the *Dysgedydd*, Rev. Herber Evans, says, "That although bred and born within ten miles of Cwm-Aman, he had never heard of this ridiculous superstition."

CHAPTER II.
EARLY LIFE UNTIL HIS ENTRANCE INTO THE MINISTRY.

> Birth and Early Hardships—Early Church Fellowship—Beginning to Learn—Loses an Eye—A Singular Dream—Beginning to Preach—His First Sermon—Is Baptized—A New Church Fellowship—The Rev. Timothy Thomas—Anecdotes—A Long Season of Spiritual Depression—Is ordained as Home Missionary to Lleyn—Commencement of Success as a Preacher—Remarks on Success—Marries—Great Sermon at Velinvole—A Personal Reminiscence of Welsh Preaching.

Christmas Evans is not the first, in point of time, in the remarkable procession of those men whose names we might mention, and of whom we shall find occasion in this volume to speak, as the great Welsh preachers. And there may be some dispute as to whether he was the first in point of eminence; but he is certainly the one of the four whose name is something more than a tradition. John Elias, Williams of Wern, and Davies of Swansea, have left behind them little beside the legendary rumour of their immense and pathetic power. This is true, especially, of David Davies of Swansea; and yet, Dr. Rees, his successor, and a very competent authority, says: "In some respects he was superior to all his distinguished contemporaries." But the name of Christmas Evans is, perhaps, the most extensively known of any,—just as the name of Bunyan has a far more extensive intimacy than the equally honourable names of Barrow and Butler; and there is a similar reason for this. Christmas Evans, in the pulpit, more nearly approached the great Dreamer than any pulpit master of whom we have heard; many of his sermons appear to have been long-sustained parables, and pictures alive with allegorical delineation of human character.

CHRISTMAS EVANS was born at a place called Esgairwen (Ysgarwen), in the parish of Llandysul, in Cardiganshire; he was born on Christmas Day—and hence his Christian name—in 1766. His parents, Samuel and Johanna Evans, were in the poorest circumstances; his father was a shoemaker, and although this profession has included such a number of men remarkable for their genius and high attainments, it has never found the masters of the craft greatly remarkable for the possession of gold or gear. His mother, by her maiden name Lewis, came from a respectable family of freeholders in the parish; but the father of Christmas died when he was a child,—and these were hard days of poverty, almost destitution, for the poor struggling widow and her family,—so her brother, James Lewis, of Bwlchog, in the parish of

Llanfihangel-ar-Arth, took little Christmas home to his farm, engaging to feed and clothe him for such labour on the farm as the poor boy might be able to perform. Here he stayed six years,—six miserable years; his uncle was a hard, cruel man, a selfish drunkard. Christmas used to say of him, in after years, "It would be difficult to find a more unconscionable man than James Lewis in the whole course of a wicked world." During these, which ought to have been the most valuable years of his life, no care was taken of his heart, his mind, or his morals; in fact, he had neither a friend nor a home. At the age of seventeen he could not read a word, he was surrounded by the worst of examples, and he became the subject of a number of serious accidents, through which he narrowly escaped with his life. Once he was stabbed in a quarrel, once he was nearly drowned, and with difficulty recovered; once he fell from a high tree with an open knife in his hand, and once a horse ran away with him, passing at full speed through a low and narrow passage. There is an erroneous impression that, in those days, he was a great boxer, and that he lost his eye in a fight; the truth is quite different; he was not a boxer, and never fought a battle in his life. He lost his eye after his conversion, when he and some other young men were attempting the work of mutual help, in making up for lost time, by evening meetings, for various works of instruction; a number of his former companions waylaid him at night, beat him unmercifully, and one struck him with a stick over the eye. In after years, when some one was jesting before Robert Hall at Welsh preachers, upon his mentioning Christmas Evans, the jester said, "And he only has one eye!" "Yes, sir," he answered, "but that's a piercer; an eye, sir, that could light an army through a wilderness in a dark night." So that in his sightless eye, Christmas Evans, like the one-eyed Spiridion, the noble witness in the Nicean Council, really "bore in his body a mark of the Lord Jesus." But we are anticipating.

At about seventeen years of age, he left his bad uncle and his more servile employments; still continuing the occupation of a farming lad, he went to Glanclettwr; afterwards he lived at Penyralltfawr, at Gwenawlt, and then at Castellhywel. Thus the days of his youth passed; he looks like a poor, neglected, and forsaken lad. Of books he knew nothing,—he had no men of intelligence around him with whom to converse, and his condition in life doomed him to association with all that was low and brutal. And yet, strange as it may seem, as his friend and earliest biographer, Mr. Rhys Stephen, has testified, even then, as in the instance of the rugged young Samson, "the Spirit of the Lord began to move him at times." It is not credible that, however crushed down beneath the weight of such abject circumstances, the boy could have been exactly what the other boys and men round him were; restless feelings, and birth-throes of emotion and thought, make themselves known in most of us before they assume a shape in consciousness: it is natural that it should have been so with him. With a life of seriousness, which resulted in Church membership, and which appears to have taken place when he was about seventeen years of age, commenced his life of mental improvement,—the first humble beginnings of intellectual effort. It is singular that the Church with which he first united, at Llwynrhydowain, originally Presbyterian, and of considerable importance in the early history of Welsh Nonconformity, approached very nearly, when Evans united with it, to Unitarianism. Its pastor was the Rev. David Davies; he was an Arian, an eminent bard, a scholar, an admirable and excellent man, who has left behind him a very honourable reputation. Such a man as Mr. Davies was, he would be likely to be interested in the intelligent and intellectual state of the youth of his Church and congregation. The slight accounts we possess of the avidity with which Christmas Evans and his companions commenced their "pursuit of knowledge under difficulties," is very animating and pleasing; they combined together with the desire to obtain the earliest and most necessary means of mental acquisitiveness, such as reading and writing, a desire for the acquisition of religious knowledge, and what may be spoken of as some of the higher branches of study. But we will employ Christmas Evans's own words:—

> "During a revival which took place in the Church under the care of Mr. David Davies, many young people united themselves with that people, and I amongst them. What became of the major part of these young converts, I have never known; but I hope God's grace followed them as it did me, the meanest of the whole. One of the fruits of this awakening was the desire for religious knowledge that fell upon us. Scarcely one person out of ten could, at this time, and in those neighbourhoods, read at all, even in the language of the country. We bought Bibles and candles, and were accustomed to meet together in the evening, in the barn of Penyralltfawr; and thus, in about one month, I was able to read the Bible in my mother tongue. I was vastly delighted with so much learning. This, however, did not satisfy me, but I borrowed books, and learnt a little English. Mr. Davies, my pastor, understood that I thirsted for knowledge, and took me to his school, where I stayed for six months. Here I went through the Latin Grammar; but so low were my circumstances that I could stay there no longer."

To preach, as we all know, has often been an object of ambition with young converts, and the novices in the vestibule of knowledge of the spiritual life; such an ambition seems very early to have stirred in the heart of young Christmas. We have already mentioned how it was that he so cruelly lost the use of an eye; it illustrates the singular brutality of the time and neighbourhood; an inoffensive lad, simply because he renounced the society of profane drunkards, and was laudably busying himself with the affairs of a higher life, was set upon in the darkness of the night by six young ruffians, unmercifully beaten with sticks, and the sight of an eye destroyed. It was the night after this calamity that he had a dream; and the dream of the night reveals the bent of his day dreams. He dreamt that the Day of Judgment was come, that he saw the world in a blaze; with great confidence he called out, "Jesus, save me!" And he thought he saw the Lord turn towards him and say, "It was thy intention to preach the Gospel, but it is now too late, for the Day of Judgment is come." But this vision of the night clung to him when he awoke; perhaps he feared that the loss of the eye would interfere with his acceptance as a minister. Certainly the dream had an influence on his future career,—so had many other dreams. It was always his belief that he had received some of his most important impressions from dreams: nothing, apparently, no amount of reason or argument, could persuade him to the contrary. To preach the Gospel became an ardent desire now with this passionately imaginative and earnest youth; but there were serious hindrances in the way. There appears to have been a kind of law in the Church with which he was connected at Llwynrhydowain, that no member of the Church should be permitted to preach until he had passed through a college course. It is very remarkable that two of the greatest preachers who have adorned the pulpit of Wales should have been admitted into Church fellowship together on the same evening,—David Davies, afterwards of Swansea, whose name we have already mentioned, and Christmas Evans. It was always the regret and complaint of their first pastor, that the Church law to which we have referred, deprived his Church of the two most eminent men it had ever produced. There were, no doubt, other reasons; but it is singular, now, to notice the parallelism of the gifted pair, for they also preached their first sermon, within a week of each other, in the same cottage. Cottage preaching was then of much more importance than it now seems to our ecclesiastical and æsthetic apprehensions; and the congregations which assembled in those old Welsh cottages were such as to try the mental and spiritual strength of a young preacher. How Davies acquitted himself, and how he ran his course, we may notice by-and-bye; our present concern is with Christmas Evans. Perhaps our readers will not entertain a depreciating opinion of the youth, when they hear him very candidly confess that the substance of his first sermon was taken from Beveridge's "Thesaurus Theologicus," a book borrowed, probably, from his pastor. But a Mr. Davies, who must have been a reading man although a farmer, heard it, was very much impressed by it, but went home and found it; so that the poor boy's reputation as a preacher seemed gone. "Still," said the good man, "I have some hope of the son of Samuel the shoemaker, because the prayer was as good as the sermon." But perhaps he would not have thought so hopefully of the young man had he then known, what Christmas afterwards confessed, that the prayer, too, was very greatly committed to memory from a collection of prayers by a well-known clergyman, Griffith Jones of Llanddowror.

Such was the first public effort of this distinguished preacher; like the first effort of his great English contemporary, Robert Hall, we suppose it would be regarded as a failure. Meantime, we have to notice that the spiritual life of the youth was going on; he began to be dissatisfied with the frame of theologic sentiment of the Church to which he belonged. He heard preachers who introduced him to the more grand, scriptural, and evangelical views of Christian truth. The men of that time did not play at preaching; the celebrated David Morris, father of the yet more celebrated Ebenezer Morris; the great Peter Williams, Jones of Llangan, Thomas Davies of Neath,—such men as these appear to have kindled in his mind loftier views of the person and the work of Christ. Also, a man named Amos, who had been a member of the same Church with Christmas Evans, had left that communion, and joined that of the Baptists. A close study of the Word of God led Christmas also to a change of convictions as to the meaning and importance of the rite of baptism. A similar change of theologic opinion was passing through the mind of his young friend and fellow-member, David Davies, who finally united himself with the Independent communion. Christmas Evans says, "I applied to the Baptist Church at Aberduar, where I was in due time received; I was then about twenty years and six months old. I was baptized by the Rev. Timothy Thomas."

As the names of successive persons and pastors pass before our eyes, and appear in these pages, it is at once affecting, humbling, and elevating, to think of men of whom our ears have scarcely ever heard, but who, in their day, were men "of whom the world was not worthy," and whose "record is now on high." Such a man, beyond all question, was this Timothy Thomas, the son of an eminent father, the brother of men who, if not as eminent as himself, were yet worthy of the noble relationship. He was a Welsh gentleman, lived on a farm, an extended lease of which he held, and which enabled him to preach and fulfil the work of a pastor without any monetary reward. He appears to have devoted himself, his time, his energy, and his property to the work of the ministry. His farm was a splendid one in the vale of the Teivy. Mr. Rhys Stephen, who knew him, speaks of his gallant bearing, his ingenuous spirit, and of his princely magnanimity; he would ride thirty or forty miles on a Saturday, through the remote wilds of Caermarthenshire and Cardiganshire, to be ready for the services on the Sunday. His gentlemanly bearing overcame and beat down mobs which sometimes assembled for the purpose of insulting and assailing him. Mr. Stephen mentions one singular instance, when Mr. Thomas was expected to administer the ordinance of baptism, and, as was not unusual in those days, in the natural baptistry of the river. A mob had assembled together for the purpose of insulting and annoying the service, the missiles of offence in their hands; when, suddenly, a well-dressed gentleman, mounted on a noble horse, rode over the village bridge; he hastily alighted, gave his bridle to a bystander, walked briskly into the middle of the little flock; the inimical members of the mob set him down for a magistrate at the least, and expected that he would give the word to disperse; but instead of doing so, he took the nearest candidate by the hand, and walked himself down into the stream, booted and spurred as he was. Before the mob had done gaping, he had done this part of his work; after this, however, he stood upon the brink of the stream, still in his wet attire, and preached one of his ardent sermons. He certainly conciliated the homage of the opposing forces, and left them under the impression that the "dippers," as the Baptists were generally called, had certainly one gentleman among them. We do not know how our Baptist brethren would like to submit to this kind of service, but it certainly seems to resemble more closely the baptism of Enon, near to Salem, and that of the Ethiopian prince by Philip, than some we have seen.

The anecdotes of this Timothy Thomas are too good and too numerous to be entirely passed by. Once he was preaching in the enchanting neighbourhood near Llandeilo, to which we referred in the first chapter—the neighbourhood of Grongar Hill, and Golden Grove; the neighbourhood of Dyer, Steele, and Jeremy Taylor. It was a still Sabbath morning in the summer, and in that lovely spot immense crowds were gathered to hear him. He had administered baptism, and preached, without interruption, when someone came up to him and told him, with startled fear and trepidation, that the clergyman,—the rector,—on his way to the church, had been detained, utterly unable to pass through the crowd, through the greater part of the service. Instantly, with admirable tact and catholicity, he exclaimed: "I understand that the respected clergyman of the parish has been listening patiently to me for the last hour; let us all go to the church and return the compliment by hearing him." The church, and the churchyard as well, were instantly crowded; the clergyman was delighted with the catholic spirit displayed by the Baptist minister, and of course not a word further was said about the trespass which had been committed.

Timothy Thomas was a noble specimen of what has been called the "muscular Christian;" he had great courage. Once, when travelling with his wife, and set upon by four ruffians, he instantly, with his single stick, floored two, but broke his stick in the very act of conquest. Immediately he flew to a hedge and tore up a prodigious stake, and was again going forth to victory, when the scoundrels, having had enough of this bishop of the Church militant, took to flight and left him in undisputed possession of the field. A remarkable man this,—a sort of Welsh chieftain; a perfect gentleman, but half farmer, half preacher. In the order of Church discipline, a man was brought up before him, as the pastor, for having knocked down an Unitarian. "Let us hear all about it," said the pastor. "To tell all the truth about it, sir," said the culprit, "I met Jack the miller at the sign of the Red Dragon, and there we had a single glass of ale together." "Stop a bit," said the minister; "I hope you paid for it." "I did, sir." "That is in your favour, Thomas," said the pastor; "I cannot bear those people who go about tippling at other people's expense. Go on, Thomas." "Well, sir, after a little while we began quietly talking about religion, and about the work of Jesus Christ. Jack said that He was only a man, and then he went on to say shocking things, things that it was beyond the power of flesh and blood to bear." "I daresay," said the pastor; "but what did he say?" "He actually said, sir, that the blood of Christ had no more power in it than the blood of a beast. I could not stand that any more, so I knocked him down." "Well, brother," said the minister, "I cannot say that you did the right thing, but I quite believe that I should have done so too. Go, and sin no more."

But with all these marks of a strong character, the lines of Timothy Thomas's faith were clear and firm.

Such was the man who received Christmas Evans into the Church of which he became so bright and shining an ornament. This noble man survived until his eighty-sixth year; he died at Cardigan, in 1840. He was asked, sometimes, how many he had baptized during his lifetime, and he would reply, brusquely, "About two thousand;" at other times, he would be more particular, and say, "I have baptized at least two thousand persons. Yes," he would add tenderly, "and thirty of them have become ministers of the Gospel; and it was I who baptized Christmas Evans,"—sometimes adding naïvely, "I did it right, too,—according to the apostolic practice, you know."

Thus we are brought to the interesting and important turning-point in the life of Christmas Evans. He had united himself with the Baptist communion. Our readers will clearly perceive, that he was a young man who could not be hidden, and it was soon discovered that the work of the ministry was to be his destination. As to his internal state, upon which a ministerial character must always depend, these early years of his religious life were times and seasons of great spiritual depression. Such frames of feeling depend, perhaps, not less, or more, upon certain aspects of religious truth, than they do upon the peculiarities of temperament; a nervous imagination is very exhausting, and brings the physical frame very low; moreover, exalted ideas, and ideals, produce very depressing appreciations of self. He thought himself a mass of ignorance and sin; he desired to preach, but he thought that such words as his must be useless to his hearers: then, as to the method of preaching, he was greatly troubled. He thought by committing his sermons to memory he forfeited the gift of the Holy Spirit; so he says he changed his method, took a text without any premeditation, and preached what occurred to him at the time; "but," he continues, "if it was bad before, it was worse now; so I thought God would have nothing to do with me as a preacher."

The young man was humbled; he entered every pulpit with dread; he thought that he was such an one that his mere appearance in the pulpit would be quite sufficient to becloud the hearts of his hearers, and to intercept the light from heaven. Then it seems he had no close friend to whom he could talk; he was afraid lest, if he laid bare the secrets of his heart, he should seem to be only a hypocrite; so he had to wrap up the bitter secrets of his soul in his own heart, and drink of his bitter cup alone. Is this experience singular? Is not this the way in which all truly great, and original preachers have been made?—Luther, Bunyan, Dr. Payson, Robert Hall,—how many beside? Such men have attained high scholarships, and fellowships, in the great university of human nature; like Peter, pierced to the heart themselves, they have "pricked" the hearts, the consciences, of the thousands who have heard them. Thus, more than from the lore of classical literatures, they have had given to them "the tongue of the learned," which has enabled them to speak "a word in season to those who were wearied;" thus, "converted" themselves, they have been able to "strengthen their brethren."

Evans passed through a painful experience; the young man was feeling his way. He was unconscious of the powers within him, although they were struggling for expression; and so, through his humility and lowly conceptions of himself, he was passing on to future eminence and usefulness.

Lleyn was the first place where he appears to have felt his feet. Lleyn at that time had not even the dignity of being a village; it is a little inland hamlet out of Caernarvon Bay; Nevin is its principal village; perhaps if the reader should seek out Lleyn, even upon a tolerable map of Caernarvonshire, he will have a difficulty in finding it. It seems to have been a hamlet of the promontory, on a grand coast, surrounded by magnificent hills, or overhanging mountains; we have never visited it, but those who have done so speak of it as possessing the charms of peculiar wildness: on the one side, precipitous ravines, shut in by the sea; on the other, walls of dark mountains,—forming the most complete picture of isolation possible to imagine. Here is said to be the last resting-place of Vortigern, who fled hither to escape the rage of his subjects, excited by his inviting the Saxons to Britain. A curious tradition holds that the mountains are magnetic, and masters of vessels are said to be careful not to approach too near the coast, fearing the effect upon their compasses; this is believed to be the effect of a strong undercurrent setting in all along the coast, dangerous to vessels, and apt to lead them out of their course. Such was Lleyn, the first field of labour on which this melancholy and brooding youth was to exercise his ministry.

Evans had attended the Baptist Association at Maesyberllan in Brecknockshire, in 1790; he was persuaded there to enter upon the ministry in this very obscure district, and he was ordained as a missionary to work among the humble Churches in that vicinity. It does not appear that, in his own neighbourhood, he had as yet attained to any reputation for peculiar power, or that there were any apparent auguries and prognostications of his future usefulness. It is curious to notice, almost so soon as he began his work in this his first distinct field of labour, he appears like a man new made; for this seems to have been the place where the burden of which Bunyan speaks, rolled from this Christian's back; here a new life of faith began to glow in him, and he knew something of what it is to have the "oil of joy for mourning, and the garment of praise instead of the spirit of heaviness." A little success is very encouraging; depreciation is frequently the parent of depression; success is often a fine old strengthening wine; and how often we have had occasion to admire men who have wrought on at life's tasks bravely and cheerfully, although success never came and sat down by their side, to cheer and encourage them; one sometimes wonders what they would have done had their efforts and words received the garland and the crown. Well, perhaps not so much; these things are more wisely ordered than we know. Only this also may be remarked, that, perhaps, the highest order of mind and heart can do almost as well without success as with it,—will behave beautifully if success should come, will behave no less beautifully even if success should never come.

At Lleyn, Christmas Evans tasted the first prelibations of a successful ministry; a wondrous power attended his preaching, numbers were gathered into the Church. "I could scarcely believe," he says, "the testimony of the people who came before the Church as candidates for membership, that they were converted through my ministry; yet I was obliged to believe, though it was marvellous in my eyes. This made me thankful to God, and increased my confidence in prayer; a delightful gale descended upon me as from the hill of the New Jerusalem, and I felt the three great things of the kingdom of heaven, righteousness, and peace, and joy in the Holy Ghost." Indeed, very unusual powers seemed to attend him. He says, "I frequently preached out of doors at nightfall," and the singing, and the praising seem to have touched him very tenderly; he frequently found his congregations bathed in tears and weeping profusely. Preaching was now to him, as he testifies, a very great pleasure,—and no wonder; quite a remarkable revival of religious feeling woke up wherever he went. When he first entered Lleyn, the religious life was very cold and feeble; quite wonderful was the change.

After a time, exhausted with his work in these villages, he accepted an invitation to visit the more remote parts of South Wales. When ministers, like Christmas Evans, are enfeebled in health, they recreate themselves by preaching; the young man was enfeebled, but he started off on his preaching tour; he could not obtain a horse, so he walked the whole way, preaching in every village or town through which he passed. Very frequently large numbers of the same congregation would follow after him the next day, and attend the services fifteen or twenty times, although many miles apart. So he went through the counties of Cardigan, Pembroke, Caernarvon, Glamorgan, Monmouth, and Brecknock, stopping and holding services at the innumerable villages lying on his way. The fame that a wonderful man of God had appeared spread through South Wales on the wings of the wind, and an appointment for Christmas Evans to preach was sufficient to attract thousands to the place. While he yet continued at Lleyn as itinerant missionary, in that short time he had acquired perhaps a greater popularity than any other preacher of that day in Wales.

We have not said that, during the first years of his residence at Lleyn, he married Catherine Jones, a young lady a member of his own Church,—a pious girl, and regarded as in every way suitable for his companion. It will be seen that, so far from diminishing, it seemed rather to increase his ardour; he frequently preached five times during the Sabbath, and walked twenty miles; his heart appeared to be full of love, he spoke as in the strains of a seraph. No wonder that such labour and incessant excitement told upon his health, it was feared even that he might sink into consumption; but surely it was a singular cure suggested for such a disease, to start off on the preaching tour we have described.

At last, however, in an unexpected moment, he became great. It was at one of those wonderful gatherings, an Association meeting, held at Velinvoel, in the immediate neighbourhood of Llanelly. A great concourse of people were assembled in the open air. There was some hitch in the arrangements. Two great men were expected, but still some one or other was wanted to break the ice—to prepare the way. On so short a notice, notwithstanding the abundant preaching power, no one was found willing to take the vacant place. Christmas Evans was there, walking about on the edge of the crowd—a tall, bony, haggard young man, uncouth, and ill-dressed. The master of the ceremonies for the occasion, the pastor of the district, was in an agony of perplexity to find his man,—one who, if not equal to the mightiest, would yet be sufficient for the occasion. In his despair, he went to our old friend, Timothy Thomas; but he, declining for himself, said abruptly, "Why not ask that one-eyed lad from the North? I hear that he preaches quite wonderfully." So the pastor went to him. He instantly consented. Many who were there afterwards expressed the surprise they felt at the communication going on between the pastor and the odd-looking youth. "Surely," they said, "he can never ask that absurdity to preach!" They felt that an egregious mistake was being committed; and some went away to refresh themselves, and others to rest beneath the hedges around, until the great men should come; and others, who stayed, comforted themselves with the assurance that the "one-eyed lad" would have the good sense to be very short. But, for the young preacher, while he was musing, the fire was burning; he was now, for the first time, to front one of those grand Welsh audiences, the sacred *Eisteddfod* of which we have spoken, and to be the preacher of an occasion, which, through all his life after, was to be his constant work. Henceforth there was to be, perhaps, not an Association meeting of his denomination, of which he was not to be the most attractive preacher, the most longed-for and brilliant star.

He took a grand text: "And you, that were sometime alienated and enemies in your mind by wicked works, yet now hath He reconciled, in the body of His flesh, through death, to present you holy, and unblamable, and unreprovable in His sight." Old men used to describe afterwards how he justified their first fears by his stiff, awkward movements; but the organ was, in those first moments, building, and soon it began to play. He showed himself a master of the instrument of speech. Closer and closer the audience began to gather near him. They got up, and came in from the hedges. The crowd grew more and more dense with eager listeners; the sermon became alive with dramatic representation. The throng of preachers present confessed that they were dazzled with the brilliance of the language, and the imagery, falling from the lips of this altogether unknown and unexpected young prophet. Presently, beneath some appalling stroke of words, numbers started to their feet; and in the pauses—if pauses were permitted in the paragraphs—the question went, "Who is this? who have we here?" His words went rocking to and fro; he had caught the "*hwyl*,"—he had also caught the people in it; he went swelling along at full sail. The people began to cry, "*Gogoniant!*" (Glory!) "*Bendigedig!*" (Blessed!) The excitement was at its highest when, amidst the weeping, and rejoicing of the mighty multitude, the preacher came to an end. Drawn together from all parts of Wales to the meeting, when they went their separate ways home they carried the memory of "the one-eyed lad" with them.

Christmas Evans was, from that moment, one of the most famous preachers in the Principality. Lord Byron tells us how he woke up one morning and found himself famous. In those days, a new great Welsh preacher was quite as famous a birth in the little country of Wales as the most famous reputation could be in the literary world of England.

We can conceive it all; for, about thirty-five years since, we were spectators of some such scene. It was far in the depths of the dark mountains beyond

Abersychan, that we were led to a large Welsh service; but it was in a great chapel, and it was on a winter's night. The place was dimly lit with candles. There were, we remember, three preachers. But whilst the first were pursuing their way, or the occasional hymns were being chanted, our companion said to us, "But I want you to hear that little hump-backed man, behind there; he will come next." We could scarcely see the little hump-backed man, but what we saw of him did not predispose our minds to any very favourable impressions, or prophecies of great effects. In due time he came forward. Even as soon as he presented himself, however, there was an evident expectation. The people began more certainly to settle themselves; to crane their necks forward; to smile their loving smile, as upon a well-known friend, who would not disappoint them; and to utter their sighs and grunts of satisfaction. He was as uncouth a piece of humanity as we have ever seen, the little hump-backed man, thin and bony. His iron-grey hair fell over his forehead with no picturesque effect, nor did his eyes seem to give any indication of fire; and there was a shuffling and shambling in his gait, giving no sign of the grace of the orator. But, gradually, as he moved along, and before he had moved far, the whole of that audience was subject to his spell of speech. His hair was thrown back from his forehead; his features were lighted up. Hump-backed! You neither saw it, nor thought of it. His wiry movement seemed informed by dignity and grandeur. First, there came forth audible gaspings, and grunts of approval and pleasure. His very accent, whether you knew his language or not, compelled tears to start to the eyes. Forth came those devout gushings of speech we have mentioned, which, in Wales, are the acclamations which greet a preacher; and, like Christmas Evans with the close of his first grand sermon, the little hump-backed man sat down, victorious over all personal deformity, amidst the weeping and rejoicing of the people. We have always thought of that circumstance as a wonderful illustration of the power of the mind over the body.

Christmas returned to Lleyn, but not to remain there long. The period of his ministry in that neighbourhood was about two years, and during that time the religious spirit of the neighbourhood had been deeply stirred. It is most likely that the immediate cause which led to his removal may be traced to the natural feeling that he was fitted for a much more obvious and extended field of labour. Lleyn was a kind of mission station, its churches were small, they had long been disorganised, and it was not likely that, even if they woke at once into newness of life, they could attain to ideas of liberality and Church order, on which the growth and advance and perpetuity of the Churches could alone be founded; and then it was very likely discovered that the man labouring among them would be demanded for labours very far afield; it is awkward when the gifts of a man make him eminently acceptable to shine and move as an evangelist, and yet he is expected to fill the place, and be as steady in pastoral relations as a pole star!

CHAPTER III.
THE MINISTRY IN THE ISLAND OF ANGLESEA.

Journey to Anglesea—Cildwrn Chapel, and Life in the Cildwrn Cottage—Poverty—Forcing his Way to Knowledge—Anecdote, "I am the Book"—A Dream—The Sandemanian Controversy—Jones of Ramoth—"Altogether Wrong"—The Work in Peril—Thomas Jones of Rhydwilym—Christmas's Restoration to Spiritual Health—Extracts from Personal Reflections—Singular Covenant with God—Renewed Success—The Great Sermon of the Churchyard World—Scenery of its Probable Delivery—Outline of the Sermon—Remarks on the Allegorical Style—Outlines of Another Remarkable Sermon, "The Hind of the Morning"—Great Preaching but Plain Preaching—Hardships of the Welsh Preacher.

In 1792 Christmas Evans left Lleyn. He speaks of a providential intimation conveyed to him from the Island of Anglesea; the providential intimation was a call to serve all the Churches of his order in that island for seventeen pounds a year! and for the twenty years during which he performed this service, he never asked for more. He was twenty-six years of age when he set forth, on his birthday, Christmas Day, for his new and enlarged world of work. He travelled like an Apostle,—and surely he travelled in an apostolic spirit,—he was unencumbered with this world's goods. It was a very rough day of frost and snow,

"The way was long, the wind was cold."

He travelled on horseback, with his wife behind him; and he arrived on the evening of the same day at Llangefni. On his arrival in Anglesea he found ten small Baptist Societies, lukewarm and faint; what amount of life there was in them was spent in the distraction of theological controversy, which just then appeared to rage, strong and high, among the Baptists in North Wales. He was the only minister amongst those Churches, and he had not a brother minister to aid him within a hundred and fifty miles; but he commenced his labours in real earnest, and one of his first movements was to appoint a day of fasting and prayer in all the preaching places; he soon had the satisfaction to find a great revival, and it may with truth be said "the pleasure of the Lord prospered in his hand."

Llangefni appears to have been the spot in Anglesea where Christmas found his home. Llangefni is a respectable town now; when the preaching apostle arrived there, near a hundred years since, its few scattered houses did not even rise to the dignity of a village. Cildwrn Chapel was here the place of his ministrations, and here stood the little cottage where Christmas and his wife passed their plain and simple days. Chapel and cottage stood upon a bleak and exposed piece of ground. The cottage has been reconstructed since those days, but upon the site of the queer and quaint old manse stands now a far more commodious chapel-keeper's house. As in the Bedford vestry they show you still the chair in which John Bunyan sat, so here they show a venerable old chair, Christmas Evans's chair, in the old Cildwrn cottage; it is deeply and curiously marked by the cuttings of his pocket-knife, made when he was indulging in those reveries and daydreams in which he lived abstracted from everything around him.

The glimpses of life we obtain from this old Cildwrn cottage do not incline us to speak in terms of very high eulogy of the Voluntary principle, as developed in Anglesea in that day; from the description, it must have been a very poor shanty, or windy shieling; it is really almost incredible to think of such a man in such a home. The stable for the horse or pony was a part of the establishment, or but very slightly separated from it; the furniture was very poor and scanty: a bed will sometimes compensate for the deprivations and toils of the day when the wearied limbs are stretched upon it, but Christmas Evans could not, as James Montgomery has it, "Stretch the tired limbs, and lay the head, upon his own delightful bed;" for, one of his biographers says, the article on which the inmates, for some time after their settlement, rested at night, could be designated a bed only by courtesy; some of the boards having given way, a few stone slabs did some necessary service. The door by which the preacher and his wife entered the cottage was rotted away, and the economical congregation saved the expense of a new door by nailing a tin plate across the bottom; the roof was so low that the master of the house, when he stood up, had to exercise more than his usual forethought and precaution.

Here, then, was the study, the furnace, forge, and anvil whence were wrought out those noble ideas, images, words, which made Christmas Evans a household name throughout the entire Principality. Here he, and his Catherine, passed their days in a life of perfect naturalness—somewhat too natural, thinks the reader—and elevated piety. Which of us, who write, or read these pages, will dare to visit them with the indignity of our pity? Small as his means were, he looks very happy, with his pleasant, bright, affectionate, helpful and useful wife; he grew in the love and honour of the people; and to his great pulpit eminence, and his simple daily life, have been applied, not unnaturally, the fine words of Wordsworth—

> "So did he travel on life's common way
> In cheerful lowliness; and yet his heart
> The mightiest duties on itself did lay."

And there was a period in Wordsworth's life, before place, and fame, and prosperity came to him, when the little cottage near the Wishing Gate, in Grasmere, was not many steps above that of the Cildwrn cottage of Christmas Evans. The dear man did not care about his poverty,—he appears never either to have attempted to conceal it, nor to grumble at it; and one of his biographers applies to him the pleasant words of Jean Paul Richter, "The pain of poverty was to him only as the piercing of a maiden's ear, and jewels were hung in the wound."

It was, no doubt, a very rough life, but he appears to have attained to the high degree of the Apostle,—"having food and raiment, let us be therewith content;" and he was caught up, and absorbed in his work: sermons, and material for sermons, were always preparing in his mind; he lived to preach, to exercise that bardic power of his. That poor room was the study; he had no separate room to which to retire, where, in solitude, he could stir, or stride the steeds of thought or passion.

During those years, in that poor Cildwrn room, he mastered some ways of scholarship, the mention of which may, perhaps, surprise some of our readers. He made himself a fair Hebraist; no wonder at that, he must have found the language, to him, a very congenial tongue; we take it that, anyhow, the average Welshman will much more readily grapple with the difficulties of Hebrew than the average Englishman. Then he became so good a Grecian, that once, in a bookseller's shop, upon his making some remarks on Homer in the presence of a clergyman, a University man, which drew forth expressions of contempt, Christmas put on his classical panoply, and so addressed himself to the shallow scholar, that he was compelled, by the pressure of engagements, to beat a surprisingly quick retreat.

Very likely the slender accoutrements of his library would create a sneer upon the lips of most of the scholars of the modern pulpit: his lexicons did not rise above Parkhurst,—and *we* will be bold to express gratitude to that forgotten and disregarded old scholar, too; Owen supplied him with the bones of theological thought, the framework of his systematic theology; and whatever readers may think of his taste, Dr. Gill largely drew upon his admiration and sympathy, in the method of his exposition. But, when all was said and done, he was the Vulcan himself, who wrought the splendid fancies of the Achilles' shield,—say, rather, of the shield of Faith; he did not disdain books, but books with him were few, and his mind, experience, and observation were large.

A little while ago, we heard a good story. A London minister of considerable notoriety, never in any danger of being charged with a too lowly estimate of himself, or his powers, was called to preach an anniversary sermon, on a week evening, some distance from London. Arrived at the house of the brother minister, for whom he had undertaken the service, before it commenced, he requested to be shown into the study, in which he might spend some little time in preparation: the minister went up with him.

"So!" said the London Doctor, as he entered, and gazed around, "this is the place where all the mischief is done; this is your furnace, this is the spot from whence the glowing thoughts, and sparks emanate!"

"Yes," said his host, "I come up here to think, and prepare, and be quiet; one cannot study so well in the family."

The Doctor strode up and down the room, glancing round the walls, lined with such few books as the modest means of a humble minister might be supposed to procure.

"Ah!" said the Doctor, "and these are the books, the alimentary canals which absorb the pabulum from whence you reinvigorate the stores of thought, and rekindle refrigerated feeling."

"Yes, Doctor," said the good man, "these are my books; I have not got many, you see, for I am not a rich London minister, but only a poor country pastor; you have a large library, Doctor?"

The great man stood still; he threw a half-indignant and half-benignant glance upon his humble brother, and he said, "*I* have no library, *I* do not want books, *I* am *the* Book!"

Christmas Evans, so far as he could command the means,—but they were very few,—was a voracious reader; and most of the things he read were welded into material for the imagination; but much more truly might he have said, than the awful London dignitary and Doctor, "I have no books, I am the book." His modesty would have prevented him from ever saying the last; but it was nevertheless eminently and especially true, he *was* the book. There was a good deal in him of the self-contained, self-evolving character; and it is significant of this, that, while probably he knew little, or nothing, of our great English classical essayists, John Foster and his Essays were especially beloved by him; far asunder as were their spheres, and widely different their more obvious and manifested life, there was much exceedingly alike in the structure of their mental characters.

We have already alluded to the dream-life of Christmas Evans; we should say, that if dreams come from the multitude of business, the daily occupation, the ordinary life he lived was well calculated to foster in him the life of dreams. Here is one,—a strange piece, which shows the mind in which he lived:—"I found myself at the gate of hell, and, standing at the threshold, I saw an opening, beneath I which was a vast sea of fire, in wave-like motion. Looking at it, I said, 'What infinite virtue there must have been in the blood of Christ to have quenched, for His people, these awful flames!' Overcome with the feeling, I knelt down by the walls of hell, saying, 'Thanks be unto Thee, O great and blessed Saviour, that Thou hast dried up this terrible sea of fire!' Whereupon Christ addressed me: 'Come this way, and I will show you how it was done.' Looking back, I beheld that the whole sea had disappeared. Jesus passed over the place, and said: 'Come, follow Me.' By this time, I was within what I thought were the gates of hell, where there were many cells, out of which it was impossible to escape. I found myself within one of these, and anxious to make my way out. Still I felt wonderfully calm, as I had only just been conversing with Jesus, and because He had gone before me, although I had now lost sight of Him. I got hold of something, with which I struck the corner of the place in which I stood, saying, 'In the name of Jesus, open!' and it instantly gave way; so I did with all the enclosures, until I made my way out into the open field. Whom should I see there but brethren, none of whom, however, I knew, except a good old deacon, and their work was to attend to a nursery of trees; I joined them, and laid hold of a tree, saying, 'In the name of Jesus, be thou plucked up by the root!' And it came up as if it had been a rush. Hence I went forth, as I fancied, to work miracles, saying, 'Now I know how the Apostles wrought miracles in the name of Christ!'"

It was during the earlier period of Christmas Evans's ministry at Anglesea, that a great irruption took place in the island, and, indeed, throughout the Principality; and the Sandemanian controversy shook the Churches, and especially the Baptist Churches, almost beyond all credibility, and certainly beyond what would have been a possibility, but for the singular power of the chief leader, John Richard Jones, of Ramoth. Christmas Evans himself fell for some time beneath the power of Sandemanian notions. Our readers, perhaps, know enough of this peculiar form of faith and practice, to be aware that the worst thing that can be said of it is, that it is a religious ice-plant, religion in an ice-house,—a form chiefly remarkable for its rigid ritualistic conservation of what are regarded as the primitive forms of apostolic times, conjoined to a separation from, and a severe and cynical reprobation of, all other Christian sects.

Christmas Evans says of himself at this period: "The Sandemanian heresy affected me so far as to quench the spirit of prayer for the conversion of sinners, and it induced in my mind a greater regard for the smaller things of the kingdom of heaven, than for the greater. I lost the strength which clothed my mind with zeal, confidence, and earnestness in the pulpit for the conversion of souls to Christ. My heart retrograded, in a manner, and I could not realize the testimony of a good conscience. Sabbath nights, after having been in the day exposing and vilifying, with all bitterness, the errors that prevailed, my conscience felt as if displeased, and reproached me that I had lost nearness to, and walking with, God. It would intimate that something exceedingly precious was now wanting in me; I would reply, that I was acting in obedience to the Word; but it continued to accuse me of the want of some precious article. I had been robbed, to a great degree, of the spirit of prayer, and of the spirit of preaching."

And the man who headed and gave effect to this Sandemanian movement, which was regarded as a mighty reform movement, was Jones of Ramoth. No doubt a real and genuine character enough, a magnificent orator, a master of bitter wit, and vigorous declamation. That is a keen saying with which Richard Hooker commences his "Ecclesiastical Polity:" "He that goeth about to persuade a multitude, that they are not so well governed as they ought to be, shall never want attentive and favourable hearers; because they know the manifold defects whereunto every kind of regiment is subject; but the secret lets and difficulties, which in public proceedings are innumerable and inevitable, they have not ordinarily the judgment to consider." This seems to have been the work, and this the effect, of John Richard Jones: very much the sum and substance of his preaching grew to be a morbid horror of the entire religious world, and a supreme contempt— one of his memorialists says, a superb contempt—for all preachers except himself, especially for all itinerant preachers. In fact, Ramoth Jones's influence in Anglesea might well be described in George MacDonald's song, "The Waesome Carl:"—

> "Ye're a' wrang, and a' wrang,
> And a'thegither a' wrang;
> There's no a man aboot the toon
> But's a'thegither a' wrang.
>
> "The minister wasna fit to pray,
>   And let alane to preach;
> He nowther had the gift o' grace,
>   Nor yet the gift o' speech.
>
> "He mind't him o' Balaam's ass,
>   Wi' a differ ye may ken:
> The Lord He opened the ass's mou',
>   The minister opened's ain.
>
> "Ye're a' wrang, and a' wrang,
> And a'thegither a' wrang;

> There's no a man aboot the toon
> But's a'thegither a' wrang."

Compared with the slender following of the Sandemanian schism now,—for we believe it has but six congregations in the whole United Kingdom,—it seems strange to know that it laid so wonderful a hold upon the island of Anglesea. It did, however; and that it did was evidently owing to the strong man whose name we have mentioned. He was a self-formed man, but he was a man, if not of large scholarship, of full acquaintance with Latin, Greek, and Hebrew; he was a skilful musician; he understood the English language well, but of the Welsh he was a great master. But his intelligence, we should think, was dry and hard; his sentiments were couched in bitter sarcasm: "If," said he, "every Bible in the world were consumed, and every word of Scripture erased from my memory, I need be at no loss how to live a religious life, according to the will of God, for I should simply have to proceed in all respects in a way perfectly contrary to the popular religionists of this age, and then I could not possibly be wrong." He was very arrogant and authoritative in tone and manner, supercilious himself, and expecting the subordination of others. He was so bitter and narrow, that one naturally supposes that some injustice had embittered him. Some of his words have a noble ring. But he encouraged a spirit far other than a charitable one wherever his word extended; and it has been not unnaturally said, that the spread of this Sandemanian narrowness in Anglesea, realized something of the old Scotch absurdity of having two Churches in the same cottage, consisting of Janet in one apartment, and Sandy in the other; or of that other famed Scottish Church, which had dwindled down to two members, old Dame Christie, and Donald, but which seemed at last likely to dwindle yet farther into one, as Christie said she had "sair doubts o' Donald."

The work of Christmas Evans, so far successful, seemed likely to be undone; all the Churches seemed inoculated by these new and narrow notions, and Christmas Evans himself appears, as we have seen, to have been not altogether unscathed. There is something so plausible in this purism of pride; and many such a creed of pessimism is the outgrowth of indifference born, and nurtured, upon decaying faith,—a faith which, perhaps, as in the instance of Ramoth Jones and his Sandemanian teachers, continued true to Christ, so far as that is compatible with utter indifference to humanity at large, and an utter separation from the larger view of the Communion of Saints.

There was, however, a grand man, who stood firm while ministers and Churches around him were reeling, Thomas Jones, of Glynceiriog, in Denbighshire; he is said to have been the one and only minister, at all known to the public, who remained in his own denomination firm, and, successfully in his own spirit, withstood, and even conquered, in this storm of new opinion. And this Thomas Jones did not stand like an insensible stone or rock, but like a living oak, braving the blasts of veering opinion. Most men think in crowds,—which is only to say they are the victims of thoughtless plausibilities. This Thomas Jones appears to have known what he believed; he was eminent for his politeness, and greatly deferential in his bearing; but with all this, his courtesy was the courtesy of the branch which bows, but retains its place. He was a man of marvellous memory, and Christmas Evans used to say of him, that wherever Thomas Jones was, no Concordance would be necessary. He was a great master in the study of Edwards "On the Freedom of the Will," and his method of reading the book was characteristic; he would first seize a proposition, then close the book, and close his eyes, and turn the proposition round and round that it might be undisturbed by anything inside the treatise, or outside of it, and in this way he would proceed with the rigorous demonstration. He was a calm and dignified knight in the tournament of discussion; and, before his lance, more vehement but less trained thinkers and theologians went down.

Thus it was that he preached a great Association sermon at Llangevni, in 1802, which dealt the Sandemanian schism a fatal blow; the captivity beneath the spell of the influence of Ramoth Jones was broken, and turned as streams in the south. While the sermon was being preached, Christmas Evans said, "This Thomas Jones is a monster of a man!" Then the great revival sprang up,—the ice reign was over; but shortly after, he was called away to Rhydwilym, in Caermarthenshire. Young as he was, when John Elias heard of his departure, he said, "The light of the north is removed." He died full of years, full of honours, full of love; closing a life, says one, of quiet beauty, which perhaps has never been surpassed, at Rhydwilym, in 1850.

This irruption of Sandemanian thought, as we have said and seen, affected the spiritual life and earnest usefulness of Christmas Evans. It is well we should place this passing flower upon the memory of Jones of Rhydwilym, for he, it seems, broke the spell and dissolved the enchantment, and bade, in the heart of Christmas Evans, the imprisoned waters once more to flow forth warm, and rejoicing, in the life and enthusiasm of love. May we not say, in passing, that some such spell, if not beneath the same denomination of opinion, holds many hearts in bondage among the Churches in our time?

The joy which Christmas Evans felt in his deliverance, realizes something of the warm words of the poet of the *Messiah*—

> "The swain in barren deserts, with surprise
> Sees lilies spring, and sudden verdure rise;
> And starts, amidst the thirsty wilds, to hear
> New falls of water murmuring in his ear."

"I was weary," he says, referring to this period, "of a cold heart towards Christ, and His sacrifice, and the work of His Spirit—of a cold heart in the pulpit, in secret prayer, and in the study. For fifteen years previously, I had felt my heart burning within, as if going to Emmaus with Jesus. On a day ever to be remembered by me, as I was going from Dolgelly to Machynlleth, and climbing up towards Cadair Idris, I considered it to be incumbent upon me to pray, however hard I felt in my heart, and however worldly the frame of my spirit was. Having begun in the name of Jesus, I soon felt, as it were, the fetters loosening, and the old hardness of heart softening, and, as I thought, mountains of frost and snow dissolving and melting within me. This engendered confidence in my soul in the promise of the Holy Ghost. I felt my whole mind relieved from some great bondage; tears flowed copiously, and I was constrained to cry out for the gracious visits of God, by restoring to my soul the joys of His salvation; and that He would visit the Churches in Anglesea that were under my care. I embraced in my supplications all the Churches of the saints, and nearly all the ministers in the Principality by their names. This struggle lasted for three hours; it rose again and again, like one wave after another, or a high flowing tide, driven by a strong wind, until my nature became faint by weeping and crying. Thus I resigned myself to Christ, body and soul, gifts and labours—all my life—every day, and every hour that remained for me; and all my cares I committed to Christ. The road was mountainous and lonely, and I was wholly alone, and suffered no interruption in my wrestlings with God.

"From this time, I was made to expect the goodness of God to Churches, and to myself. Thus the Lord delivered me and the people of Anglesea from being carried away by the flood of Sandemanianism. In the first religious meetings after this, I felt as if I had been removed from the cold and sterile regions of spiritual frost, into the verdant fields of Divine promises. The former striving with God in prayer, and the longing anxiety for the conversion of sinners, which I had experienced at Lëyn, were now restored. I had a hold of the promises of God. The result was, when I returned home, the first thing that arrested my attention was, that the Spirit was working also in the brethren in Anglesea, inducing in them a spirit of prayer, especially in two of the deacons, who were particularly importunate that God would visit us in mercy, and render the Word of His grace effectual amongst us for the conversion of sinners."

And to about this time belongs a most interesting article, preserved among his papers, "a solemn covenant with God," made, he says, "under a deep sense of the evil of his own heart, and in dependence upon the infinite grace and merit of the Redeemer." It is a fine illustration of the spirit and faith of the man in his lonely communions among the mountains.

Covenant with God.

I. I give my soul and body unto Thee, Jesus, the true God, and everlasting life; deliver me from sin, and from eternal death, and bring me into life everlasting. Amen.—C. E.

II. I call the day, the sun, the earth, the trees, the stones, the bed, the table, and the books, to witness that I come unto Thee, Redeemer of sinners, that I may obtain rest for my soul from the thunders of guilt and the dread of eternity. Amen.—C. E.

III. I do, through confidence in Thy power, earnestly entreat Thee to take the work into Thine own hand, and give me a circumcised heart, that I may love Thee; and create in me a right spirit, that I may seek thy glory. Grant me that principle which Thou wilt own in the day of judgment, that I may not then assume pale-facedness, and find myself a hypocrite. Grant me this, for the sake of Thy most precious blood. Amen.—C. E.

IV. I entreat Thee, Jesus, the Son of God, in power grant me, for the sake of Thy agonizing death, a covenant interest in Thy blood which cleanseth; in Thy righteousness, which justifieth; and in Thy redemption, which delivereth. I entreat an interest in Thy blood, for Thy *blood's* sake, and a part in Thee, for Thy Name's sake, which Thou hast given among men. Amen.—C. E.

V. O Jesus Christ, Son of the living God, take, for the sake of Thy cruel death, my time, and strength, and the gifts and talents I possess; which, with a full purpose of heart, I consecrate to Thy glory in the building up of Thy Church in the world, for Thou art worthy of the hearts and talents of all men. Amen.—C. E.

VI. I desire Thee, my great High Priest, to confirm, by Thy power from Thy High Court, my usefulness as a preacher, and my piety as a Christian, as two gardens nigh to each other; that sin may not have place in my heart to becloud my confidence in Thy righteousness, and that I may not be left to any foolish act that may occasion my gifts to wither, and I be rendered useless before my life ends. Keep Thy gracious eye upon me, and watch over me, O my Lord, and my God for ever! Amen.—C. E.

VII. I give myself in a particular manner to Thee, O Jesus Christ the Saviour, to be preserved from the falls into which many stumble, that Thy name (in Thy cause) may not be blasphemed or wounded, that my peace may not be injured, that Thy people may not be grieved, and that Thine enemies may not be hardened. Amen.—C. E.

VIII. I come unto Thee, beseeching Thee to be in covenant with me in my ministry. As Thou didst prosper Bunyan, Vavasor Powell, Howell Harris, Rowlands, and Whitfield, O do Thou prosper me. Whatsoever things are opposed to my prosperity, remove them out of the way. Work in me everything approved of God for the attainment of this. Give me a heart "sick of love" to Thyself, and to the souls of men. Grant that I may experience the power of Thy Word before I deliver it, as Moses felt the power of his own rod, before he saw it on the land and waters of Egypt. Grant this, for the sake of Thine infinitely precious blood, O Jesus, my hope, and my all in all. Amen.—C. E.

IX. Search me now, and lead me into plain paths of judgment. Let me discover in this life what I am before Thee, that I may not find myself of another character when I am shown in the light of the immortal world, and open my eyes in all the brightness of eternity. Wash me in Thy redeeming blood. Amen.—C. E.

X. Grant me strength to depend upon Thee for food and raiment, and to make known my requests. O let Thy care be over me as a covenant-privilege betwixt Thee and myself, and not like a general care to feed the ravens that perish, and clothe the lily that is cast into the oven; but let Thy care be over me as one of Thy family, as one of Thine unworthy brethren. Amen.—C. E.

XI. Grant, O Jesus, and take upon Thyself the preparing of me for death, for Thou art God; there is no need but for Thee to speak the word. If possible, Thy will be done; leave me not long in affliction, nor to die suddenly, without bidding adieu to my brethren, and let me die in their sight, after a short illness. Let all things be ordered against the day of removing from one world to another, that there be no confusion nor disorder, but a quiet discharge in peace. O grant me this, for the sake of Thine agony in the garden. Amen.—C. E.

XII. Grant, O blessed Lord, that nothing may grow and be matured in me to occasion Thee to cast me off from the service of the sanctuary, like the sons of Eli; and for the sake of Thine unbounded merit, let not my days be longer than my usefulness. O let me not be like lumber in a house in the end of my days, in the way of others to work. Amen.— C. E.

XIII. I beseech Thee, O Redeemer, to present these my supplications before the Father; and oh, inscribe them in Thy Book with Thine own immortal pen, while I am writing them with my mortal hand in my book on earth. According to the depths of Thy merit, Thine undiminished grace, and Thy compassion, and Thy manner unto Thy people, O attach Thy Name in Thine Upper Court to these unworthy petitions; and set Thine Amen to them, as I do on my part of the covenant. Amen.—CHRISTMAS EVANS, *Llangevni, Anglesea, April* 10, 18—.

Is not this an amazing document? It is of this time that he further writes:— "I felt a sweet peace and tranquillity of soul, like unto a poor man that had been brought under the protection of the Royal Family, and had an annual settlement for life made upon him; and from whose dwelling painful dread of poverty and want had been for ever banished away." We have heard of God-intoxicated men; and what language can more appropriately describe a covenant-engagement so elevated, so astonishing, and sublime?

Now, apparently strengthened as by a new spirit, with "might in the inner man," he laboured with renewed energy and zeal; and new and singular blessings descended upon his labours. In two years, his ten preaching places in Anglesea were increased to twenty, and six hundred converts were added to the Church under his own immediate care. It seemed as if the wilderness and the solitary place were glad for him, and the desert rejoiced and blossomed as the rose.

Probably, Christmas Evans's name had been scarcely announced, or read, in England, until his great Graveyard Sermon was introduced to a company of friends, by the then celebrated preacher, Dr. Raffles, of Liverpool. As the story has been related, some persons present had affected contempt for Welsh preaching. "Listen to me," said Raffles, "and I will give to you a specimen of Welsh eloquence." Upon those present, the effect was, we suppose, electrical. He was requested to put it in print; and so the sermon became very extensively known, and has been regarded, by many, as the preacher's most astonishing piece.

To what exact period of Evans's history it is to be assigned cannot be very well ascertained, but it is probably nearly sixty years since Raffles first recited it; so that it belongs, beyond a doubt, to the early Anglesea days. It was, most likely, prepared as a great bardic or dramatic chant for some vast Association meeting, and was, no doubt, repeated several times, for it became very famous. It mingles something of the life of an old Mystery Play, or Ober-Ammergau performance; but as to any adequate rendering of it, we apprehend that to be quite impossible. Raffles was a rhetorician, and famous as his version became, the good Doctor knew little or nothing of Welsh, nor was the order of his mind likely very accurately to render either the Welsh picture or the Welsh accent. His periods were too rounded, the language too fine, and the pictures too highly coloured.

It was about the same time that, far away from Anglesea, among the remote, unheard-of German mountains of Baireuth, a dreamer of a very different kind was visited by some such vision of the world, regarded as a great churchyard. Jean Paul Richter's churchyard, visited by the dead Christ, was written in Siebinckas, for the purpose of presenting the misty, starless, cheerless, and spectral outlook of the French atheism, which was then spreading out, noxious and baleful, over Europe.

Very different were the two men, their spheres, and their avocations; overwhelming, solemn, and impressive as is the vision of Jean Paul, it certainly would have said little to a vast Welsh congregation among the dark hills. Christmas Evans's piece is dramatic; his power of impersonation and colloquy in the pulpit was very great; and the reader has to conceive all this, while on these colder pages the scenes and the conversations go on. It appears to have been first preached in a small dell among the mountains of Carnarvonshire. The spot was exquisitely romantic; it was a summer's season, the grass was in its rich green, brooks were purling round, and the spot hemmed in by jagged crags and the cliffs of tall mountains; a beautiful spot, but an Englishman spoke of it as "beauty sleeping on the lap of terror."

A preliminary service, of course, went on,—hymns, the sounding of the slow, plaintive minor melody from thousands of tongues, rising and loitering, and lingering among the neighbouring acclivities, before they finally fade off into silence; then there is reading, and prayer, singing again, and a short sermon before Christmas Evans comes. He has not attained to the full height of his great national fame as yet; he is before the people, however, "the one-eyed man of Anglesea,"—the designation by which he was to be known for many years to come. He stands six feet high, his face very expressive, but very calm and quiet; but a great fire was burning within the man. He gave out some verses of a well-known Welsh hymn, and while it was being sung took out a small phial from his waistcoat-pocket, wetting the tips of his fingers and drawing them over his blind eye; it was laudanum, used to deaden the excruciating pain which upon some occasions possessed him.

He gave out his text from Romans v. 15: "If through the offence of one many be dead, much more the grace of God, and the gift by grace, which is by one man, Jesus Christ, hath abounded unto many." Naturally, he does not begin at once, but spends a little time, in clearly-enunciated words, in announcing two things,—the universal depravity and sinfulness of men, and the sighing after propitiation. *Mene! Tekel!* he says, is written on every human heart; wanting, wanting, is inscribed on heathen fanes and altars, on the laws, customs, and institutions of every nation, and on the universal consciousness of mankind; and bloody sacrifices among pagan nations show the handwriting of remorse upon the conscience,—a sense of guilt, and a dread of punishment, and a fear which hath torment.

As he goes on the people draw nearer, become more intense in their earnest listening; they are rising from their seats, their temporary forms. Some are in carriages; there is a lady leaning on her husband's shoulder, he still sitting, she with outstretched neck gazing with obviously strange emotion at the preacher; some of the people are beginning to weep. There is an old evangelical clergyman who has always preached the Gospel, although laughed at by his squire, and quite unknown by his Bishop; he is rejoicing with a great joy to hear his old loved truths set forth in such a manner; he is weeping profusely.

Christmas Evans, meantime, is pursuing his way, lost in his theme. Now his eye lights up, says one who knew him, like a brilliantly-flashing star, his clear forehead expands, his form dilates in majestic dignity; and all that has gone before will be lost in the white-heat passion with which he prepares to sing of Paradise lost, and Paradise regained. One of his Welsh critics says: "All the stores of his energy, and the resources of his voice, which was one of great compass, depth, and sweetness, seemed reserved for the closing portions of the picture, when he represented the routed and battered hosts of evil retreating from the cross, where they anticipated a triumph, and met a signal, and irretrievable overthrow." Thus prepared, he presented to his hearers the picture of

"THE WORLD AS A GRAVEYARD."

> "Methinks," exclaimed the impassioned preacher, "I find myself standing upon the summit of one of the highest of the everlasting hills, permitted from thence to take a survey of the whole earth; and all before me I see a wide and far-spread burial-ground, a graveyard, over which lie scattered the countless multitudes of the wretched and perishing children of Adam! The ground is full of hollows, the

yawning caverns of death; and over the whole scene broods a thick cloud of darkness: no light from above shines upon it, there is no ray of sun or moon, there is no beam, even of a little candle, seen through all its borders. It is walled all around, but it has gates, large and massive, ten thousand times stronger than all the gates of brass forged among men; they are one and all safely locked,—the hand of Divine Law has locked them; and so firmly secured are the strong bolts, that all the created powers even of the heavenly world, were they to labour to all eternity, could not drive so much as one of them back. How hopeless is the wretchedness to which the race is doomed! into what irrecoverable depths of ruin has sin plunged the people who sit there in darkness, and in the shadow of death, while there, by the brazen gates, stands the inflexible guard, brandishing the flaming sword of undeviating Law!

"But see! In the cool of the day, there is one descending from the eternal hills in the distance: it is Mercy! the radiant form of Mercy, seated in the chariot of Divine Promise. She comes through the worlds of the universe; she pauses here to mark the imprisoned and grave-like aspect of our once fair world; her eye affected her heart as she beheld the misery, and heard the cry of despair, borne upon the four winds of heaven; she could not pass by, nor pass on; she wept over the melancholy scene, and she said, 'Oh that I might enter! I would bind up their wounds, I would relieve their sorrows, I would save their souls!' An embassy of angels, commissioned from Heaven to some other world, paused at the sight; and Heaven forgave that pause. They saw Mercy standing by the gate, and they cried, 'Mercy, canst thou not enter? Canst thou look upon that world and not pity? Canst thou pity and not relieve?' And Mercy, in tears, replied, 'I can see, and I can pity, but I cannot relieve.' 'Why dost thou not enter?' inquired the heavenly host. 'Oh,' said Mercy, 'Law has barred the gate against me, and I must not, and I cannot unbar it.' And Law stood there watching the gate, and the angels asked of him, 'Why wilt thou not suffer Mercy to enter?' And he said, 'No one can enter here and live;' and the thunder of his voice outspoke the wailings within. Then again I heard Mercy cry, 'Is there no entrance for me into this field of death? may I not visit these caverns of the grave; and seek, if it may be, to raise some at least of these children of destruction, and bring them to the light of day? Open, Justice, Open! drive back these iron bolts, and let me in, that I may proclaim the jubilee of redemption to the children of the dust!' And then I heard Justice reply, 'Mercy! surely thou lovest Justice too well to wish to burst these gates by force of arm, and thus to obtain entrance by lawless violence. I cannot open the door: I am not angry with these unhappy, I have no delight in their death, or in hearing their cries, as they lie upon the burning hearth of the great fire, kindled by the wrath of God, in the land that is lower than the grave. But *without shedding of blood there is no remission.*'

"So Mercy expanded her wings, splendid beyond the brightness of the morning when its rays are seen shooting over mountains of pearl,—and Mercy renewed her flight amongst the unfallen worlds; she re-ascended into the mid air, but could not proceed far, because she could not forget the sad sight of the Graveyard-World, the melancholy prison. She returned to her native throne in the Heaven of heavens; it was a glorious high throne, unshaken and untarnished by the fallen fate of man and angels. Even there she could not forget what she had witnessed, and wept over, and she weighed the woes of the sad world against the doom of eternal Law; she could not forget the prison and the graveyard, and she re-descended with a more rapid and radiant flight, and she stood again by the gate, but again was denied admission. And the two stood there together, Justice and Mercy; and Justice dropped his brandishing sword while they held converse together; and while they talked, there was silence in heaven.

"'Is there then no admission on any terms whatever?' she said. 'Ah, yes,' said Justice; 'but then they are terms which no created being can fulfil. I demand atoning death for the Eternal life of those who lie in this Graveyard; I demand Divine life for their ransom.' And while they were talking, behold there stood by them a third Form, fairer than the children of men, radiant with the glory of heaven. He cast a look upon the graveyard. And He said to Mercy, 'Accept the terms.' 'Where is the security?' said Justice. 'Here,' said Mercy, pointing to the radiant Stranger, 'is my bond. Four thousand years from hence, demand its payment on Calvary. To redeem men,' said Mercy, 'I will be incarnate in the Son of God, I will be the Lamb slain for the life of this Graveyard World.'

"The bond was accepted, and Mercy entered the graveyard leaning on the arm of Justice. She spoke to the prisoners. Centuries rolled by. So went on the gathering of the firstfruits in the field of redemption. Still ages passed away, and at last the clock of prophecy struck the fulness of time. The bond, which had been committed to patriarchs and prophets, had to be redeemed; a long series of rites and ceremonies, sacrifices and oblations, had been instituted to perpetuate the memory of that solemn deed.

"At the close of the four thousandth year, when Daniel's seventy weeks were accomplished, Justice and Mercy appeared on the hill of Calvary; angels and archangels, cherubim and seraphim, principalities and powers, left their thrones and mansions of glory, and bent over the battlements of heaven, gazing in mute amazement and breathless suspense upon the solemn scene. At the foot of Calvary's hill was beheld the Son of God. 'Lo, I come,' He said; 'in the bond it is written of me.' He appeared without the gates of Jerusalem, crowned with thorns, and followed by the weeping Church. It was with Him the hour and the power of darkness; above Him were all the vials of Divine wrath, and the thunders of the eternal Law; round Him were all the powers of darkness,—the monsters of the pit, huge, fierce and relentless, were there; the lions as a great army, gnashing their teeth ready to tear him in pieces; the unicorns, a countless host, were rushing onwards to thrust him through; and there were the bulls of Bashan roaring terribly; the dragons of the pit unfolding themselves, and shooting out their stings; and dogs, many, all round the mountain.

"And He passed through this dense array, an unresisting victim led as a lamb to the slaughter. He took the bond from the hand of Justice, and, as He was nailed to the cross, He nailed it to the cross; and all the hosts of hell, though invisible to man, had formed a ring around it. The rocks rent, the sun shrank from the scene, as Justice lifted his right hand to the throne, exclaiming, 'Fires of heaven, descend and consume this sacrifice!' The fires of heaven, animated with living spirit, answered the call, 'We come! we come! and, when we have consumed that victim, we will burn the world.' They burst, blazed, devoured; the blood of the victim was fast dropping; the hosts of hell were shouting, until the humanity of Emmanuel gave up the ghost. The fire went on burning until the ninth hour of the day, but when it touched the Deity of the Son of God it expired; Justice dropped the fiery sword at the foot of the cross; and the Law joined with the prophets in witnessing to the righteousness which is by faith in the Son of God, for all had heard the dying Redeemer exclaim, 'It is finished!' The weeping Church heard it, and lifting up her head cried too, 'It is finished!' Attending angels hovering near heard it, and, winging their flight, they sang, 'It is finished!' The powers of darkness heard the acclamations of the universe, and hurried away from the scene in death-like feebleness. He triumphed over them openly. The graves of the old Burial-ground have been thrown open, and gales of life have blown over the valley of dry bones, and an exceeding great army has already been sealed to our God as among the living in Zion; for so the Bond was paid and eternal redemption secured."

This was certainly singular preaching; it reads like a leaf or two from Klopstock. We may believe that the enjoyment with which it was heard was rich and great, but we suppose that the taste of our time would regard it as almost intolerable. Still, there are left among us some who can enjoy the *Pilgrim's Progress*, and the *Fairy Queen*, and we do not see how, in the presence of those pieces, a very arrogant exception can be taken to this extraordinary sermon.

A more serious objection, perhaps, will be taken to the nomenclature, the symbolic language in which the preacher expressed his theology. It literally represented the theology of Wales at the time when it was delivered; the theology was stern and awful; the features of God were those of a stern and inflexible Judge; nature presented few relieving lights, and man was not regarded as pleasant to look upon. Let the reader remember all this, and perhaps he will be more tolerant to the stern outline of this allegory; it is pleasant, now, to know that we have changed all that, and that everywhere, and all around us, God, and nature, and man are presented in rose-hued lights, and all conditions of being are washed by rosy and pacific seas; we see nothing stern or awful now, either in nature or in grace, in natural or in supernatural things; Justice has become gentlemanly, and Law, instead of being stern and terrible, is bland, and graceful, and beautiful as a woman's smile!

In Christmas Evans's day, it was not quite so. As to objections to the mode of preaching, as in contrast with that style which adopts only the sustained argument, and the rhetorical climax and relation, we have already said that Christmas must be tried by quite another standard; we have already said that he was a bard among preachers, and belonged to a nation of bards. It was a kind of primeval song, addressed to people of primeval instincts; but, whatever its merits or demerits may be, it fairly represents the man and his preaching. It does not, indeed, reflect the style of the modern mind; but, there are many writers, and readers at present, who are carrying us back to the mediæval times, and the monastic preachers of those ages, and among them we find innumerable pieces of the same order of sustained allegory which we have just quoted from Christmas Evans. What is it but to say, that the simple mind is charmed with pictures,—it must have them; and such sermons as abound in them, have power over it?

We believe we have rendered this singular passage with such fairness that the reader may be enabled to form some idea of its splendour. When it was repeated to Robert Hall, he pronounced it one of the finest allegories in the language. When Christmas Evans was on a visit to Dr. Raffles, the Doctor recited to him his own version, and, apparently with some amazement, said, "Did you actually say all that?" "Oh, yes," said Christmas, "I did say all that, but I could never have put it into such English." And this we are greatly disposed to regard as impairing the bold grandeur and strength of the piece; any rendering of it into English must, as it seems to us, add to its prettiness, and therefore divest it of its power.

Probably to the same period of the preacher's history belongs another sermon, which has always seemed to us a piece of undoubted greatness. It is upon the same subject, the Crucifixion of Christ. We should think that its delivery would, at any time, from such lips as his, produce equally pathetic emotions. The allegory is not so sustained, but it is still full of allegorical allusions derived from Scriptural expression.

"THE HIND OF THE MORNING.

> "It is generally admitted that the twenty-second Psalm has particular reference to Christ. This is evident from His own appropriation of the first verse upon the cross: 'My God! my God! why hast Thou forsaken Me?' The title of that Psalm is '*Aijeleth Shahar*,' which signifies 'A Hart, or the Hind of the Morning.' The striking metaphors which it contains are descriptive of Messiah's peculiar sufferings. He is the Hart, or the Hind of the Morning, hunted by the Black Prince, with his hell-hounds—by Satan, and all his allies. The 'dogs,' the 'lions,' the 'unicorns,' and

the 'strong bulls of Bashan,' with their devouring teeth, and their terrible horns, pursued Him from Bethlehem to Calvary. They beset Him in the manger, gnashed upon Him in the garden, and well-nigh tore Him to pieces upon the cross. And still they persecute Him in His cause, and in the persons and interests of His people.

"The faith of the Church anticipated the coming of Christ, 'like a roe or a young hart,' with the dawn of the day promised in Eden; and we hear her exclaiming in the Canticles—'The voice of my beloved! behold, He cometh, leaping upon the mountains, and skipping upon the hills!' She heard Him announce His advent in the promise, 'Lo, I come to do Thy will, O God!' and with prophetic eye, saw Him leaping from the mountains of eternity to the mountains of time, and skipping from hill to hill throughout the land of Palestine, going about doing good. In the various types and shadows of the law, she beheld Him 'standing by the wall, looking forth at the windows, showing Himself through the lattice;' and then she sang—'Until the day break and the shadows flee away, turn, my beloved, and be thou like the roe or the young hart upon the mountains of Bether!' Bloody sacrifices revealed Him to her view, going down to the 'vineyards of red wine;' whence she traced Him to the meadows of Gospel ordinances, where 'He feedeth among the lilies'—to 'the gardens of cucumbers,' and 'the beds of spices;' and then she sang to Him again—'Make haste'—or, flee away—'my beloved! be thou like the roe or the young hart among the mountains of spices.'

"Thus she longed to see Him, first 'on the mountain of Bether,' and then 'on the mountain of spices.' On both mountains she saw Him eighteen hundred years ago, and on both she may still trace the footsteps of His majesty, and His mercy. The former, He hath tracked with His own blood, and His path upon the latter is redolent of frankincense and myrrh.

"Bether signifies division. This is the craggy mountain of Calvary; whither the 'Hind of the Morning' fled, followed by all the wild beasts of the forest, and the bloodhounds of hell; summoned to the pursuit, and urged on, by the prince of perdition; till the victim, in His agony, sweat great drops of blood—where He was terribly crushed between the cliffs, and dreadfully mangled by sharp and ragged rocks—where He was seized by Death, the great Bloodhound of the bottomless pit—whence He leaped the precipice, without breaking a bone; and sunk in the dead sea, sunk to its utmost depth, and saw no corruption.

"Behold the 'Hind of the Morning' on that dreadful mountain! It is the place of skulls, where Death holds his carnival in companionship with worms, and hell laughs in the face of heaven. Dark storms are gathering there—convolving clouds, charged with no common wrath. Terrors set themselves in battle-array before the Son of God; and tempests burst upon Him which might sweep all mankind in a moment to eternal ruin. Hark! hear ye not the subterranean thunder? Feel ye not the tremor of the mountain? It is the shock of Satan's artillery, playing upon the Captain of our Salvation. It is the explosion of the magazine of vengeance. Lo, the earth is quaking, the rocks are rending, the graves are opening, the dead are rising, and all nature stands aghast at the conflict of Divine mercy with the powers of darkness. One dread convulsion more, one cry of desperate agony, and Jesus dies—an arrow has entered into His heart. Now leap the lions, roaring, upon their prey; and the bulls of Bashan are bellowing; and the dogs of perdition are barking; and the unicorns toss their horns on high; and the devil, dancing with exultant joy, clanks his iron chains, and thrusts up his fettered hands in defiance towards the face of Jehovah!

"Go a little farther upon the mountain, and you come to 'a new tomb hewn out of the rock.' There lies a dead body. It is the body of Jesus. His disciples have laid it down in sorrow, and returned, weeping, to the city. Mary's heart is broken, Peter's zeal is quenched in tears, and John would fain lie down and die in his Master's grave. The sepulchre is closed up, and sealed, and a Roman sentry placed at its entrance. On the morning of the third day, while it is yet dark, two or three women come to anoint the body. They are debating about the great stone at the mouth of the cave. 'Who shall roll it away?' says one of them. 'Pity we did not bring Peter, or John with us.' But, arriving, they find the stone already rolled away, and one sitting upon it, whose countenance is like lightning, and whose garments are white as the light. The steel-clad, iron-hearted soldiers lie around him, like men slain in battle, having swooned with terror. He speaks: 'Why seek ye the living among the dead? He is not here; He is risen; He is gone forth from this cave victoriously.'

"It is even so! For there are the shroud, and the napkin, and the heavenly watchers; and when He awoke, and cast off His grave-clothes, the earthquake was felt in the city, and jarred the gates of hell. 'The Hind of the Morning' is up earlier than any of His pursuers, 'leaping upon the mountains, and skipping upon the hills.' He is seen first with Mary at the tomb; then with the disciples in Jerusalem; then with two of them on the way to Emmaus; then going before His brethren into Galilee; and, finally, leaping upon the top of Olivet to the hills of Paradise; fleeing away to 'the mountain of spices,' where He shall never more be hunted by the Black Prince and his hounds.

"Christ is perfect master of gravitation, and all the laws of nature are obedient to His will. Once He walked upon the water, as if it were marble beneath His feet; and now, as He stands blessing His people, the glorious Form, so recently nailed to the cross, and still more recently cold in the grave, begins to ascend like 'the living creature' in Ezekiel's vision, 'lifted up from the earth,' till nearly out of sight; when 'the chariots of God, even thousands of angels,' receive Him, and haste to the celestial city, waking the thrones of eternity with this jubilant chorus—'Lift up your heads, O ye gates! and be ye lifted up, ye everlasting doors! and the King of glory shall come in!'

"Christ might have rode in a chariot of fire all the way from Bethlehem to Calvary; but he preferred riding in a chariot of mercy, whose lining was crimson, and whose ornament the malefactor's cross. How rapidly rolled his wheels over the hills and the plains of Palestine, gathering up everywhere the children of affliction, and scattering blessings like the beams of the morning! Now we find Him in Cana of Galilee, turning water into wine; then treading the waves of the sea, and hushing the roar of the tempest; then delivering the demoniac of Gadara from the fury of a legion of fiends; then healing the nobleman's son at Capernaum; raising the daughter of Jairus, and the young man of Nain; writing upon the grave of Bethany, 'I am the resurrection and the life;' curing the invalid at the pool of Bethesda; feeding the five thousand in the wilderness; preaching to the woman by Jacob's well, acquitting the adulteress, and shaming her accusers; and exercising everywhere, in all his travels, the three offices of Physician, Prophet, and Saviour, as he drove on towards the place of skulls.

"Now we see the chariot surrounded with enemies—Herod, and Pilate, and Caiaphas, and the Roman soldiers, and the populace of Jerusalem, and thousands of Jews who have come up to keep the Passover, led on by Judas and the devil. See how they rage and curse, as if they would tear him from his chariot of mercy! But Jesus maintains his seat, and holds fast the reins, and drives right on through the angry crowd, without shooting an arrow, or lifting a spear upon his foes. For in that chariot the King must ride to Calvary—Calvary must be consecrated to mercy for ever. He sees the cross planted upon the brow of the hill, and hastens forward to embrace it. No sacrifice shall be offered to Justice on this day, but the one sacrifice which reconciles heaven and earth. None of these children of Belial shall suffer to-day. The bribed witnesses, and clamorous murderers, shall be spared—the smiters, the scourgers, the spitters, the thorn-plaiters, the nail drivers, the head-shakers—for Jesus pleads on their behalf: 'Father, forgive them! they know not what they do. They are ignorant of Thy grace and truth. They are not aware of whom they are crucifying. Oh, spare them! Let Death know that he shall have enough to do with *me* to-day! Let him open all his batteries upon *me*! *My* bosom is bare to the stroke. *I* will gather all the lances of hell in *my* heart!'

"Still the chariot rushes on, and 'fiery darts' are thick and fast, like a shower of meteors, on Messiah's head, till He is covered with wounds, and the blood flows down His garments, and leaves a crimson track behind Him. As He passes, He casts at the dying malefactor a glance of benignity, and throws him a passport into Paradise, written with His own blood; stretches forth His sceptre, and touches the prison-door of death, and many of the prisoners came forth, and the tyrant shall never regain his dominion over them; rides triumphant over thrones and principalities, and crushes beneath his wheels the last enemy himself, and leaves the memorial of his march engraven on the rocks of Golgotha!

"Christ is everywhere in the Scriptures spoken of as a Blessing; and whether we contemplate His advent, His ministry, His miracles, His agony, His crucifixion, His interment, His resurrection, or His ascension, we may truly say, 'All His paths drop fatness.' All His travels were on the road of mercy; and trees are growing up in His footsteps, whose fruit is delicious food, and 'whose leaves are for the healing of the nations.' He walketh upon the south winds, causing propitious gales to blow upon the wilderness till songs of joy awake in the solitary place, and the desert blossoms as the rose.

"If we will consider what the prophets wrote of the Messiah, in connection with the evangelical history, we shall be satisfied that none like Him, either before or since, ever entered our world, or departed from it. Both God and man—at once the Father of eternity and the Son of time, He filled the universe, while He was embodied upon earth, and ruled the celestial principalities and powers, while He wandered, a persecuted stranger, in Judea. 'No man,' saith He, 'hath ascended up to heaven, but He that came down from heaven, even the Son of man who is in heaven.'

"Heaven was no strange place to Jesus. He talks of the mansions in His Father's house as familiarly as one of the royal family would talk of Windsor Castle where he was born; and saith to His disciples, 'I go to prepare a place for you; that where I am there ye may be also.' The glory into which He entered was His own glory—the glory which He had with the Father before the world was. He had an original and supreme right to the celestial mansions; and He acquired a new and additional claim by His office as Mediator. Having suffered for our sins, He 'ought to enter into His glory.' He ought, because He is 'God, blessed for ever;' He ought, because He is the representative of His redeemed people. He has taken possession of the kingdom in our behalf, and left on record for our encouragement this cheering promise, 'To him that overcometh will I grant to sit with me in my throne; even as I also have overcome, and am set down with my Father in His throne.'

"The departure of God from Eden, and the departure of Christ from the earth, were two of the sublimest events that ever occurred, and fraught with immense consequences to our race. When Jehovah went out from Eden, He left a curse upon the place for man's sake, and drove out man before him into an accursed earth. But when Jesus descended from Olivet, He lifted the curse with Him, and left a blessing behind Him—sowed the world with the seed of eternal blessings; 'and instead of the thorn shall come up the fir-tree; and instead of the briar shall come up the myrtle-tree; and it shall be to the Lord for a name, and an everlasting sign, that shall not be cut off.' He ascended to intercede for sinners, and reopen Paradise to His people; and when He shall come the second time, according to the promise, with all His holy angels, then shall we be 'caught up to meet the Lord in the air, and so shall we ever be with the Lord.'

"'The Lord is gone up with a shout!' and has taken our redeemed nature with Him. He is the Head of the Church, and is the representative at the right hand of the Father. 'He hath ascended on high; He hath led captivity captive; He hath received gifts for men; yea, for the rebellious also, that God may dwell among them.' 'Him hath God exalted, with His own right hand, to be a Prince and a Saviour, to give repentance to Israel, and remission of sins.' This is the Father's recognition of His 'Beloved Son,' and significant acceptance of his sacrifice. 'Wherefore God also hath highly exalted Him, and given Him a name which is above every name; that at the name of Jesus every knee should bow, of things in heaven, and things in the earth, and things under the earth; and that every tongue should confess that Jesus Christ is Lord, to the glory of God the Father.'

"The evidence of our Lord's ascension is ample. He ascended in the presence of many witnesses, who stood gazing after Him till a cloud received Him out of their sight. And while they looked steadfastly toward heaven, two angels appeared to them, and talked with them of what they had seen. Soon afterward, on the day of Pentecost, He fulfilled, in a remarkable manner, the promise which He had made to His people: 'If I go away I will send you another Comforter, who shall abide with you for ever.' Stephen, the first of His disciples that glorified the Master by martyrdom, testified to his murderers, 'Lo, I see the heavens opened, and the Son of man standing on the right hand of God!' And John, the 'beloved disciple,' while an exile 'in Patmos, for the word of God, and the testimony of Jesus

Christ,' beheld Him 'in the midst of the throne, as a Lamb that had been slain!' These are the evidences that our Lord is in heaven; these are our consolations in the house of our pilgrimage.

"The Apostle speaks of the *necessity* of this event, 'Whom the heaven *must* receive.'

"Divine necessity is a golden chain reaching from eternity to eternity, and encircling all the events of time. It consists of many links all hanging upon each other; and not one of them can be broken without destroying the support of the whole. The first link is in God, 'before the world was;' and the last is in heaven, when the world shall be no more. Christ is its Alpha, and Omega, and Christ constitutes all its intervenient links. Christ in the bosom of the Father, receiving the promise of eternal life, before the foundation of the world, is the beginning; Christ in His sacrificial blood, atoning for our sins, and pardoning and sanctifying all them that believe, is the middle; and Christ in heaven, pleading the merit of His vicarious sufferings, making intercession for the transgressors, drawing all men unto Himself, presenting the prayers of His people, and preparing their mansions, is the end.

"There is a necessity in all that Christ has done as our Mediator, in all that He is doing on our behalf, and all that he has engaged to do—the necessity of Divine love manifested, of Divine mercy exercised, of Divine purposes accomplished, of Divine covenants fulfilled, of Divine faithfulness maintained, of Divine justice satisfied, of Divine holiness vindicated, and of Divine power displayed. Christ felt this necessity while He tabernacled among us, often declared it to His disciples, and acknowledged it to the Father in the agony in the Garden.

"Behold Him wrestling in prayer, with strong crying and tears: 'Father, save me from this hour! If it be possible, let this cup pass from me!' Now the Father reads to Him His covenant engagement, which He signed and sealed with His own hand before the foundation of the world. The glorious Sufferer replies, 'Thy will be done! For this cause came I unto this hour. I will drink the cup which Thou hast mingled, and not a dreg of any of its ingredients shall be left for my people. I will pass through the approaching dreadful night, under the hidings of Thy countenance, bearing away the curse from my beloved. Henceforth repentance is hidden from my eyes!' Now, on His knees, He reads the covenant engagements of the Father, and adds, 'I have glorified Thee on the earth. I have finished the work which Thou gavest Me to do. Now glorify Thou Me, according to Thy promise, with Thine own Self, with the glory which I had with Thee before the world was. Father, I will also that they whom Thou hast given Me be with Me where I am, that they may behold My glory. Thine they were, and Thou hast given them to Me, on condition of My pouring out My soul unto death. Thou hast promised them, through My righteousness and meritorious sacrifice, the kingdom of heaven, which I now claim on their behalf. Father, glorify My people, with Him whom Thou lovedst before the foundation of the world!'

"This intercession of Christ for His saints, begun on earth, is continued in heaven. This is our confidence and joy in our journey through the wilderness. We know that our Joshua has gone over into the land of our inheritance, where He is preparing the place of our habitation for Israel; for it is His will that all whom He has redeemed should be with Him for ever!

"And there is a text which speaks of the period when the great purposes of our Lord's ascension shall be fully accomplished: 'Until the times of the restitution of all things.'

"The period here mentioned is 'the dispensation of the fulness of time,' when 'the fulness of the Gentiles shall come in,' and 'the dispersed of Judah' shall be restored, and Christ shall 'gather together in Himself all things in heaven and in earth,' overthrow his enemies, establish his everlasting kingdom, deliver the groaning creation from its bondage, glorify His people with Himself, imprison the devil with his angels in the bottomless pit, and punish with banishment from His presence them that obey not the Gospel.

"To this glorious consummation, the great travail of redemption, and all the events of time, are only preparatory. It was promised in Eden, and the promise was renewed and enlarged to Abraham, to Isaac, and to

Jacob. It was described in gorgeous oriental imagery by Isaiah, and 'the sweet Psalmist of Israel;' and 'spoken of by all the Prophets, since the world began.' Christ came into the world to prepare the way for His future triumph—to lay on Calvary the 'chief corner-stone' of a temple, which shall be completed at the end of time, and endure through all eternity. He began the great restitution. He redeemed His people with a price, and gave them a pledge of redemption by power. He made an end of sin, abolished the Levitical priesthood, and swallowed up all the types and shadows in Himself. He sent home the beasts, overthrew the altars, and quenched the holy fire; and, upon the sanctifying altar of His own divinity, offered His own sinless humanity, which was consumed by fire from heaven. He removed the seat of government from Mount Zion, in Jerusalem, to Mount Zion above, where He sits—'a Priest upon His throne,' drawing heaven and earth together, and establishing 'the covenant of peace between them both.'

"Blessed be God! we can now go to Jesus, the Mediator; passing by millions of angels, and all 'the spirits of just men made perfect;' till we 'come to the blood of sprinkling, which speaketh better things than that of Abel.' And we look for that blessed day, when 'this gospel of the kingdom' shall be universally prevalent; 'and all shall know the Lord, from the least even to the greatest;' when there shall be a 'new heaven, and a new earth, wherein dwelleth righteousness;' when both the political, and the moral aspects of our world shall be changed; and a happier state of things shall exist than has ever been known before,— when the pestilence, the famine, and the sword shall cease to destroy, and 'the saints of the Most High shall possess the kingdom' in 'quietness, and assurance for ever.' Then cometh the end, when Emmanuel 'shall destroy in this mountain the veil of the covering cast over all people, and swallow up death in victory!'"

Such sermons as we have quoted surely convey a living and distinct idea of the kind of power which made the man remarkable. It is, from every aspect, very unlike the preaching to which we are now accustomed, and which, therefore, finds general favour with us; it is dogmatic in the last degree; nothing in it is tentative, or hypothetical, yet the dogmatism is not that of a schoolman, or a casuist; it is the dogmatism of burning conviction, of a profound and unquestioning faith in the veracity of New Testament truth, and the corresponding light and illustration from the Old. In these sermons, and others we shall place before our readers, there is nothing pretty, no nice metaphysical or critical analysis, no attempt to carve giants' heads on cherry-stones. He realized his office as a preacher, not as one set apart to minister to intellectual luxury, or vanity, but to stand, announcing eternal truth. The people to whom he spoke were not *dilettantic*, he was no *dilettante*. We can quite conceive,—and therefore these remarks,—that the greater number even of the more eminent men in our modern pulpit will regard the style of Christmas Evans with contempt. We are only setting it forth in these pages. Evidently it told marvellously on the Principality; it "searched Jerusalem with candles;" those who despise it had better settle the question with Christmas Evans himself, and show the superiority of their method by their larger ministerial usefulness.

The worth and value of great preaching and great sermons must depend upon the measure to which they represent the preacher's own familiarity with the truths he touches, and proclaims. The history of the mind of Christmas Evans is, from this point of view, very interesting. We can only get at it from the papers found after his death; but they reveal the story of the life, walk, and triumph of faith in his mind and heart. He kept no journal; but still we have the record of his communions with God amongst the mountains,—acts of consecration to God quite remarkable, which he had thought it well to commit to paper, that he might remind himself of the engagements he had made. It was after some such season that he said to a brother minister, "Brother, the doctrine, the confidence, and strength I feel will make people dance with joy in some parts of Wales;" and then, as the tears came into his eyes whilst he was speaking, he said again, "Yes, brother!"

Little idea can be formed of the Welsh preacher from the life of the minister in England. The congregations, we have seen, lay wide, and scattered far apart. Often, in Wales ourselves, we have met the minister pursuing his way on his horse, or pony, to his next "publication;" very often, his Bible in his hand, reading it as he slowly jogged along. So Christmas Evans passed his life, constantly, either on foot or on horseback, urging his way; sometimes through a country frowning as if smitten by a blow of desolation, and at others, laughing in loveliness and beauty; sometimes through the hot summer, when the burning beams poured from the craggy mountains; sometimes in winter, through the snow and rain and coldest inclemency, to fulfil his engagements. For the greater part of his life his income was never more than thirty pounds a year, and for the first part only about from ten to seventeen. It looks a wretched sum; but we may remember that Luther's income was never much more; and, probably, what seems to us a miserable little income, was very much further removed from want, and even poverty, than in other, less primitive, circumstances is often an income of hundreds. Certainly, Christmas Evans was never in want; always, not only comfortable, but able even to spare, from his limited means, subscriptions to some of the great societies of the day.

CHAPTER IV.
THE MINISTRY IN ANGLESEA (CONTINUED).

Christmas Evans as a Bishop over many Churches—As a Moderator in Public Meetings—Chapel-building and all its Difficulties to Christmas Evans—Extensive Travelling for Chapel-debts—Especially in South Wales—The Cildwrn Cottage again—A Mysterious Life of Poverty but of Hospitality—Catherine's Troubles—Story of a Hat—Wayfaring—Insatiability for Sermons in the Welsh—The Scenery of a Great Sermon—The Demoniac of Gadara—A Remarkable Illustration of the Varied Method of the Preacher—A Series of Illustrations of his Power of Allegoric Painting—The Four Methods of Preaching—The Seeking of the Young Child—Satan walking in Dry Places—Christmas Evans in Another Light—Lengthy Letter to a Young Minister—Contributions to Magazines—To be accursed from Christ—Dark Days of Persecution—Threatened with Law for a Chapel Debt—Darker Days—Loss of his Wife—Other Troubles—Determines to leave Anglesea.

The few glimpses we are able to obtain of the life and ministry in Anglesea, assure us of the supreme influence obtained by Christmas Evans, as was natural, over all the Churches of his order throughout that region. And in a small way, in a circle far removed from the noise of ideas, and the crowds and agitations of the great world, incessant activity was imposed upon him,—so many Societies under his care, so many meeting-houses to be erected, and funds to be procured for their erection, so many cases of Church discipline, so many co-pastors appointed, and set apart to work with him—who, however, were men mostly in business, had their own domestic affairs to manage, and for all the help they could give, needed helping and guidance; who had to receive instructions from him as to what they were to do, and whither they were to go,—so that, in fact, he was here, in Anglesea, a pastor of pastors, a bishop, if ever any pastor deserved that designation; an overseer of many Churches, and of many ministers. And hence, as a matter of course, in all ministerial meetings, and other smaller gatherings, he was usually at once not merely the nominal president, but the presiding spirit.

Rhys Stephen suggests a good many ludicrous aspects to the monthly meetings, and other such gatherings; indeed, they were of a very primitive description, and illustrative of what we should call a very rude, and unconventional state of society. Order was maintained, apparently, very much after the patriarchal or patristic fashion. All the preachers he called by their Christian names, and he would certainly have wondered what stranger happened to be in the place had any one addressed him as Mr. Evans; "Christmas Evans," before his face and behind his back, was the name by which he was known not only throughout all Anglesea, but, by-and-by, throughout the entire Principality.

Affectionate familiarity sometimes pays the penalty in diminished reverence, and in a subtraction from the respect due to a higher gift or superior position. Christmas appears to have been equal to this dilemma, and to have sustained with great natural dignity the post of Moderator, without surrendering his claim upon the affection of his colleagues. In such a meeting, some humble brother would rise to speak a second time, and, perhaps, not very pointedly, to the question; then the Moderator in the pulpit, gathering up his brows, would suddenly cut across the speaker with, "William, my boy, you have spoken before: have done with it;" or, "Richard, *bach*, you have forgotten the question before the meeting: hold your tongue."

On one occasion, a minister from South Wales, although a native of Anglesea, happening to be present, and rising evidently with the intention of speaking, Christmas, who suffered no intrusion from the south into their northern organizations, instantly nipped the flowers of oratory by crying out, "Sit down, David, sit down."

Such instances as these must seem very strange, even *outré*, to our temper, taste, and ideas of public meetings; but they furnish a very distinct idea of time, place, and circumstances, and give a not altogether unbeautiful picture of a state of society when, if politeness and culture had not attained their present eminence, there was a good deal of light and sweetness, however offensive it might seem to our intellectual Rimmels and Edisons.

Perhaps in every truly great and apostolic preacher, the preaching power, although before men the most conspicuous, is really the smallest part of the preacher's labour, and presents the fewest claims for homage and honour. We have very little, and know very little, of the Apostle Paul's sermons and great orations, mighty as they unquestionably were; he lives to us most in his letters, in his life, and its many martyrdoms. Ah, we fancy, if Christmas Evans had but to preach, to stay at home and minister to his one congregation, what a serene and quiet life it would have been, and how happy in the humble obscurity of his Cildwrn cottage!

But all his life in Anglesea seems to have been worried with chapel-debts. Chapels rose,—it was necessary that they should rise; people in scattered villages thronged to hear the Word; many hundreds appear to have crowded into Church fellowship, chapels had to be multiplied and enlarged; but, so far as we are able to read his biography, Christmas appears to have been the only person on whom was laid the burden of paying for them. Certainly he had no money: his wealth was in his eloquence, and his fame; and the island of Anglesea appears to have been by no means indisposed to lay these under contribution. A chapel had to be raised, and

Christmas Evans was the name upon which the money was very cheerfully lent for its erection; but by-and-by the interest pressed, or the debt had to be paid: what could be done then? He must go forth into the south, and beg from richer Churches, and from brethren who, with none of his gifts of genius or of holiness, occupied the higher places in the sanctuary.

Our heart is very much melted while we read of all the toils he accomplished in this way. Where were his sermons composed? Not so much in his lowly cottage home as in the long, lonely, toilsome travels on his horse through wild and unfrequented regions, where, throughout the long day's journey, he perhaps, sometimes, never met a traveller on the solitary road. For many years, it is said, he went twice from his northern bishopric to the south, once to the great Association, wherever that might be, and where, of course, he was expected as the chief and most attractive star, but once also with some chapel case, a journey which always had to be undertaken in the winter, and which was always a painful journey. Let us think of him with affection as we see him wending on, he and his friendly horse, through wild snows, and rains, and bleak storms of mountain wind.

Scarcely do we need to say he had a highly nervous temperament. The dear man had a very capricious appetite, but who ever thought of that? He was thrown upon himself; but the testimony is that he was a man utterly regardless of his own health, ridiculously inattentive to his dress, and to all his travelling arrangements. These journeys with his chapel case would usually take some six weeks, or two months. It was no dainty tour in a railway train, with first-class travelling expenses paid for the best carriage, or the best hotel.

A man who was something like Christmas Evans, though still at an infinite remove from him in the grandeur of his genius, a great preacher, William Dawson—Billy Dawson, as he is still familiarly called—used to say, that in the course of his ministry he found himself in places where he was sometimes treated like a bishop, and sometimes like an apostle; sometimes a great man would receive, and make a great dinner for him, and invite celebrities to meet him, and give him the best entertainment, the best room in a large, well-furnished house, where a warm fire shed a glow over the apartment, and where he slept on a bed of down,—and this was what he called being entertained like a bishop; but in other places he would be received in a very humble home, coarse fare on the table, a mug of ale, a piece of oatmeal cake, perhaps a slice of meat, a poor, unfurnished chamber, a coarse bed, a cold room,—and this was what he called being entertained like an apostle.

We may be very sure that the apostolic entertainment was that which usually awaited Christmas Evans at the close of his long day's journey. Not to be looked upon with contempt either,—hearty and free; and, perhaps, the conversation in the intervals between the puff of the pipe was what we should rather relish, than the more timorous and equable flow of speech in the finer mansion. This is certain, however, that the entertainment of Christmas Evans, in most of his excursions, would be of the coarsest kind.

And this was far from the worst of his afflictions; there were, in that day, persons of an order of character, unknown to our happier, more Christian, and enlightened times,—pert and conceited brethren, unworthy to unloose the latchet of the great man's shoes, but who fancied themselves far above him, from their leading a town life, and being pastors over wealthier Churches. Well, they have gone, and we are not writing their lives, for they never had a life to write, only they were often annoying flies which teased the poor traveller on his way. On most of these he took his revenge, by fastening upon them some *sobriquet*, which he fetched out of that imaginative storehouse of his,—from the closets of compound epithet; these often stuck like a burr to the coat of the character, and proved to be perhaps the best passport to its owner's notoriety through the Principality. Further than this, we need not suppose they troubled the great man much; uncomplainingly he went on, for he loved his Master, and he loved his work. He only remembered that a certain sum must be found by such a day to pay off a certain portion of a chapel-debt; he had to meet the emergency, and he could only meet it by obtaining help from his brethren.

In this way he travelled from North to South Wales forty times; he preached always once every day in the week, and twice on the Lord's Day. Of course, the congregations everywhere welcomed him; the collections usually would be but very small; ministers and officers, more usually, as far as was possible, somewhat resented these calls, as too frequent and irregular. He preached one of his own glorious sermons, and then—does it not seem shocking to us to know, that he usually stood at the door, as it were, hat in hand, to receive such contributions as the friends might give to him? And he did this for many years, until, at last, his frequent indisposition, in consequence of this severity of service, compelled him to ask some friend to take his place at the door; but in doing this he always apologised for his delegation of service to another, lest it should seem that he had treated with inattention and disrespect those who had contributed to him of their love and kindness.

And so a number of the Welsh Baptist chapels, in Anglesea and North Wales, rose. There was frequently a loud outcry among the ministers of the south, that he came too often; and certainly it was only the marvellous attractions of the preacher which saved him from the indignity of a refusal. His reply was always ready: "What can I do? the people crowd to hear us; it is our duty to accommodate them as well as we can; all we have we give; to you much is given, you can give much; it is more blessed to give than receive," etc., etc. Then sometimes came more plaintive words; and so he won his way into the pulpit, and, once there, it was not difficult to win his way to the people's hearts. It was what we suppose may be called the age of chapel cases. How many of our chapels in England have been erected by the humiliating travels of poor ministers?

Christmas Evans was saved from one greater indignity yet, the encountering the proud rich man, insolent, haughty, and arrogant. It is not a beautiful chapter in the history of voluntaryism. In the course of these excursions, he usually succeeded in accomplishing the purpose for which he set forth; probably the contributions were generally very small; but then, on many occasions, the preacher had so succeeded in putting himself on good terms with all his hearers that most of them gave something.

It is said that on one occasion not a single person passed by without contributing something: surely a most unusual circumstance, but it was the result of a manœuvre. It was in an obscure district, just then especially remarkable for sheep-stealing; indeed, it was quite notorious. The preacher was aware of this circumstance, and, when he stood up in the immense crowd to urge the people to liberality, he spoke of this crime of the neighbourhood; he supposed that amidst that large multitude it was impossible but that some of those sheep-stealers would be present: he addressed them solemnly, and implored them, if present, not to give anything to the collection about to be made. It was indeed a feat rather worthy of Rowland Hill than illustrative of Christmas Evans, but so it was; those who had no money upon them borrowed from those who had, and it is said that, upon that occasion, not a single person permitted himself to pass out without a contribution.

The good man, however, often felt that a burden was laid upon him, which scarcely belonged to the work to which he regarded himself as especially set apart. Perhaps he might have paraphrased the words of the Apostle, and said, "The Lord sent me not to attend to the affairs of your chapel-debts, but to preach the gospel." There is not only pathos, but truth in the following words; he says, "I humbly think that no missionaries in India, or any other country, have had to bear such a burden as I have borne, because of chapel-debts, and *they* have not had besides to provide for their own support, as I have had to do through all my life in Anglesea; London committees have cared for *them*, while I, for many years, received but seventeen pounds per annum for all my services. The other preachers were young, and inexperienced, and the members threw all the responsibility upon me, as children do upon a father; my anxiety often moved me in the depths of the night to cry out unto God to preserve His cause from shame. God's promises to sustain His cause in the world greatly comforted me. I would search for the Divine promises to this effect, and plead them in prayer, until I felt as confident as if every farthing had been paid. I laboured hard to institute weekly penny offerings, but was not very successful; and after every effort there remained large sums unpaid in connection with some of the chapels which had been built without my consent."

Poor Christmas! As we read of him he excites our wonder.

"Passing rich with forty pounds a year."

looks like positive wealth as compared with the emoluments of our poor preacher; and yet the record is that he was given to hospitality, and he contributed his sovereign, and half-sovereign, not only occasionally, but annually, where his richer neighbours satisfied their consciences with far inferior bequests. How did the man do it? He had not married a rich wife, and he did not, as many of his brethren, eke out his income by some farm, or secular pursuit; a very common, and a very necessary thing to do, we should say, in Wales.

But, no doubt, Catherine had much to do with his unburdened life of domestic quiet; perhaps,—it does not appear, but it seems probable—she had some little money of her own; she had what to her husband was incomparably more valuable, a clear practical mind, rich in faith, but a calm, quiet, household faith. Lonely indeed her life must often have been in the solitary cottage, into which, assuredly, nothing in the shape of a luxury ever intruded itself. It has been called, by a Welshman, a curious anomaly in Welsh life, the insatiable appetite for sermons, and the singular, even marvellous, disregard for the temporal comforts of the preacher. Christmas, it seems to us, was able to bear much very unrepiningly, but sometimes his righteous soul was vexed. Upon one occasion, when, after preaching from home, he not only received less for his expenses than he naturally expected, but even less than an ordinary itinerant fee, an old dame remarked to him, "Well, Christmas, *bach*, you have given us a wonderful sermon, and I hope you will be paid at the resurrection," "Yes, yes, *shan fach*," said the preacher, "no doubt of that, but what am I to do till I get there? And there's the old white mare that carries me, what will she do? for her there will be no resurrection."

Decidedly the Welsh of that day seemed to think that it was essential to the preservation of the purity of the Gospel that their ministers should be kept low. Mr. D. M. Evans, in his Life of Christmas Evans, gives us the anecdote of a worthy and popular minister of this time, who was in the receipt of exactly twenty pounds a year; he received an invitation from another Church, offering him three pounds ten a month. This miserable lover of filthy lucre, like another Demas, was tempted by the dazzling offer, and intimated his serious intention of accepting "the call." There was a great commotion in the neighbourhood, where the poor man was exceedingly beloved; many of his people remonstrated with him on the sad exhibition he was giving of a guilty love of money; and, after much consideration, the leading deacon was appointed as a deputation to wait upon him, and to inform him, that rather than suffer the loss of his removal on account of money considerations, they had agreed to advance his salary to twenty guineas, or twenty-one pounds! Overcome by such an expression of his people's attachment, says Mr. Evans, he repented of his incontinent love of money, and stayed.

A strange part-glimpse all this seems to give of Welsh clerical life, not calculated either to kindle, or to keep in a minister's mind, the essential sense of self-respect. The brothers of La Trappe, St. Francis and his preaching friars, do not seem to us a more humiliated tribe than Christmas and his itinerating "little *brethren* of the poor." We suppose that sometimes a farmer would send a cheese, and another a few pounds of butter, and another a flitch of bacon; and, perhaps, occasionally, in the course of his travels,—we do not know of any such instances, we only suppose it possible, and probable,— some rich man, after an eloquent sermon, would graciously patronize the illustrious preacher, by pressing a real golden sovereign into the apostle's hand.

One wonders how clothes were provided. William Huntingdon's "Bank of Faith" seems to us, in comparison with that of Christmas Evans, like the faith of a man who wakes every morning to the sense of the possession of a million sterling at his banker's,—in comparison with *his* faith, who rises sensible that, from day to day, he has to live as on the assurance, and confidence of a child.

Certainly, Wales did not contain at that time a more unselfish, and divinely thoughtless creature than this Christmas Evans; and then he had no children. A man without children, without a child, can afford to be more careless and indifferent to the world's gold and gear. The coat, no doubt, often got very shabby, and the mothers of Israel in Anglesea, let us hope, sometimes gathered together, and thought of pleasant surprises in the way of improving the personal appearance of their pastor; but indeed the man was ridiculous in his disregard to all the circumstances of dress and adornment. Once, when he was about to set forth on a preaching tour, Catherine had found her mind greatly exercised concerning her husband's hat, and, with some difficulty, she had succeeded in equipping that noble head of his with a new one. But upon the journey there came a time when his horse needed to drink; at last he came to a clear, and pleasant pond, or brook, but he was at a loss for a pail; now what was to be done? Happy thought, equal to any of those of Mr. Barnand! he took the hat from off his head, and filled it with water for poor old Lemon. When he returned home, Catherine was amazed at the deterioration of the headgear, and he related to her the story. A man like this would not be likely to be greatly troubled by any defections in personal adornment.

Wordsworth has chanted, in well-remembered lines, the name and fame of him, whom he designates, for his life of probity, purity, and poverty,—united in the pastoral office, in his mountain chapel in Westmoreland,—Wonderful Robert Walker. Far be it from us to attempt to detract from the well-won honours of the holy Westmoreland pastor; but, assuredly, as we think of Christmas Evans, he too seems to us even far more wonderful; for there was laid upon him, not merely the thought for his own pulpit and his own family, but the care of all the Churches in his neighbourhood.

And so the end is, that during these years we have to follow him through mountain villages, in which the silence and desolation greet him, like that he might have found in old Castile, or La Mancha,—through spots where ruined old castles and monasteries were turned into barns, and hay and straw stowed away within walls, once devoted either to gorgeous festivity or idolatry,—through wild and beautiful scenes; narrow glen and ravine, down which mountain torrents roared and foamed,—through wild mountain gorges, far, in his day, from the noise and traffic of towns,—although in such spots Mr. Borrow found the dark hills strangely ablaze with furnaces, seeming to that strange traveller, so he said, queerly enough, "like a Sabbath in hell, and devils proceeding to afternoon worship,"—past simple, and unadorned, and spireless churches, hallowed by the prayers of many generations; and through churchyards in which rests the dust of the venerable dead. We can see him coming to the lonely Methodist chapel, rising like a Shiloh, bearing the ark, like a lighthouse among the high hills—strolling into a solitary cottage as he passes, and finding some ancient woman, in her comfortable kitchen, over her Welsh Bible, and concordance, neither an unpleasant nor an unusual sight;—never happier, we will be bold to say, than when, keeping his own company, he traverses and travels these lone and solitary roads and mountain by-paths, not only through the long day, but far into the night, sometimes by the bright clear moonlight, among the mountains, and sometimes through the "villain mists," their large sheets rolling up the mountain sides bushes and trees seen indistinctly like goblins and elves, till—

> "In every hollow dingle stood,
> Of wry-mouth fiends a wrathful brood."

So we think of him pressing on his way; no doubt often drenched to the skin, although uninjured in body; sometimes through scenes novel and grand, where the mountain looks sad with some ruin on its brow, as beneath Cader Idris (the chair or throne of Idris), where the meditative wanderer might conceive he saw some old king, unfortunate and melancholy, but a king still, with the look of a king, and the ancestral crown on his forehead.

We may be sure he came where corpse-candles glittered, unquenched by nineteenth-century ideas, along the road; for those travelling times were much nearer to the days of Twm ór Nant, who, when he kept turnpike, was constantly troubled by hearses, and mourning coaches, and funeral processions on foot passing through his gate. Through lonely places and alder swamps, where nothing would be heard but the murmuring of waters, and the wind rushing down the gullies,—sometimes falling in with a pious and sympathetic traveller, a lonely creature, "Sorry to say, Good-bye, thank you for your conversation; I haven't heard such a treat of talk for many a weary day." Often, passing through scenes where the sweet voice of village bells mingled with the low rush of the river; and sometimes where the rocks rolled back the echoes like a pack of dogs sweeping down the hills. "Hark to the dogs!" exclaimed a companion to Mr. Borrow once. "This pass is called *Nant yr ieuanc gwn*, the pass of the young dogs; because, when one shouts, it answers with a noise resembling the crying of hounds."

What honour was paid to the name and memory of the earnest-hearted and intrepid Felix Neff, the pastor of the Higher Alps; but does not the reader, familiar with the life of that holy man, perceive much resemblance in the work, the endurance, and the scenery of the toil, to that of Christmas Evans? May he not be called the pastor of our English Engadine?

All such lives have their grand compensations; doubtless this man had his, and *great* compensations too; perhaps, among the minor ones, we may mention his ardent reception at the great Association gatherings. At these his name created great expectations; there he met crowds of brethren and friends, from the remote parts of the Principality, by whom he was at once honoured and loved. We may conceive such an occasion; the "one-eyed man of Anglesea" has now been for many years at the very height of his popularity; his name is now the greatest in his denomination; this will be one of his great occasions, and his coming has been expected for many weeks. No expectation hanging upon the appearance of Jenny Lind, or Christine Nielson, or Sims Reeves, on some great musical festivity, can reach, in our imagination, the expectations of these poor, simple villagers as they think of the delight they will experience in listening to their wonderful and well-loved prophet.

So, along all the roads, there presses an untiring crowd, showing that something unusual is going on somewhere. The roads are all picturesque and lively with all sorts of people, on foot, on horseback, in old farm carts, and even in carriages; all wending their way to the largest and most central chapel of the neighbourhood. It is the chief service. It is a Sabbath evening; the congregation is wedged together in the spacious house of God; it becomes almost insupportable, but the Welsh like it. The service has not commenced, and a cry is already raised that it had better be held in an adjoining field; but it is said this would be inconvenient. The doors, the windows, are all thrown open; and so the time goes on, and the hour for the commencement of the service arrives. All eyes are strained as the door opens beneath the pulpit, and the minister of the congregation comes in, and makes his way, as well as he can, for himself and his friend, the great preacher—there he is! that tall, commanding figure,—that is he, the "one-eyed man of Anglesea."

A murmur of joy, whisperings of glad congratulation, which almost want to burst into acclamations, pass over the multitude. And the service commences with prayer, singing, reading a chapter, and a short sermon,—a very short one, only twenty minutes. There are crowds of preachers sitting beneath the pulpit, but they, and all, have come to hear the mighty minstrel—and the moment is here. A few more verses of a hymn, during which there is no little commotion, in order that there may be none by-and-bye, those who have been long standing changing places with those who had been sitting. There, he is up! he is before the people! And in some such circumstances he seems to have first sung that wonderful song or sermon,

THE DEMONIAC OF GADARA.

The text he announced was—*"Jesus said unto him, Go home unto thy friends, and tell them how great things the Lord hath done for thee, and hath had compassion on thee."*

The introduction was very simple and brief; but, before long, the preacher broke loose from all relations of mere comment and explanation, and seemed to revel in dramatic scenery, and pictorial imagination, and, as was so usual with him in such descriptions, increasing, heightening, and intensifying the picture, by making each picture, each scene, to live even in the kind of enchantment of a present demoniacal possession. He began by describing the demoniac as a castle garrisoned with a legion of fiends, towards which the great Conqueror was approaching over the Sea of Tiberias, the winds hushing at His word, the sea growing calm at His bidding. Already He had acquired among the devils a terrible fame, and His name shook the garrison of the entire man, and the infernal legion within, with confusion and horror.

> "I imagine," he said, "that this demoniac was not only an object of pity, but he was really a terror to the country. So terrific was his appearance, so dreadful and hideous his screams, so formidable, frightful, and horrid his wild career, that all the women in that region were so much alarmed that none of them dared go to market, lest he should leap upon them like a panther on his prey.
>
> "And what made him still more terrible was the place of his abode. It was not in a city, where some attention might be paid to order and decorum (though he would sometimes ramble into the city, as in this case). It was not in a town,

or village, or any house whatever, where assistance might be obtained in case of necessity; but it was among the tombs, and in the wilderness—not far, however, from the turnpike road. No one could tell but that he might leap at them, like a wild beast, and scare them to death. The gloominess of the place made it more awful and solemn. It was among the tombs—where, in the opinion of some, all witches, corpse-candles, and hobgoblins abide.

"One day, however, Mary was determined that no such nuisance should be suffered in the country of the Gadarenes. The man must be clothed, though he was mad and crazy. And if he should at any future time strip himself, tie up his clothes in a bundle, throw them into the river, and tell them to go to see Abraham, he must be tied and taken care of. Well, this was all right; no sooner said than done. But, so soon as the fellow was bound, although even in chains and fetters, Samson-like he broke the bands asunder, and could not be tamed.

"By this time, the devil became offended with the Gadarenes, and, in a pout, he took the demoniac away, and drove him into the wilderness. He thought the Gadarenes had no business to interfere, and meddle with his property; for he had possession of the man. And he knew that 'a bird in the hand is worth two in the bush.' It is probable that he wanted to send him home; for there was no knowing what might happen now-a-days. But there was too much matter about him to send him as he was; therefore, he thought the best plan would be to persuade him to commit suicide by cutting his throat. But here Satan was at a nonplus—his rope was too short. He could not turn executioner himself, as that would not have answered the design he has in view, when he wants people to commit suicide; for the act would have been his own sin, and not the man's. The poor demoniac, therefore, must go about to hunt for a sharp stone, or anything that he could get. He might have been in search of such an article, when he returned from the wilderness into the city, whence he came, when he met the Son of God.

"Jesus commanded the unclean spirit to come out of the man. And when he saw Jesus he cried out, and fell down before him, and with a loud voice said, 'What have I to do with thee, Jesus, Thou Son of God most high? I beseech Thee, torment me not.'

"Here is the devil's confession of faith. The devils believe and tremble, while men make a mock of sin, and sport on the brink of eternal ruin. To many of the human race, Christ appears as a root out of dry ground. They see in Him neither form nor comeliness, and there is no beauty in Him that they should desire Him. Some said He was the carpenter's son, and would not believe in Him; others said He had a devil, and that it was through Beelzebub, the chief of the devils, that He cast out devils: some cried out, 'Let Him be crucified;' and others said, 'Let His blood be on us and on our children.' As the Jews would not have Him to reign over them, so many, who call themselves Christians, say that He is a mere man; as such, He has no right to rule over their consciences, and demand their obedience, adoration, and praise. But the devils know better—they say, Jesus is the Son of God most high.

"Many of the children of the devil, whose work they do, differ very widely from their father in their sentiments respecting the person of Christ.

"Jesus commanded the legion of unclean spirits to come out of the man. They knew that out they must go. But they were like Irishmen—very unwilling to return to their own country. They would rather go into hogs' skins than to their own country. And He suffered them to go into the herd of swine. Methinks that one of the men who fed the hogs, kept a better look out than the rest of them and said, 'What ails the hogs? Look sharp there, boys—keep them in—make good use of your whips! Why don't you run? Why, I declare, one of them has gone over the cliff! There, there, Morgan, goes another! Drive them back, Tom.' Never was there such a running, and whipping, and hallooing; but down go the hogs, before they are aware of it.

"One of them said, 'They are all gone!'

"'No, sure not all gone into the sea!'

"'Yes, every one of them, the *black hog* and all. They are all drowned! the devil is in them! What shall we do now? What can we say to the owners?'

"'What can we say?' said another; 'we must tell the truth—that is all about it. We did our best—all that was in our power. What could any man do more?'

"So they went their way to the city, to tell the masters what had happened.

"'John, where are you going?' exclaimed one of the masters.

"'Sir, did you know the demoniac that was among the tombs there?'

"'Demoniac among the tombs! Where did you leave the hogs?'

"'That madman, sir—'

"'Madman! Why do you come home without the hogs?'

"'That wild and furious man, sir, that mistress was afraid of so much—'

"'Why, John, I ask you a plain and simple question—why don't you answer me? Where are the hogs?'

"'That man who was possessed with the devils, sir—'

"'Why, sure enough, you are crazy! You look wild! Tell me your story, if you can, let it be what it may.'

"'Jesus Christ, sir, has cast the unclean spirits out of the demoniac; they are gone into the swine; and they are all drowned in the sea; for I saw the tail of the last one!'

"The Gadarenes went out to see what was done, and finding that it was even so, they were afraid, and besought Jesus to depart from them.

"How awful must be the condition of those men who love the things of this world more than Jesus Christ.

"The man out of whom the unclean spirits were cast, besought Jesus that he might be with Him. But He told him to return to his own house, and show how great things God had done unto him. And he went his way, and published, throughout the whole city of Decapolis, how great things Jesus had done unto him. The act of Jesus casting so many devils out of him, was sufficient to persuade him that Jesus was God as well as man.

"I imagine I see him going through the city, crying—'Oh yes! Oh yes! Oh yes! please to take notice of me, the demoniac among the tombs. I am the man who was a terror to the people of this place—that wild man, who would wear no clothes, and that no man could bind. Here am I now, in my right mind. Jesus Christ, the Friend of sinners, had compassion on me. He remembered me when I was in my low estate—when there was no eye to pity, and no hand to save. He cast out the devils and redeemed my soul from destruction.'

"Most wonderful must have been the surprise of the people, to hear such proclamation. The ladies running to the windows, the shoemakers throwing their lasts one way, and their awls another, running out to meet him and to converse with him, that they might be positive that there was no imposition, and found it to be a fact that could not be contradicted. 'Oh, the wonder of all wonders! Never was there such a thing,' must, I think, have been the general conversation.

"And while they were talking, and everybody having something to say, homeward goes the man. As soon as he comes in sight of the house, I imagine I see one of the children running in, and crying, 'Oh, mother! father is coming—he will kill us all!'

"'Children, come all into the house,' says the mother. 'Let us fasten the doors. I think there is no sorrow like my sorrow!' says the broken-hearted woman. 'Are all the windows fastened, children?'

"'Yes, mother.'

"'Mary, my dear, come from the window—don't be standing there.'

"'Why, mother, I can hardly believe it is father! That man is well dressed.'

"'Oh yes, my dear children, it is your own father. I knew him by his walk, the moment I saw him.'

"Another child stepping to the window, says, 'Why, mother, I never saw father coming home as he comes to-day. He walks on the footpath, and turns round the corner of the fence. He used to come towards the house as straight as a line, over fences, ditches, and hedges; and I never saw him walk as slowly as he does now.'

"In a few moments, however, he arrives at the door of the house, to the great terror and consternation of all the inmates. He gently tries the door, and finds no admittance. He pauses a moment, steps towards the window, and says in a low, firm, and melodious voice, 'My dear wife, if you will let me in, there is no danger. I will not hurt you. I bring you glad tidings of great joy.' The door is reluctantly opened, as it were between joy and fear. Having deliberately seated himself, he says: 'I am come to show you what great things God has done for me. He loved me with an everlasting love. He redeemed me from the curse of the law, and the threatenings of vindictive justice. He saved me from the power and dominion of sin. He cast the devils out of my heart, and made that heart, which was a den of thieves, the temple of the Holy Spirit. I cannot tell you how much I love my Saviour. Jesus Christ is the foundation of my hope, the object of my faith, and the centre of my affections. I can venture my immortal soul upon Him. He is my best friend. He is altogether lovely—the chief among ten thousand. He is my wisdom, righteousness, sanctification, and redemption. There is enough in Him to make a poor sinner rich, and a miserable sinner happy. His flesh and blood is my food,—His righteousness my wedding garment, and His blood is efficacious to cleanse me from all my sins. Through Him I can obtain eternal life; for He is the brightness of the Father's glory, and the express image of His Person: in whom dwelleth all the fulness of the Godhead bodily. He deserves my highest esteem, and my warmest gratitude. Unto Him who loved me with an eternal love, and washed me in His own blood, unto Him be the glory, dominion, and power, for ever and ever! For He has rescued my soul from hell. He plucked me as a brand from the burning. He took me out of the miry clay, and out of a horrible pit. He set my feet upon a rock, and established my goings, and put in my mouth a new song of praise, and glory to Him! Glory to Him for ever! Glory to God in the highest! Glory to God for ever and ever! Let the whole earth praise Him! Yea, let all the people praise Him!' How sweet was all this, the transporting joy of his wife!

"It is beyond the power of the strongest imagination to conceive the joy and gladness of this family. The joy of seafaring men delivered from shipwreck; the joy of a man delivered from a burning house; the joy of not being found guilty at a criminal bar; the joy of receiving pardon to a condemned malefactor; the joy of freedom to a prisoner of war, is nothing in comparison to the joy of him who is delivered from going down to the pit of eternal destruction. For it is a joy unspeakable and full of glory."

The effect of this sermon is described as overwhelmingly wonderful. The first portion, in which he pictured the mysterious and terrible being, the wild demoniac, something of a wild beast, and something of a fiend, made the people shudder. Then, shifting his scene, the catastrophe of the swine, the flight of the affrighted herdsmen, the report to the master, and the effect of the miracle on the populace, was rendered with such dramatic effect, the preacher even laughing himself, as he painted the rushing swine, hurrying down the steep place into the lake, especially the "black hog," and all,—for they all understood the point of that allusion,—that beneath the grim grotesqueness of the scene, laughter ran over the whole multitude. But the pathos of the family scene! Mary embracing her restored husband; and the restored maniac's experience, and hymn of praise. The place became a perfect Bochim; they wept like mourners at a funeral. Shouts of prayer and praise mingled together. One who heard that wonderful sermon says, that, at last, the people seemed like the inhabitants of a city which had been shaken by an earthquake, that, in their escape, rushed into the streets, falling upon the earth screaming, and calling upon God!

This sermon has never been printed; indeed, it is obvious that it never could be prepared for the press. It defies all criticism; and the few outlines we have attempted to present are quite inadequate to reproduce it. All who heard it understood, that it was a picture of a lunatic, and demon-haunted world; and it was beneath the impression of this, that passionate cries, universal, thankful, penitent murmurs rose; whilst amidst loud "Amens!" and sobs, and tears, some petitions ascended: "O Lord, who didst walk on the sea, that Thou mightest meet the Gadarene, cast out some demons from our midst to-night."

Although the demoniac of Gadara is not, in the strict sense of the word, an allegory, yet it is allegoric throughout; a fine piece of shadowy painting, in which unconverted, and converted men, and women might realize something of their own personal history, and the means by which they would "come to themselves."

And, no doubt, the chief charm, and most original characteristic of the preacher, was his power of sustained allegory; some incident, even some passing expression in Scripture, some prophetic figure of speech, was turned round and round by him, beaten out, or suggested a series of cartoon paintings, until it became like a chapter from the "Pilgrim's Progress." It has seemed to us, that his translators have been singularly unfortunate in rendering these excursions of his fancy into English; our most vivid impressions of them have been derived from those who had heard them, in all their freshness, from the preacher's own wonderful lips. We will attempt to transfer one or two of these allegories to our pages. It must have been effective to have heard him describe the necessity of Divine life, spiritual power, to raise a soul from spiritual death. This may be called

"THE FOUR METHODS OF PREACHING.

"He beheld," he said, "such a one as Lazarus lying in the cave, locked in the sleep of death; now how shall he be raised? how shall he be brought back to life? Who will roll away for us the stone from this sepulchre? First came one, who went down to the cave with blankets, and salt, to rub with the fomentations of duty, to appeal to the will, to say to the sleeping man, that he could if he would; chafing and rubbing the cold and inert limbs, he thinks to call back the vital warmth; and then retiring, and standing some distance apart, he says to the other spectators, 'Do you not see him stir? Are there no signs of life? Is he not moving?' No, he lies very still, there is no motion. How could it be otherwise? how could a sense of moral duty be felt by the man there?—*for the man was dead*!

"The first man gave up in despair. And then came the second. 'I thought you would never do it,' he said; 'but if you look at me, you will see a thing. No,' he said, 'your treatment has been too gentle.' And he went down into the cave with a scourge. Said he, 'The man only wants severe treatment to be brought back to life. I warrant me I will make him feel,' he said. And he laid on in quick succession the fervid blows, the sharp threatenings of law and judgment, and future danger and doom; and then he retired to some distance. 'Is he not waking?' he said. 'Do you not see the corpse stir?' No! A corpse he was before the man began to lay on his lashes, and a corpse he continued still;— *for the man was dead*!

"'Ah,' said another, advancing, 'but I have wonderful power. You, with your rubbing, and your smiting, what can you do? but I have it, for I have two things.' And he advanced, and he fixed an electric battery, and disposed it so that it touched the dead man, and then, from a flute which he held, he drew forth such sweet sounds that they charmed the ears which were listening; and whether it was the battery, or whether it was the music, so it was, that effect seemed to be produced. 'Behold,' said he, 'what the refinements of education and cultivation will do!' And, indeed, so it was, for the hair of the dead man seemed to rise, and his eye-balls seemed to start and dilate; and see! he rises, starts up, and takes a stride down the cave. Ah, but it is all over; it was nothing but the electricity in the battery; and he sank back again flat on the floor of the cave;—*for the man was dead*!

"And then, when all were filled with despair, there came One, and stood by the entrance of the cave; but He was the Lord and Giver of life, and standing there, He said, 'Come from the four winds, O breath, and breathe upon this slain one, that he may live. Christ hath given thee life. Awake, thou that sleepest.' And the man arose; he shook off his grave-clothes; what he needed had come to him now—*life*! Life is the only cure for death. Not the prescriptions of duty, not the threats of punishment and damnation, not the arts and the refinements of education, but new, spiritual, Divine *life*."

The same manner appears in the way in which he traces the story of a soul seeking Christ, under the idea of the Wise Men following the leading star in

"SEEKING THE YOUNG CHILD."

We have remarked before that the preacher's descriptions of Oriental travel were always Welsh, and this could not arise so much from ignorance, for he was fairly well read in the geography, and, perhaps, even in the topography, of the Holy Land; but he was quite aware that Oriental description would be altogether incomprehensible to the great multitude of his auditors. He described, therefore, the Wise Men, not as we, perhaps, see them, on their camels, solemnly pacing the vast sandy desert, whose sands reflected the glow of the silvery star. They passed on their way through scenes, and villages, which might be recognised by the hearers, anxiously enquiring for the young Child. Turnpikes, if unknown in Palestine, our readers will, perhaps, remember as one of the great nuisances of even a very short journey in Wales in Christmas's day.

"The wise men came up to the gate,—it was closed; they spoke to the keeper, inquiring, 'Do you know anything of the Child?'

"The gatekeeper came to the door, saying, in answer to the question, 'You have threepence to pay for each of the asses.'

"They explained, 'We did not know there was anything to pay; here is the money; but tell us, do you know anything of the young Child?'

"No, the keeper did not even know what they meant. For they know nothing on the world's great highway of the Child sent for the redemption of man. But he said, 'You go on a little farther, and you will come to a blacksmith's shop; he has all the news, he knows everything, and he will be sure to be able to tell you all you want to know.'

"So they paced along the road, following the star, till they came to the blacksmith's shop; and it was very full, and the blacksmith was very busy, but they spoke out loudly to him, and said, 'Where is the young Child?'

"'Now,' said the blacksmith, 'it is of no use shouting that way; you must wait, you see I am busy; your asses cannot be shod for a couple of hours.'

"'Oh, you mistake us,' said the wise men; 'we do not want our asses shod, but we want you to tell us, you, who know everything hereabouts, where shall we find the young Child.'

"'I do not know,' said the blacksmith. For the world, in its bustle and trade, knows nothing, and cares nothing about the holy Child Jesus. 'But look you,' he said, 'go on, and you will come to the inn, the great public-house; everybody from the village goes there, they know all the news there.'

"And so, with heavy hearts, they still pursued their way till they came to the inn; at the door, still resting on their asses, they inquired if any one knew of the Child, the wonderful Child.

"But the landlord said, 'Be quick! Evan, John, where are you? bring out the ale—the porter—for these gentlemen.'

"'No,' they said, 'we are too anxious to refresh ourselves; but tell us, hereabouts has been born the wonderful Child; He is the desire of all the nations; look there, we have seen His Star, we want to worship Him. Do you know?'

"'Not I,' said the landlord. For pleasure knows nothing of Him through whom the secrets of all hearts are revealed. 'Plenty of children born hereabouts,' said the landlord; 'but I know nothing of Him whom you seek.' And he thought them a little mad, and was, moreover, a little cross because they would not dismount and go into the inn. 'However,' he said, 'there is an old Rabbi lives in a lane hard by here; I think I have heard him say something about a Child that should be born, whose name should be called Wonderful. See, there is the way, you will find the old man.'

"So again they went on their way; and they stopped before the house of the old Rabbi, and knocked, and the door was opened; and here they left their asses by the gate, and entered in; and they found the old Rabbi seated with his Hebrew books, and chronicles about him, and he was strangely attired with mitre and vestment. And now, they thought, they would be sure to learn, and that their journey might be at an end. And they told him of the Star, and that the young Child was born who should be King of the Jews, and they were come to worship Him.

"'Ah, yes,' he said, 'He is coming, and you shall see Him, but not now. You shall behold Him, but not nigh. See, it is written here—a Star shall rise out of Jacob. And when He comes it will be here He will show Himself. Go back, and when He comes I will send word and let you know.' For even religious people, and Churches, cannot always guide seekers after God to Him whom to know is life eternal.

"But they were not satisfied, and they said, 'No, no, we cannot return; He is born, He is here!'

"'There has been a great mistake made,' said the Rabbi; 'there have been some who have said that He is born, but it is not so.'

"'But who has said it?' they inquired.

"And then he told them of another priestly man, who lived near to the river hard by; and to him they went, and inquired for the young Child.

"'Yes, yes,' he said, when they pointed him to the Star, 'yes, through the tender mercies of our God, the Dayspring from on high hath visited us; to give light to them that sit in darkness and the shadow of death; to guide our steps into the way of peace.'

"And so he guided them to the manger, and the Star rested and stood over the place where the young Child was, while they offered their gifts of gold, and frankincense, and myrrh."

Sometimes the preacher, in another version which we have seen, appears to have varied the last guide, and to have brought the wise men, by a singular, and perfectly inadmissible anachronism, to the man in the camel's hair by the river's brink, who said, "Behold, the Lamb of God, who taketh away the sins of the world!"

But one of the most effective of these sustained allegories, was founded on the text which speaks of the evil "spirit walking through dry places, seeking rest, and finding none." We believe we were first indebted for it, to the old dame who entertained us nearly forty years since in the Caerphilly Cottage.

SATAN WALKING IN DRY PLACES.

The preacher appears to have been desirous of teaching the beautiful truth, that a mind preoccupied, and inhabited by Divine thoughts, cannot entertain an evil visitor, but is compelled to betake himself to flight, by the strong expulsive power of Divine affections. He commenced, by describing Satan as a vast and wicked, although invisible spirit,—somehow, as Milton might have described him; and the preacher was not unacquainted with the grand imagery of the "Paradise Lost," in which the poet describes the Evil One, when he tempts, with wandering feet, the dark, unbottomed, infinite abyss, and, through the palpable obscure, seeks to find out his uncouth way. Christmas described him, as spreading his airy flight on indefatigable wings, determined to insinuate himself, through the avenues of sense, to some poor soul, and lure it to destruction. And, with this end, flying through the air, and seeking for a dwelling-place, he found himself moving over one of those wide Welsh moors, the preacher so well knew, and had so often travelled; and his fiery, although invisible glance, espied a young lad, in the bloom of his days, and the strength of his powers, sitting on the box of his cart, driving on his way to the quarries for slate or lime.

'"'There he is,' said Satan; 'his veins are full of blood, his bones are full of marrow. I will cast my sparks into his bosom, and set all his passions on fire; I will lead him on, and he shall rob his master, and lose his place, and find another, and rob again, and do worse; and he shall go on from worse to worse, and then his soul shall sink, never to rise again, into the lake of fire.' But just then, as he was about to dart a fiery temptation into the heart of the youth, the evil one heard him sing,

"'Guide me, O Thou great Jehovah,
　Pilgrim through this barren land;
I am weak, but Thou art mighty,
　Hold me by Thy powerful hand;
　　Strong deliverer,
Be Thou still my Strength and Shield.'

'Oh, but this is a dry place,' said the fiery dragon as he fled away.

"But I saw him pass on," said the preacher, "hovering, like a hawk or a vulture, in the air, and casting about for a suitable place where he might nestle his black wings; when, at the edge of the moor, he came to a lovely valley; the hills rose round it, it was a beautiful, still, meadow-like spot, watered by a lovely stream; and there, beneath the eaves of a little cottage, he saw a girl, some eighteen years of age, a flower among the flowers: she was knitting, or sewing at the cottage door. Said Satan, 'She will do for me; I will whisper the evil thought in her heart, and she shall turn it over, and over again, until she learns to love it; and then the evil thought shall be an evil deed; and then she shall be obliged to leave her village, and go to the great town, and she shall live a life of evil, all astray from the paths of my Almighty Enemy. Oh, I will make her mine, and then, by-and-bye, I will cast her over the precipices, and she shall sink, sink into the furnace of divine wrath.' And so he hastened to approach, and dart into the mind of the maiden; but while he was approaching, all the hills and crags seemed to break out into singing, as her sweet voice rose, high and clear, chanting out the words,

"'Jesus, lover of my soul,
　Let me to Thy bosom fly,
While the nearer waters roll,

While the tempest still is high.
Other refuge have I none,
   Hangs my helpless soul on Thee;
Leave, ah, leave me not alone,
   Still support, and comfort me.'

'This is a very dry place, too,' said the dragon, as he fled away.

"And so he passed from the valley among the hills, but with hot rage. 'I will have a place to dwell in!' he said; 'I will somehow leap over the fences, and the hedges, of the purpose, and covenant, and grace of God. I do not seem to have succeeded with the young, I will try the old;' for passing down the village street, he saw an old woman; she, too, was sitting at the door of her cot, and spinning on her little wheel. 'Ah!' said Satan, 'it will be good to lay hold of her grey hairs, and make her taste of the lake that burneth with fire and brimstone.' And he descended on the eaves of the cot; but as he approached near, he heard the trembling, quavering voice of the aged woman murmuring to herself lowly, 'For the mountains shall depart, and the hills be removed, but My kindness shall not depart from thee, neither shall the covenant of My peace be removed, saith the Lord, that hath mercy on thee.' And the words hurt the evil one, as well as disappointed him; they wounded him as he fled away, saying, 'Another dry place!'

"Ah, poor Devil!" exclaimed the preacher, "and he usually so very successful! but he was quite unsuccessful that day. And, now, it was night, and he was scudding about, like a bird of prey, upon his black wings, and pouring forth his screams of rage. But he passed through another little Welsh village, the white cottages gleaming out in the white moonlight on the sloping hillside. And there was a cottage, and in the upper room there was a faint light trembling, and 'Oh,' said the Devil to himself, 'Devil, thou hast been a very foolish Devil to-day, and there, in that room, where the lamplight is, old Williams is slowly, surely wasting away. Over eighty, or I am mistaken; not much mind left; and he has borne the burden and heat of the day, as they call it. Thanks to me, he has had a hard time of it; he has had very few mercies to be thankful for; he has not found serving God, I think, a very profitable business. Come, cheer up, Devil, it will be a grand thing if thou canst get him to doubt a bit, and then to despair a bit, and then to curse God, and die; that will make up for this day's losses.'

"Then he entered the room; there was the old man lying on the poor bed, and his long, thin, wasted hands and fingers lying on the coverlid; his eyes closed, the long silvery hair falling over the pillow. Now, Satan, make haste, or it will be too late; the hour is coming, there is even a stir in every room in the house: they seem to know that the old man is passing. But as Satan himself moved before the bed, to dart into the mind of the old man, the patriarch rose in bed, stretched forth his hands, and pinned his enemy to the wall, as he exclaimed, 'Though I walk through the valley of the shadow of death, I will fear no evil: for Thou art with me, Thy rod and Thy staff they comfort me; Thou preparest a table before me, in *the presence of mine enemy*; Thou anointest my head with oil, my cup runneth over; goodness and mercy, all the days of my life, dwell in the house of my God for ever.' Oh, *that* was a fearfully dry place! The old man sank back, it was all over; those words beat Satan down to the bottom of his own bottomless pit, glad to escape from such confusion and shame, and exclaiming, 'I will return to the place from whence I came, for this is too dry for me.'"

This will, no doubt, be thought, by many, to be strange preaching; many would even affect to despise it,—perhaps would even regard it as a high compliment were we to say, they would feel exceedingly puzzled even if, by way of a change, they were called upon to use it. It appears, however, to have been a style exceedingly fascinating to the Welsh mind of that day; it told, it stirred up suggestions, awakened thoughts, and reclaimed and converted character; and we need not, therefore, stay to attempt any vindication of it.

We have inserted these very characteristic illustrations here, because they appear to have belonged to the Anglesea period. Such, then, was the teaching, the preaching, the truth, which, while it was his own truth, and sustained his own mind, gave to him such power, at once, amongst the Churches to which he immediately administered, and made him the object of such attraction, when visiting distant neighbourhoods.

It might have been thought—it has usually been the case, in the instances of other men—that such excursions as those we have described, would have interfered with the great success of his work in the ministry as a preacher, and with his efficiency as a pastor. That they did not, substantially, is clear from many evidences. There can be no doubt that his sermons were no off-hand productions; there was a careful, rigid, and patiently conscientious weighing of their material. All those which we possess, abundantly show this; and he entered with all his heart, and mind, and strength into the work of preaching; but he never had an easy sphere; and yet, would his sermons have been greater had he been placed where the circle of his labour would have been narrower, and the means of his support more ready, and sufficient, and ample? Most likely not; but he weighed the entire work of the ministry in a manner which seems to us, sometimes, more like the sound thoughtfulness, and consideration of the theological Principal of a college, than a popular, or itinerant preacher. As an illustration of this, we may insert the following, very lengthy, but admirable letter to a young minister, written, we believe, some time nearer the close of his career than that we have just depicted:—

> "DEAR BROTHER,—1. Consider, in the first place, the great importance, to a preacher, of a blameless life. You must, like Timothy, 'flee youthful lusts,' as you would escape from beasts of prey; for there are kinds of beasts, living in the wilderness of man's corruption, that will charm, by means of their beauteous colours, those that walk among their haunts; there is no safety but by keeping from them, and adhering to such as live by faith, and watch, and pray. It will be well for you, while you travel through the coppice of youth, to keep from all appearance of evil. May you have grace to pass through the coppice of forbidden trees, without cutting your name into the bark of one of them, or you may be upbraided, at critical times, by those who may wish to prove that you are not better than themselves; even the *iota*, inserted by your hand, may be produced after many years.
>
> "2. I remember the words of Luther, that *reading, prayer*, and *temptation* are necessary to strengthen, and to purify the talents of a minister. Read, to extend your general knowledge, especially as to the plan of redemption, according to the Scriptures, in all its parts, from the election to the glorification; that you may, like a spiritual watchmaker, know all the relative cog-wheels, and be able to open them in the pulpit, and to connect them all by faith, hope, and charity, that they may occupy their own places, and exhibit their true results on the dial-plate; thus proving yourself a workman that needeth not to be ashamed, rightly dividing the word of truth. Be not like that thrasher, who presumptuously took his watch to pieces in the barn, and

could not put it together again, but was obliged to carry it home in his handkerchief. The messengers of God, described in the book of Revelations, are full of eyes behind, and before. You must use prayer to fetch strength out of Christ, like the homer to carry home the manna in, or the water-pot of the woman of Samaria. Without the prayer of faith, the preacher will have 'nothing to draw with,' from the well that is deep,—even *the deep things of God.* Temptation is requisite, to prove the nature of the metal of the preacher's character, and doctrine,—'approved of God.' The piece of gold, in every true minister's ministry, must be tried in some furnace, prepared by Divine Providence. He must, therefore, do the work of an evangelist, fulfil his ministry, endure hardness, and affliction, and thus prove himself a good soldier of Jesus Christ.

"3. Avail yourself, in the morning of your days, of every opportunity to acquire knowledge useful for the ministry. Let it be your constant aim, to turn every stream and rivulet of knowledge in the right direction, to facilitate the work of the ministry, for the good of souls, and the glory of God; as the bee, in all her excursions amongst the flowers of the gardens, and the hedges, gathers honey to enrich the hive, as the common treasury of the industrious race. Always have a book to read, instead of indulging in vain conversations. Strive to learn English, as you cannot have academical training. Learn your own mother-tongue well. Learn to write a good hand by frequent practice. Avoid vain conversation, instead of growth in knowledge. Remember this, that you cannot commit some loved sin in private, and perform the work of the ministry, in public, with facility and acceptance. For a preacher to fall into sin, be it a secret one, and to live in it, is as fatal, ultimately, as the cutting of Samson's hair. Be strong in the grace that is in Christ Jesus against all corruption.

"4. With regard to the composition of your sermons: first, let the matter be evangelical. The doctrine of the Gospel is a mould from heaven, and not changed. It puts its own impress and shape on the professor that is melted into it, so that his justification, sanctification, and all his salvation, flow from the merits of Christ; and all through God's grace, and not of ourselves. The gospel, as a glass, should be kept clean and clear in the pulpit, that the hearers may see the glory of Christ, and be changed to the same image. Every duty is to be urged by evangelical motives. 'Let us have grace,' etc.

"Hereby we can serve God in all the duties of the kingdom of heaven. The whole is summed up in living by faith, which worketh by love, to him that died for us, and rose again for our justification. Secondly, let your divisions be natural to the text. Take care that your interpretation accord with the contexts. Two or three general heads; avoid many. Four or five remarks you may make on each head; see that they are fairly in the truth of the text. Thirdly, I am not inclined to make inferences, or applications, from the whole. When the preacher has expended his strength, or ingenuity, in endeavouring to impress, and apply the truth to the minds of his hearers, application seems to me to be doing again what has been effected already. The blacksmith does not put the horse-shoe in the fire, after he has nailed it to the hoof; and the cook does not spread the cloth again, when dinner is over. Fourthly, beware of long sermons, as well as long prayers. When there is but one preacher, he should not preach for more than an hour; when there are two, both should not be more than an hour and a half, that the worship may close within two hours; whenever this time is passed, coolness and fatigue ensue. To put three ministers to preach (in one meeting) is a modern corruption, and likely to make some progress in Wales; while the English, generally, have but one sermon in one service. They excel us herein; for we do not read that, on the day of Pentecost, Peter, James, and John, preached after each other; but Peter, '*one* of the twelve,' delivered that successful sermon. When we lose sight of the Scriptures, and common sense, we are driven to extremes, though it be with the kindly purpose of respecting strange ministers, by putting them to preach.

"5. Attend, also, my young brother, to your outward appearance in the pulpit. Beware of a proud, haughty appearance, with wandering eyes, and unfeeling countenance, so that the people utterly fail to see the man of God in you. We must, in order hereunto, have something like unto Moses, when he had been on the mount with God, that will indicate seriousness, love to souls, a spirit of prayer, zeal for Christ, and longing for the salvation of men; like unto those who have felt the fear of perdition ourselves, and the infinite value of salvation by God's grace; and that we wrestle with God in order to be useful to souls. These things must be imprinted on our appearance and deportment, having transformed us, in some measure, to a heavenly form and habit. Our outward conversation should be consistent herewith, or men will despise us as hypocrites, without the fear of God.

"6. Avoid, my dear brother, all foolish bodily gestures.

"7. We now come to the part of the subject upon which you are most anxious to have my thoughts: that refers *to the delivery of your sermons*. It is difficult to put general rules of rhetoric into execution. After reading all that has been said by Blair, Williams, Fuller, and the Archbishop of Cambray (Fenelon), who have spoken at length of Cicero and Demosthenes, it is easy, by endeavouring to follow them, to lose the spirit of the work, and thus, by seeking the form, to forfeit the life. Preach the gospel of the grace of God intelligibly, affectionately, and without shame—all the contents of the great box, from predestination to glorification. It was the closing, and concealing, of this box that occasioned the opening of the venomous Mohammedan box, as well as that of Popery, together with all the vain legality that is to be found among Protestants, established and dissenting. It may be said, that they seek justification; but it is by the deeds of the law. The locking up, and the losing, of the doctrine of grace, through the merits of Christ, utterly destroyed the Jewish Church; for it was in the chest, which they locked up by their false interpolations of Scripture, that the 'things which belong to their peace' were contained; 'but now,' says the Redeemer, 'they are concealed from their eyes;' shut up under unbelief. 'The things that pertain to their peace' belong also to our peace, as Gentiles. The Deity of Christ, etc.; Redemption, etc. Excuse this digression, for the river of God's throne moved me along.

"We were upon the best mode of delivering sermons for edification. It is not easy to reduce the rules of prudence into practice. I have seen some men, of the highest powers, who understood Greek better than their mother-tongue, attempting to preach according to rule, and to them the pulpit was like unto Gilboa; they neither affected themselves, nor their hearers. The difficulty was, the bringing of their regulations into natural practice. I saw one of those men, the most eminent for learning and genius, who found the right way, under the influence of a mighty fervency that descended upon him in the pulpit, so that his voice became utterly different from what it used to be, and his tongue at liberty, as though something was cut that had hitherto restrained his tongue, and affections, from natural exercise.

"Here you have the sum, and substance, and mystery of all rules:—1. Let the preacher influence himself; let him reach his own heart, if he would reach the hearts of others; if he would have others feel, he must feel himself. Dry shouting (or vociferation) will not do this. The shout of a man who does not himself feel the effect of what he says, hardens, instead of softening; locks, instead of opening the heart. 2. The elevation, and fire of the voice must accord with the fervency of the matter in the heart. A person said to me once, 'Mr. Evans, you have not studied Dr. Blair's Rhetoric.' That man, with his rules, was always as dry as Gilboa. 'Why do you say so,' replied I, 'when you just now saw hundreds weeping under the sermon? That could not be, had I not first of all been influenced myself, which, you know, is the substance, and mystery, of all rules for speaking.' Wherever there is effect, there is life; and rules, without life, have no power. Now, brother, follow the natural course of affection, and voice. Raise not the voice while the heart is dry; but let the heart and affections shout first; let it commence within. Take this comparison:—Go to the blacksmith's shop; he first puts the piece of iron in the fire, and there is no sound of striking the anvil; he collects together the coals for heat; then he tells the boy, 'Blow!' while he masterfully manages the shovel, adjusting the coals, and asking sundry questions. He calmly looks at the fire heating the iron, and does not yet take hold of the hammer, nor order his assistants to use the sledge; but at length, seeing that the iron has attained the proper malleability, he takes it out, covered with sparkling fire, puts it on the anvil, handles the hammer, and orders his workman to take the larger one, and fashions it according to his pleasure; and so on, all day long. Here, observe, he does not beat the iron in order to make it hot, for without first heating it, the beating process is in vain. Equally vain is the hammer of vociferation, unless the matter is brought home with warmth into our hearts. We have often sought to produce effect, and to influence our hearers, much as though the smith merely put the iron in fire, and barely warmed it; it is contrary to the nature of things to use the hammer while the material is not duly tempered. Thus I have frequently, brother, found myself in preaching. You have, above, the mystery of all effective speaking, in Parliament, at the bar, and in the pulpit; remembering the difference in the subjects, and the sources of heat. In the pulpit, we speak of the deep things of God; and we are to pray for, and to expect warmth from the Divine Spirit. You complain that you cannot get your voice into a manageable key, and yet to speak with liveliness and power. Many, with a bad voice, well-governed, have become powerful speakers; while others, with a good voice, have, in consequence of not mastering a natural key, and not being able to move themselves, been most ineffective speakers. I would direct you to fix your voice at its natural pitch, which you may easily do; you may then, with facility, raise and lower it according to the subject in hand. If you commence in too high a key, you cannot keep it up long. First, you cannot modulate it as the occasion may require; and you fall into an unpliable, tedious monotony, and all natural cadence, and emphasis is lost. Without attuning the voice into the natural key, effective oratory is impossible. Secondly, remember, not to speak in your throat, or nostrils. If the former, you must soon become hoarse, and harsh loudness follows; the glory and vivacity are then departed, and instead of facility and cheerfulness, you have the roarings of death—the breath failing, with forced screams, and harsh whisperings. Thirdly, raise your voice to the roof of your mouth; do not close your teeth against it, neither imprison it in the nostrils, but open your mouth naturally, and keep your voice within your lips, where it will find room enough to play its high, and its low intonations, to discourse its flats, and sharps, to utter its joys, and sorrows. When you thus have your voice under control, instead of you being under its control, dragging you about in all disorder, you will find it your servant, running upon your errands, up and down, all through the camp, alternating in energy, and pliability, to the end of the sermon; and not becoming cold and weak, scarcely bearing you through, like Bucephalus, Alexander the Great's horse, which, mortally wounded, just brought his master out of the battle, and then expired. Fourthly, remember, not to press too much upon your breath, when you have attained the natural use of it, by using very long sentences, without pausing at proper places, which (pauses) will add to the effect, as well as preserve the voice; so that you will be, like the smith, ready to strike the duly-tempered metal, prepared to give the suitable emphasis at the end of the paragraph. Let the matter raise the voice, do not attempt by the voice to elevate the subject. Fifthly, use words easily understood, that the people's affections may not cool, while the mind is sent to a dictionary, to understand your terms. The great work, the exploit of a minister, is to win the heart to believe in Christ, and to love Him. Sixthly, bear in mind, also, the necessity of keeping the voice free, without (affected) restraint; give every syllable, and every letter, its full and proper sound. (It is one of the peculiarities and excellences of the Welsh language, and proves its Eastern origin.) No letter has to complain that it is (condemned to be) mute, and neglected, and has no utterance. In English, many letters have this complaint; but in Welsh, every letter, even as the knights at the round table of King Arthur, has, without preference, its own appropriate and complete sound. Seventhly, remember, also, to enunciate clearly the last syllable in every Welsh word; that will cause your most distant hearer to understand you; while, without this, much of what you say must be inevitably lost. Eighthly, in order to all this, carefully attend to the manner of the best, and ablest preachers, and imitate, not their weaknesses, but their excellences. You will observe, that some heavenly ornament, and power from on high, are visible in many ministers when under the Divine irradiation, which you cannot approach to by merely imitating their artistic excellence, without resembling them in the spiritual taste, fervency, and zeal which Christ and his Spirit 'work in them.' This will cause, not only your being like unto them in gracefulness of action, and propriety of elocution, but will also induce prayer for the anointing from the Holy One, which worketh mightily in the inward man. This is the mystery of all effective preaching. We must be endowed with power from on high: here is the grand inward secret. Without this, we (often) perceive that it is impossible, with all academic advantages, to make good preachers of young men from any college, in the Church of England, or among the dissenters, in the English or the Welsh language. A young preacher must have the mystery of being 'constrained' by 'the love of Christ'; 'the gift of God' must be kindled in him; and He alone, by the Spirit, can sustain that gift by the Holy Spirit. 'Who is sufficient for these things?' May the Lord give you, brother, a good understanding in all things; and preserve in you the heavenly gift by the Holy Ghost! may it be rekindled where it is, and contributed where it is not! Without it, we can do nothing for the glory of God, or the good of souls.

"Affectionately,
"CHRISTMAS EVANS."

Sometimes Mr. Evans occupied such slight leisure as he could command, by a contribution to the *Seren Gomer*, an extensively-circulating magazine of the Principality. Several of these papers are interesting; we select one, illustrating the bent of the writer's mind; it was published January 1821,—"An inquiry into the meaning of the singular language of the Apostle, his wish

"TO BE ACCURSED FROM CHRIST.

"'For I could wish that I were accursed (anathema) from Christ for my brethren,' etc. (Rom. ix. 3). Many things, most incredible to me, have been said in exposition of this passage; and principally, I think, from not observing that the word 'anathema' is used in two senses,—the one good, and the other bad. Barclay analyses into four acceptations; and, according to the first, it signifies that which is devoted, or set apart, to God, in a good sense. According to Parkhurst, it signifies, in Luke xxi. 5, a consecrated gift, set apart for the temple of God, and to His service alone. The word translated gifts is *anathemasi*. In the second book of Maccabees, ix. 8, the word denotes a consecrated gift. The word in the LXX., according to Parkhurst, is synonymous with the Hebrew word CHEREM, and signifies, generally, that which is entirely separated from its former condition, and use. If so, why should we not understand Paul, in the text, as expressing his ardent desire that he should be separated, *a devoted thing*, for the conversion of his brethren according to the flesh? Having gone thus far in explanation, we offer the following interpretation: 'For I could wish that

> I were *anathema*, or a gift, in my labours as an apostle, and a preacher of the Gospel, from Christ, for the spiritual benefit of my brethren according to the flesh, principally, instead of being an apostle to the Gentiles, as I am appointed; theirs is the adoption, etc.; and I could also wish that I, also, as an apostle, were an especial gift of Christ for their distinctive service.' If this be correct, there is no necessity for changing the tense of the verb from the present to the perfect, and reading, 'I could wish,' as 'I have wished;' while it saves us from putting in the Apostle's mouth a wish entirely opposed to the 'new creation,' to the plan of Divine grace, and to the glory of God; for it is certain that it is quite in opposition to all this, for a man to desire to live in sin, and to be accursed for ever,—and that cannot for a moment be predicated of the Apostle of the Gentiles. I humbly ask some learned correspondent, whether there is anything in the original text with which this exposition will not harmonize.
>
> "CHRISTMAS EVANS."

This letter led to some unsympathetic criticism, and reply. Christmas Evans wrote a vindication of his former views, which may be not uninteresting to our readers, as illustrating a phase of his intellectual character. It appeared in the *Seren Gomer* for 1822:—

> "MR. GOMER,—If you please, publish the following, in defence of my former letter on Romans ix. 3, and in reply to your correspondent, *Pen Tafar*.
>
> "It is admitted, on all hands, that the words in the question express the highest degree of love to the Jews. Let us, now, put the different expositions before the reader, and then let him judge which of them contains the greatest harmony and fitness; *i.e.*, first, to express love to the Jews; second, the best adapted to bring about their salvation; third, the most consistent with supreme love to Christ; and fourth, within the confines of sinlessness.
>
> "1. Many learned men set forth the Apostle as having formed this desire when he was an enemy to Christ. This they maintain by tracing the word *anathema* throughout the Greek Scriptures, and the Hebrew word *cherem*, of which it is the synonym. *Anathema*, they say, always signifies 'without an exception,' a separation, or devotement of a beast, a city, or something else, to irredeemable destruction

(Lev. xxvii. 29). The devoted thing was not to be redeemed, but certainly to be put to death (Gal. i. 9). '*Let him be accursed,*' says Paul of the angel that would preach another gospel. 'If any man love not the Lord Jesus Christ, let him be *anathema maranatha,*' 'accursed when the Lord cometh.' But who *can* believe that this is the meaning of the word in the passage before us? I say, with Dr. Gill, 'This never can be the signification.' What probability is there that Paul would swear, calling Jesus Christ to witness, to his ancient enmity against Him? This was notorious enough throughout the whole country. No asseveration was necessary to prove *Paul's persecuting spirit.*

"Again, how could that which he formerly had been, prove, he now having denied himself, his old persecuting spirit, and, being deeply ashamed on the account, prove his present love to the Jews? How did his former love to Satan prove his present love to the Jews?

"2. Others say that it is Paul's wish as a Christian, whatever *anathema* means. I believe it is his desire as a Christian; otherwise I see not how it could be an instance of his love to his brethren according to the flesh. Several authors maintain that Paul was willing, *for the sake of saving his nation, to part with his interest in Christ, and to perish for ever.* Peter Williams and Matthew Henry give this interpretation. But, seriously, how can a person persuade himself to believe this? Would not the Apostle, in this case, love his nation more than Christ, and be accordingly unworthy of Christ? This is opposed to a principle of our nature, which never can desire its own destruction; to the principle of grace, which loves Christ above all things on earth, and in heaven. Such a desire would make Paul a devil.

"3. Others suppose that Paul here speaks inconsiderately, in a kind of ecstasy, carried away by a stream of affection to his people. Who can believe this without giving up Paul's inspiration, even when he solemnly appeals to Christ?

"4. Another notion is, that the Apostle was willing, and desirous to be excommunicated from the Church of Christ upon earth, and to be deprived of its ordinances. How can this, again, be considered as consistent with love to Christ, and His Church? What tendency could his leaving the Church have to induce the Jews to enter it? This is contrary to the whole course of the Divine command, and promises: God will give His people an everlasting home, and place in His house.

"5. Some say, it is an *hyperbole*. To confirm this, Exod. xxxii. 32 is quoted as a case in point: '*Blot me, I pray thee, out of Thy book, which Thou hast written.*' This is not the book of eternal life, but the book of the dispensation, in which Moses was leader, and mediator. '*I would,*' he says, '*give up my office.*' God rejected the request: 'Lead the people unto the place of which I have spoken to thee.' It was not for Israel, nor a condition of forgiveness to them, but for himself, that Moses said, 'Blot my name out of Thy book.' All this gives but little assistance to understand the Apostle. The two spiritual men do not stand on the same ground. Moses seeks the obliteration of his name, unless Israel was pardoned. Paul seeks a work, and an office, in order to the forgiveness of his nation.

"6. Further, it is supposed to be proper to modify—*to soften*—the meaning of the word *anathema*, as signifying, sometimes, anything devoted to God, and that never could, afterwards, be appropriated to any other service; and here, to understand it in that softened sense, signifying that Paul was willing for the Redeemer to make him a devoted thing—a martyr for the truth, for the good of the Jewish nation. This is substantially the opinion of Thomas Charles, and Dr. Gill. Christmas Evans's theory is erected on this ground—the modified sense of the word; thus, 'I could wish myself entirely set apart, by Christ, to the service of my people, for their spiritual good; I should have been glad, had I my choice, to have been an Apostle, separated to them alone, and not to the Gentiles, with my dwelling, and labours, amongst them, and to die a martyr for the truth, even the most horrible death that could be devised, if Christ had appointed me hereto.' If 'P. T.' says this is a new interpretation of Christmas Evans's, the answer is, No, but a legitimate extension of a former one; for he did not intend, nor did his words import, the separation of martyrdom, or the most anathematised sufferings, from Paul for his kinsmen according to the flesh.

"7. Is it not plain, and does not 'P. T.' see, that this view is superior to the former five, and that it takes in, and is an improving addition to the latter of the five, as to its fitness to express the Apostle's great love to his people, without destroying his love to Christ, as well as to bring about the salvation of the Jews by proper means? How could the death of the Apostle contribute to the conversion of the Jews, unless he died *as an apostate of the circumcision?*"

It appears to have been towards the close of the Anglesea period, that he was thrown into a panic of fear, by a threat of a legal prosecution, on account of some chapel debts, for which, of course, he was regarded as responsible. "They talk," he said, "of casting me into a court of law, where I have never been, and I hope I shall never go; but I will cast them, first, into the court of Jesus Christ." We have seen that he was in the habit of putting on paper his prayers, and communions with God. It was a time of severe trial to him. He says, "I knew there was no ground of action, but, still, I was much disturbed, being, at the time, sixty years of age, and having, very recently, buried my wife." He continues, "I received the letter at a monthly meeting, at one of the contests with spiritual wickedness in high places. On my return home, I had fellowship with God, during the whole journey of ten miles, and, arriving at my own house, I went upstairs to my own chamber, and poured forth my heart before the Redeemer, who has in His hands all authority, and power." And the following seem to be the pathetic words in which he indulged:—

> "O blessed Lord! in Thy merit I confide, and trust to be heard. Lord, some of my brethren have run wild; and forgetting their duty, and obligations to their father in the Gospel, they threaten me with the law of the land. Weaken, I beseech Thee, their designs in this, as Thou didst wither the arm of Jeroboam; and soften them, as Thou didst soften the mind of Esau, and disarmed him of his warlike temper against Thy servant Jacob, after the wrestling at Penuel. So disarm them, for I do not know the length of Satan's chain in this case, and in this unbrotherly attack. But Thou canst shorten the chain as short as it may please Thee. Lord, I anticipate them in point of law. They think of casting Thine unworthy servant into the little courts here below; but I cast my cause into the High Court, in which Thou, gracious Jesus, art the High Chancellor. Receive Thou the cause of Thine unworthy servant, and send him a writ, or a notice, immediately—sending into their conscience, and summoning them to consider what they are doing. Oh, frighten them with a summons from Thy court, until they come, and bow in contrition at Thy feet; and take from their hands every revengeful weapon, and make them deliver up

every gun of scandal, and every sword of bitter words, and every spear of slanderous expressions, and surrender them all at Thy cross. Forgive them all their faults, and clothe them with white robes, and give them oil for their heads, and the organ, and the harp of ten strings, to sing, for the trampling of Satan under our feet by the God of peace.

"I went up once," he says, "and was about ten minutes in prayer; I felt some confidence that Jesus heard. I went up again with a tender heart; I could not refrain from weeping with the joy of hope that the Lord was drawing near to me. After the seventh struggle I came down, fully believing that the Redeemer had taken my cause into His hands, and that He would arrange, and manage for me. My countenance was cheerful, as I came down the last time, like Naaman, having washed himself seven times in the Jordan; or Bunyan's Pilgrim, having cast his burden at the foot of the cross, into the grave of Jesus. I well remember the place—the little house adjoining the meeting-house, at Cildwrn, where I then resided—in which this struggle took place; I can call it Penuel. No weapon intended against me prospered, and I had peace, at once, to my mind, and in my (temporal) condition. I have frequently prayed for those who would injure me, that they might be blessed, even as I have been blessed. I know not what would have become of me, had it not been for these furnaces in which I have been tried, and in which the spirit of prayer has been excited, and exercised in me."

It is scarcely necessary to add, that the threat was never executed, nor did poor Christmas, apparently, hear anything further of the matter; but we have seen how great was the trouble, and agitation it caused him, while the fear was upon him. It is very affecting to find that this great, this saintly, and earnest minister, had upon his heart, and mind, the burden of all the chapel-debts connected with his denomination in Anglesea, while he was minister there.

It might have been thought that the ministerial course of Christmas Evans would close in Anglesea, where he had laboured so long, and so effectually. He was, now, about sixty years of age, but there was little light just now, in the evening-time of his life; indeed, clouds of trouble were thickening around him. It often seems that trouble, in the ministerial life, comes exactly at that moment when the life is least able to stand, with strength, against it; and, certainly, in the life of Christmas Evans, sorrows gathered, and multiplied at the close.

Chief among these must be mentioned, beyond any doubt, the death of the beloved companion of all the Anglesea life, his good wife, Catherine; she left him in 1823. She was eminently, and admirably fitted to be the wife of such a man as Christmas. Somewhat younger than her husband, she supplied many attributes of character, to him most helpful; she was not an enthusiast, but she was a Christian, with real, deep, and devout convictions. We have no lengthy accounts of her; but little side-lights, a kind of casemented window, reveal a character at once affectionate, beautiful, and strong.

We have seen that their home was the region of self-denial, and her husband long remembered, and used to tell, how "if there happened to be on our table one thing better than the other, she would, modestly, but cheerfully and earnestly, resist all importunity to partake of it until she ascertained that there was enough for both." What a little candle such a sentence as this is, but what a light it sheds over the whole room! She did not pretend to be her husband; he filled his larger sphere, and she, in all her manifold, gentle ways, sought to give him rest. Surely she adds another name to the long catalogue of good wives. She reminds us of Lavater's wife, and some little incidents in that Cildwrn cottage call up memories from the manse of St. Peter's Church, and the shadows of the old Lindenhof of Zurich, where probably life did not put on a gayer apparel, or present more lavish and luxurious possibilities, than in the poor parsonage of Anglesea.

It is incredible, almost, to read what the good Catherine did, poor—to our thinking, miserable—as was the income of her husband. Her hand was most generous; how she did it, what committee of ways and means she called together, in her thoughtful mind, we do not know,—only, that she, constantly, found some food to give to poor children, and needy people; unblessed by children of her own, she employed her fingers in making clothes for the poor members, and families, of the Church. There was always help for the poor hungry labourer passing her cottage; the house was always open for the itinerant minister travelling on his way to some "publication," and she was always ready to minister to his necessities with her own kind hands. Her husband often thought that the glance she gave upon a text shed light upon it. She never had robust health, but she accompanied her husband on several of his longer journeys through the greater part of Wales,—ah, and some of them in the winter, through storms of rain, and snow, and hail, along dangerous roads too, across difficult ferries; and she was uniformly cheerful! What an invaluable creature, what a blessed companion! A keener observer of character, probably, from what we can gather, than her husband; a sharper eye, in general, to detect the subterfuges of selfishness and conceit.

One mighty trial she had before she died; she had, in some way, been deeply wounded, grievously injured, and hurt, and she found it hard to forgive; she agonized, and prayed, and struggled; and before she was called to eternity, she was able to feel that she had forgiven, and buried the memory of the injuries in the love and compassion of the Redeemer. Her husband had to give her up, and at a time, perhaps, when he needed her most. The illness was long, but great strength was given to her, and at last the release came. There was mourning in the Cildwrn cottage. The last night of her life she repeated a beautiful, and comfortable Welsh hymn, and then, ejaculating three times, "Lord Jesus, have mercy upon me!" she breathed forth her quiet, affectionate, and hopeful spirit, into her Saviour's hands, and left her husband all alone, to bear the burden of her departure, and other griefs, and troubles which were crowding upon him.

Other troubles,—for, in what way we need not attempt too curiously to inquire,—the pastorate gave to the poor old pastor little, or no peace. There were strong Diotrephesian troubles agitating the great preacher's life. The Churches, too, which Christmas Evans had raised, and to which, by his earnest eloquence, and active, organizing mind, he had given existence, grew restive, and self-willed beneath his guidance, refusing his advice with reference to ministers he suggested, and inviting others, whose appointment he thought unwise.

Poor Christmas! Did he ever ask himself, in these moments, when he thought of his lost Catherine, and felt the waves of trouble rising up, and beating all round him,—did he ever ask himself whether the game was worth the candle? whether he was a mere plaything in life, whom that arch old player, Death, had outplayed, and defeated? Did it ever seem to him that it was all a vanity, ending in vexation of spirit? The life most beloved had burnt out, the building he had spent long years to erect, seemed only to be furnished for discomfort, and distraction.

Did he begin to think that the wine of life was only turning into acrid vinegar, by-and-by to end with the long sleeping-draught? Of life's good things, in the worldling's sense of good, he had tasted few; most clearly he had never desired them. He had never the opportunity, nor had he ever desired to be like a Nebuchadnezzar, roaming the world like a beast, and pasturing at a dinner-table, as upon a sort of meadow-land of the stomach, sinking the soul to the cattle of the field; but he might have expected that his Church, and Churches, would be a joy, a rest, a pleasant meadow-land to him. The body was certainly crumbling to decay: would the ideas also prove like frescoes, which could be washed out by tears, or removed, and leave the soul only a desolate habitation, waiting for its doom of dust?

We do not suppose that, amidst his depressing griefs, these desolating beliefs, or unbeliefs, had any mastery over him. What did the men who tormented him know of those mighty springs of comfort, which came from those covenants he had made with God, amidst the lonely solitudes of his journeyings among the wild Welsh hills? He had not built his home, or his hopes, on the faithfulness of men, or the vitality of Churches; the roots of his faith, as they had struck downward, were now to bear fruit upward.

There was a fine healthfulness in his spirit. There is nothing in his life to lead one to think that he had ever been much intoxicated by the fame which had attended him; he appears to have been always beneath the control of the great truths in which he believed, and it was not the seductive charms of popularity for which he cared, but the power of those truths to bring light, conviction, and rest, to human souls. All his sermons look that way; all that we know of his preaching, and experience, turns in that direction.

Rose-leaves are said to act as an emetic, and have much the same effect on the constitution as senna-leaves. It is so with those sweet things which fame offers to the imagination; the conserves of its fragrance, by-and-by, become sickening. So, the robust nature of our fine old friend had to rise over grief, and disappointment, and unfriendliness, and diaconal dictation and impertinence. Only one thing he remembered. He appears to have been sustained, even as Edward Irving was, in his conviction that the truth of his message, the lamp of the ministry which he carried, gave to him a right, and a prerogative which he was not to relinquish; he had proved himself, he had proved the Spirit of God to be in him of a truth. He was not a wrangler, not disposed to maintain debates as to his rights; nor was he disposed to yield to caprice, faction, and turbulence; and so, he began to think of retiring, old as he was, from the field, the fragrance of which had proclaimed that the Lord had blessed him there.

Christmas Evans, as he draws near to the close of his work in Anglesea, only illustrates what many a far greater, and many a lesser man than he, have alike illustrated. There is a fine word among the many fine words of that great, although eccentric teacher, John Ruskin:—"It is one of the appointed conditions of the labour of man, that in proportion to the time between the seed-sowing and the harvest, is the fulness of the fruit; and that generally, therefore, the further off we place our aim, and the less we desire to be the witnesses of what we have laboured for, the more wide and rich will be the measure of our success." This was, no doubt, the consolation of Christmas; but as we look upon him, a friendly voice reminds us, that, as he leaves Anglesea, he realizes very much of Robert Browning's soliloquy of the martyred patriot:—

> "Thus I entered, and thus I go!
> In triumphs people have dropped down dead.
> Paid by the world,—what dost thou owe
> Me? God might question; now, instead,
> 'Tis God shall repay! I am safer so."

So the candlestick was removed out of its place in Anglesea, and Anglesea soon, but too late, regretted the removal. Christmas Evans, however, seems to illustrate a truth, which may be announced almost as a general law, from the time of the Saviour and his Apostles down to our own, that those who have wrought most unselfishly, and serviceably for the cause of God, and the well-being of man, had to receive their payment in themselves, and in the life to come. In proportion to the greatness of their work was the smallness of their remuneration here.

If we refer to the painful circumstances in connection with the close of the ministry of Christmas Evans at Anglesea, it is, especially, to notice how his faith survived the shock of surrounding trouble. He himself writes: "Nothing could preserve me in cheerfulness and confidence under these afflictions, but the assurance of the faithfulness of Christ; I felt assured that I had much work yet to do, and that my ministry would be instrumental in bringing many sinners to God. This arose from my trust in God, and in the spirit of prayer that possessed me; I frequently arose above all my sorrows."

And again he writes: "As soon as I went into the pulpit during this period, I forgot my troubles, and found my mountain strong; I was blessed with such heavenly unction, and longed so intensely for the salvation of men, and I felt the truth like a hammer in power, and the doctrine distilling like the honey-comb, and like unto the rarest wine, that I became most anxious that the ministers of the county should unite with me to plead the promise, 'If any two of you agree touching anything,' etc. Everything now conspired to induce my departure from the island: the unyielding spirit of those who had oppressed, and traduced me; and my own most courageous state of mind, fully believing that there was yet more work for me to do in the harvest of the Son of Man, my earnest prayers for Divine guidance, during one whole year, and the visions of my head at night, in my bed—all worked together towards this result."

Few things we know of are more sad than this story. "It was an affecting sight," says Mr. William Morgan, quoted by Mr. Rhys Stephen in his Memoir, "to see the aged man, who had laboured so long, and with such happy effects, leaving the sphere of his exertions under these circumstances; having laboured so much to pay for their meeting-houses, having performed so many journeys to South Wales for their benefit, having served them so diligently in the island, and passed through so many dangers; now some of the people withheld their contributions, to avenge themselves on their own father in the Gospel; others, while professing to be friends, did little more; while he, like David, was obliged to leave his city, not knowing whether he should ever return to see the ark of God, and his tabernacle in Anglesea again. Whatever misunderstanding there was between Mr. Evans, and some of his brethren, it is clear that his counsels ought to have been received with due acknowledgment of his age, and experience, and that his reputation should have been energetically vindicated. I am of opinion, I am quite convinced, that more strenuous exertions should have been made to defend his character, and to bear him, in the arms of love, through the archers, and not to have permitted him to fall in the street without an advocate."

The whole aim of Mr. Evans's life, as far as we have been able to read it, was to get good from heaven, in order that he might do good on earth. Clearly, he never worked with any hope of a great earthly reward for any personal worthiness; perhaps there arose a sense that he had always been unjustly remunerated, that burdens had been laid upon him he ought not to have been called upon to bear; and now the sense of injustice sought, as is so frequently the case, to vindicate itself by ingratitude. It seems so perpetually true, in the sad record of the story of human nature, that it is those who have injured us who seek yet further to hurt us.

CHAPTER V.
CONTEMPORARIES IN THE WELSH PULPIT—WILLIAMS OF WERN.

The Great Welsh Preachers unknown in England—The Family of the Williamses—Williams of Pantycelyn—Peter Williams—Evan Williams—Dr. Williams—Williams of Wern—The immense Power of his Graphic Language—Reading and Thinking—Instances of his Power of Luminous Illustration—Early Piety—A Young Preacher—A Welsh Gilboa—Admiration of, and Likeness to, Jacob Abbot—Axiomatic Style—Illustrations of Humour—The Devils—Fondness for Natural Imagery—Fondness of Solitude—Affecting Anecdotes of Dying Hours—His Daughter—His Preaching characterised—The Power of the Refrain in the Musician and the Preacher, "Unto us a Child is born."

WE pause here for a short time, in our review of the career, and character, and pulpit power of Christmas Evans, to notice some of those eminent men, who exercised, in his day, an influence over the Welsh mind. We will then notice some of those preachers, of even the wilder Wales, who preceded these men. So little is known of many of them in England, and yet their character, and labours, are so essentially and excellently instructive, that we feel this work, to those who are interested, to be not one of supererogation. The men, their country, the people among whom they moved, their work in it, the singular faith in, and love for preaching, for the words these men had to utter,—they must seem, to us, remarkable, and memorable. In this time of ours, when preaching, and all faith in preaching, is so rapidly dying out, that it may be regarded, now, as one of the chief qualifications of a candidate for the pulpit, that he cannot preach a sermon, but can "go to those who sell, and buy for himself"—this study of what was effected by a living voice, with a real live soul behind it, must seem, as a matter of mere history, noteworthy. And first among those who charmed the Welsh ear, in the time of Christmas Evans, we mention Williams of Wern.

It is not without reason, that many eminent Welshmen can only be known, and really designated after the place of their birth, or the chief scene of their labours. The family of the Williamses, for instance, in Wales, is a very large one—even the eminent Williamses; and William Williams would not make the matter any clearer; for, always with tenderest love ought to be pronounced the name of that other William Williams, or, as he is called, Williams of Pantycelyn—the obscure, but not forgotten, Watts of Wales. His hymns have been sung over the face of the whole earth, and long before missionary societies had been dreamed of, he wrote, in his remote Welsh village,

> "O'er the gloomy hills of darkness;"

and he has cheered, and comforted many a Zion's pilgrim by his sweet song,

> "Guide me, O Thou great Jehovah!"

He was born in 1717, and died in 1791. This sweet and sacred singer ought to receive more than this passing allusion. Little is known of him in England; and it is curious that Mr. Christopher's volume on "Hymn Writers and their Hymns" neither mentions his hymns, nor his name.

A writer in the *Quarterly Review*, evidently not very favourable to that denomination of religious sentiment which Williams represented, has spoken of the "unmixed pleasure" his name and character awakens: "He was a man in whom singular purity of sentiment added grace to a truly original genius." "His direction to other composers was, never to attempt to compose a hymn until they feel their souls near heaven. His precept, and his practice, in this respect, have been compared to those of Fra Angelico." Would that some competent Welsh pen would render for us, into English, more of these notes of the sweet singer of Pantycelyn.

William Williams came from the neighbourhood of Llandovery, the parish of Pritchard of the "Welshman's Candle;" he was, as his hymns would indicate, well educated; he studied for, and entered upon the medical profession; but, converted beneath the preaching of Howell Harris, in Talgarth churchyard, he turned from medicine to the work of the ministry. He was a member of the Established Church; he sought, and received ordination, and deacon's orders, but, upon application for priest's orders, he was refused. He then united himself with the Calvinistic Methodists, but still continued to labour with the great Daniel Rowlands, at Llangeitho. His sermons were, like his hymns, often sublime, always abounding in notes of sweetness. During the forty three years of his ministry, it is said, he travelled about 2,230 miles a year, making in all 95,890 miles! He wrote extensively, also, in prose. There is a handsome edition of his works in the Welsh language, and an English edition of some of his hymns. Among the most beautiful, our readers will remember—

> "Jesus, lead us with Thy power
> Safe into the promised rest."

This was William Williams of Pantycelyn.

Then, there was Peter Williams, a famous name in the Principality, and of about the same period as Williams of Pantycelyn. No man of his time did so much to cultivate religious literature in Wales. He was a great preacher, and an exemplary man; when a minister within the Church of England, he was persecuted for his opinions, and practices; and, when he left that communion, he suffered even a more bitter persecution from his Methodist brethren. His life, and his preaching, appear to have been full of romantic incidents.

Then there was Evan Williams, who is spoken of as a seraphic man, and whose life appears to justify the distinctive designation, although he died at the age of twenty-nine, very greatly in consequence of ill-usage received in persecution.

Then, in England, we are better acquainted with Daniel Williams, the founder of what is called Dr. Williams's Library; and who, in addition to this magnificent bequest, left sums of money to Wales for schools, endowments of ministers, annual grants of Bibles, and religious books, and for widows of ministers; by which Wales has received since, and receives now, the sum of about £700 a year. His ministry, however, was in London, at Hand Alley, Bishopsgate Street, nearly two hundred years since. His works are contained in six octavo volumes; but he scarcely falls beneath the intention of these pages.

Besides these, there are many others; so that, as we said above, the name of Williams represents, not only a large family, but a family remarkable for Christian usefulness in Wales. But, in this catalogue of eminent preachers, Williams of Wern, among those of his name, is singularly eminent. He had that power, to which we have referred, of using his language in such a manner, that people, in a very awful way, realized the scenes he described. Dr. Rees mentions of him, that when preaching on the resurrection of the dead, from the window of Ynysgan Chapel, Merthyr Tydvil, he so riveted the attention of the vast multitude, who were on the burying-ground before him, that when he reached the climax, all the crowd moved together in terror, imagining that the graves under their feet were bursting open, and the dead rising. Yet Williams was a singularly quiet preacher; these effects were wrought by the power of that language, so wonderfully fitted to work on the emotions of a very imaginative people, and which he knew how to play upon so well.

This great preacher had quite as remarkable an individuality as either of the eminent men, whose characters we may attempt faintly to portray. Christmas Evans, we have seen, led his hearers along through really dramatic, and pictorial representations. Davies was called the "Silver Trumpet" of Wales; his voice was an instrument of overwhelming compass, and sweetness. Elias was a man of severe, and passionate eloquence,—all the more terrible, because held in the restraint of a perfect, and commanding will. Williams differed from all three; nor must it, for a moment, be said that he "attained not to the first three." His eminence was equal to theirs, and, in his own walk, he was quite as highly esteemed; but his department of power was completely different. Perhaps, he was less the vehicle of vehement passion than either Elias, or Davies; and it was altogether apart from his purpose to use the amazing imagery of Christmas Evans. His mind was built up of compacted thought; his images were not personifications, but analogies. So far as we are able to form a conception of him, his mind appears to have moved in a pathway of self-evidencing light.

Thus, if we were to speak of these four men as constituting a quartette in the harmony of the great Welsh pulpit, we should give to John Elias the place of the deep bass; to Davies, the rich and melting soprano; to Christmas Evans the tenor; reserving, for Williams of Wern, the place of the alto. His teaching was eminently self-evolved. None of the great Welsh preachers dealt much with pen, and paper. They wrought out their sermons on horseback, or whilst moving from place to place. With Williams it was especially so. Two ministers called upon him in 1830. One of them was something of a bookworm, and he asked him if he had read a certain book which had just been published. Williams said he had not. "Have you," continued his friend, "seen so-and-so?" naming another work. "No, I have not." And, presently, a third was mentioned, and the answer was still in the negative. "I'll tell you what," said Mr. Williams, "you read too much; you do not think sufficiently. My plan in preparing sermons is to examine the connection of a passage, extract its principle, and think it over in my own mind. I never look at a Commentary, except when completely beaten."

It has often been said that, in the very proportion in which eloquence is effective, and commanding in delivery, in the degree in which it is effective as *heard*, it is impossible to be *read*; and, with some measure of exception, this is, no doubt, true. Williams, certainly, is an illustration of this general principle; yet he was, perhaps, one of the most luminous of speakers; only, this alone, without accompanying passion, does not make the orator. Take the following as an illustration of his manner. On ejaculatory prayer:—

> "Ejaculatory prayer is the Christian's breath; the secret path to his hiding-place; his express to heaven in circumstances of difficulty, and peril; it is the tuner of all his religious feelings; it is his sling, and stone, with which he slays the enemy, ere he is aware of it; it is the hiding of his strength; and, of every religious performance, it is the most convenient. Ejaculatory prayer is like the rope of a belfry; the bell is in one room, and the handle, or the end of the rope which sets it a-ringing, in another. Perhaps the bell may not be heard in the apartment where the rope is, but it is heard in its own apartment. Moses laid hold of the rope, and pulled it hard, on the shore of the Red Sea; and though no one heard, or knew anything of it, in the lower chamber,

the bell rang loudly in the upper one, till the whole place was moved, and the Lord said, 'Wherefore criest thou unto me?'"

This is luminous preaching. Unfortunately, as with others, we have very little—scarcely anything, indeed—left of Williams's pulpit talk.

William Williams was born in the year 1781, at Cwm-y-swn-ganol, in Merionethshire. There his parents occupied a farm, and were much respected. It seems, to us, an odd thing that their name was not Williams, but Probert, or Ap-Robert. He received his name of Williams from the singular practice, then prevalent in many parts of Wales, of converting, with the aid of the letter S, the Christian name of the father into the surname of the son. His father, although an orderly attendant upon Divine Worship, never made a public profession of religion; but his mother was a very pious, and exemplary member of the Calvinistic Methodist connexion.

The decisive hour of real religious conviction came to the youth when he was very young—only about thirteen years of age. Impressions deep, and permanent, were made on his mind, and heart, and at fifteen he was received into Church fellowship; but he suffered greatly from diffidence. Although it was expected of him, he could not pray either in the family, or in public, because, as he used to say, he would then be required, by all his acquaintance, to conduct himself like a perfect saint. But one night, when all the family, with the exception of his mother, and himself, had retired to rest, she engaged in prayer with him, and then said, "Now, Will, dear, do you pray," and he did so; and from this moment dated the commencement of his courage, and confidence.

It was in his twenty-second year that he entered Wrexham Academy. He was a thorough Welshman—a monoglot. He made some progress in the acquisition of English, and Greek; but he could never speak English fluently, and was advanced in life before he knew a word of it; and he used to say, "When I violate English, I am like a child that breaks a window; I do not go back to mend it, but I run away, hoping I shall not be seen." As linguists, most of his fellow-students outshone him; in the pulpit, from his very first efforts, he not only outshone them all, but it was soon seen that he was to transcend most of the teachers, and speakers of his time.

Perhaps his example will not commend itself to some of our modern writers, as to preparation for the ministry; for when he was recommended to continue longer under tuition, he said, "No—no; for if so, the harvest will be over while I am sharpening my sickle." Young as he was, he took a singular view of the leadings of Providence, which, however, eminently marks the character of the man. He received a most unanimous invitation from a large, and influential Church at Horeb, in Cardiganshire, and was just about accepting the invitation, when the smaller, and, in comparison, quite insignificant sphere of Wern was put before him, with such commendations of the importance of the work as commanded his regards. He declined Horeb, and accepted Wern.

His field of labour appears to have comprehended a cluster of villages, such as Llangollen, Rhuabon, and Rhosllanerchrugog; and in this region the greater number of his days were passed, excepting that brief period, towards the close of his life, when he became the minister of the great Welsh tabernacle in Cross Hall Street, Liverpool. But he left Wales with a heavy heart, amidst the pretty distinctly expressed dissatisfaction of the people of the Principality, who, however, still insisted on giving him his designation of Williams of Wern. Nor was he away from them long. His old Church continued unsettled, and after three years' ministry in Liverpool, he returned to Wern, to close his active, and useful life.

His pastorate consisted, really, of three places—Wern, Rhos, and Harwood. It was a singular circumstance, that whilst large crowds thronged round him at the first two places, and while his name was becoming as a sharp arrow through the whole Principality, he made little impression on Harwood. He used to say that Harwood had been of greater service to him than he had been to it; for it was "the thorn in the flesh, lest he should be exalted above measure;" and if he ever felt disposed to be lifted up when he saw the crowds gathering round him at other places, he had only to go over to, or think about Harwood, and this became an effectual check to the feelings of self-inflation, in which he might have been tempted to indulge. It was so, whilst other places, Churches, and congregations, "waited for him as for the rain, and opened their mouths wide as for the latter rain;" whilst upon other fields his "doctrine distilled as the dew," his stubborn Harwood appears to have been a kind of Welsh Gilboa, upon which no dew fell.

He was claimed as a kind of public property, and Churches at a distance seemed to think they had a right to his services, frequently very much to the irritation of his own people, to whom he might have given the consolation he once administered to a brother minister; "I understand that your people complain a good deal because you so often leave them. Well, let us be thankful that the reverse is not the case; for our own people might have tired of us, and be pleased to hear strangers, and preferred our absence, regarding us as 'a vessel wherein is no pleasure.'" Unfortunately, in such cases, congregations do not take the matter as philosophically as the old Scotchwoman, who, when she met a neighbouring clergyman one Sabbath morning, wending his way to her own kirk, expressed her surprise at meeting him there, and then. He explained that it was an exchange of services. "Eh, then," said the old woman, "*your* people will be having a grand treat the day."

Something of the nature of Williams's mind, and his method of ministration, may be gathered from his exceeding admiration of Jacob Abbot, and especially his work, "The Corner Stone." "Oh! what a pity," he said, "that we cannot preach as this man writes." But, so far as we have been able to judge from the scanty means we possess, he did preach very much after the manner of Jacob Abbot's writings. His words appear, first, to have been full of strong, seminal principles, and these were soon made clear in the light of very apt illustrations. Truly it has been said, that, first, the harper seizes his harp, and lays his hand firmly upon it, before he sweeps the strings. In an eminent manner, Williams gave to his people the sense, as soon as he commenced, that a subject was upon his heart, and mind; and he had a firm grasp of it, and from his creative mind each successive stroke was some fine, apt, happy evolution.

Illustration was his *forte*, but of a very different order from that of Christmas Evans; for instance, illustrating the contests of Christian creeds, and sects with each other, "I remember," he said, "talking with a marine, who gave to me a good deal of his history. He told me the most terrible engagement he had ever been in, was one between the ship to which he belonged, and another English vessel, when, on meeting in the night, they mistook each other for a French man-of-war. Many persons were wounded, some slain; both vessels sustained serious damage from the firing, and, when the day broke, great was their surprise to find the English flag hoisted from the masts of both vessels, and that, through mistake, they had been fighting all night against their own countrymen. It was of no avail, now, that they wept together: the mischief was done. Christians," said the preacher, "often commit the same error in this present world. One denomination mistakes another for an enemy; it is night, and they cannot see to recognise each other. What will be their surprise when they see each other in the light of another world! when they meet in heaven, after having shot at each other through the mists of the present state! How will they salute each other, when better known, and understood, after having wounded one another in the night! But they should wait till the dawn breaks, at any rate, that they may not be in danger, through any mistake, of shooting at their friends."

The Welsh language is, as we suppose our readers well know, especially rich in compact, proverbial, axiomatic expressions. The Welsh triads are an illustration of this. The same power often appears in the pulpit. The latter, and more recent, languages are unfavourable to the expression of proverbs. Williams we should suppose to have been one of the most favourable exemplifications of this power. General tradition in Wales gives him this kind of eminence—poem, and proverb united in his sentences. We have not been able to obtain many instances of this; and we fear it must be admitted, that our language only in a clumsy way translates the pithy quaintness of the Welsh, such as the following: "The door of heaven shuts from below, not from above. 'Your iniquities have separated, saith the Lord.'" "Of all the birds," he once said, "the dove is the most easily alarmed, and put to flight, at hearing a shot fired. Remember," he continued, "that the Holy Ghost is compared to a dove; and if you begin to shoot at each other, the heavenly Dove will take wing, and instantly leave you. The Holy Spirit is one of love, and peace, not of tumult, and confusion. He cannot live amongst the smoke, and noise of fired shots: if you would grieve the Holy Spirit, and compel Him to retire, you have only to commence firing at one another, and He will instantly depart." "The mind of man is like a mill, which will grind whatever you put into it, whether it be husk or wheat. The devil is very eager to have his turn at this mill, and to employ it for grinding the husk of vain thoughts. Keep the wheat of the Word in the mind; 'keep thy heart with all diligence.'"

Some of his words seem very odd, although he was a most grave, and serious man. Thus; "Our prayers often resemble the mischievous tricks of town-children, who knock at their neighbours' houses, and then run away; we often knock at Heaven's door, and then run off into the spirit of the world: instead of waiting for entrance, and answer, we act as if we were afraid of having our prayers answered." Again: "There are three devils which injure, and ravage our Churches, and congregations,—the singing devil, the pew-letting devil, and the Church officers' appointment devil: they are of the worst kind of devils, and this kind goeth not out but by prayer, and fasting." "The old ministers," he used to say, "were not much better preachers than we are, and, in many respects, they were inferior to us; but they had a success attendant upon their ministry that can now seldom be seen. They prayed more than we do. It was on his knees that Jacob became a prince; and if we would become princes, we must be more upon our knees. We should be successful as our fathers, could we be brought to the same spirit, and frame of mind."

But Williams is like Elias in this; we have had none of his sermons rendered into English, and, therefore, the descriptions we have are rather tantalizing. Mr. Parry, the Congregational minister of Llandudno, a man well fitted to judge—himself one of the most distinguished living poets in the Welsh language, and who has carried many prizes from the Eisteddfodd—says of him: "I shall never forget his eloquence. It poured forth like a swollen torrent. I cannot help referring to a sermon he preached at an annual Association at Llanerchmedd, Anglesea. The meeting was, as usual, held in the open air. The weather was very sultry; the congregation seemed drowsy. His manner, before preaching, showed considerable restlessness, and when he came to the desk, he looked rather wild. It was evident his spirit was on fire, and his mind charged brimful with ideas. He read his text in a quick, bold tone; 'But now they desire a better country, that is, a heavenly.' He poured forth such a flood of eloquent description, that he completely enchanted our feelings, and made us imagine we felt the field move under our feet. He himself thought this occasion one of the most remarkable in his life; for I spoke to him about the sermon years after. I believe it served to raise our Churches throughout the whole land."

He was a more extensive reader than any of his brethren in the ministry; a keen observer, too, in the departments of natural history, and natural philosophy. It was, indeed, much like his own method, and it illustrated the reason of his great admiration for Jacob Abbot's "Corner Stone," when he very prettily says, "The blessed Redeemer was very fond of His Father's works." He used to say, "If we understood nature better, it would help us to understand the Bible better. The kingdom of nature, and the kingdom of grace, are very like each other. There is a striking resemblance between the natural principles of the one, and the moral principles of the other." He entered with a kind of joy into the sublime moods of nature; was fond of watching the play of the lightning, and listening to the voice of the thunder. "Jesus," he used to say, "loved to look at the lily, and to listen to the birds; to speak upon the mysteries of the seed, and to draw forth principles from these things. It was no part of His plan to expound the laws of nature, although He understood them more perfectly than any one else; but He employed nature as a book of reference, to explain the great principles of the plan of salvation."

A clergyman writes of him, that "his appearance when preaching was very remarkable, and singularly beautiful. When standing in a great crowd, every soul seemed agitated to its centre, and cheeks streaming with tears. It is but justice that every one should have his likeness taken when he appears to the greatest advantage; and so Williams. His picture, on such an occasion, would be an honour to the country which reared him, a treasure to the thousands who heard him, and a name to the painter." The likeness is before us now, and in the firm, composed thoughtfulness, a kind of sad, far outlook in the eyes, and the lips which seem to wait to tremble into emotion—we think we can well realize, from the inanimate engraving, what life must have been in the speech of this extraordinary man. His mind was cast in a sweetly meditative mould. He was fond of retreating by himself among the trees, and walking beneath their shadows, as they formed a canopy over his head. He said of one such place, "I think I must love that spot through all eternity, for I have felt a degree of heaven there."

And thus he died. He had lost his wife some time before. It is very affecting to read the account of himself, and his daughter, dying together in different rooms of the same house. As he said to her, one day, "We appear to be running, with contending footsteps, to be first at the goal." They spent much time in talking together, with unruffled composure, of death, and heaven, and being "absent from the body, and present with the Lord." Every morning, as soon as he was up, found him by the bedside of his daughter.

Once he said to her, "Well, Eliza, how are you this morning?"

"Very weak, father."

"Ah!" said he, "we are both on the racecourse. Which of us do you think will get to the end first?"

"Oh, I shall, father. I think you must have more work to do yet."

"No," he said; "I think my work is nearly over."

"It may be so, father; but, still, I think I shall be the first to go."

"Perhaps," he said, "it is best it should be so, for I am more able to bear the blow. But," he continued, "do you long to see the end of the journey?"

"Oh, from my heart!" she replied.

"But why?"

"Because I shall see so many of my old friends, and my mother; and, above all, I shall see Jesus."

"Ah, well, then," he said, "tell them I am coming! tell them I am coming!"

She died first. Her last words were, "Peace! peace!" He followed her shortly after—on the 17th of March, 1840, in the fifty-ninth year of his age.

Amongst the great preachers of Wales, not one seems to have won more upon the tender love of those who knew him. Dr. Raffles said of him, "What he was as a preacher, I can only gather from the effects he produced on those who understood the language in which he spoke, but I can truly say, that every occasion on which I saw him only served to impress me more with the ardour of his piety, and the kindness of his heart. He was one of the loveliest characters it has been my lot to meet."

High strains of thought, rendered into the sweet variety, melting tenderness, and the grand strength of the language of Wales, seem to have been the characteristics of the preaching of Williams of Wern; tender, and terrible, sweetness alternating with strength. We have already said how much Welsh preaching derived, in its greatest men, from the power of varying accent; the reader may conceive it himself if ever listening to that wonderful chorus in Handel's "Messiah," which Herder, the great German, called truly the Christian Epos; but the chorus to which we refer, is that singular piece of varying pictorial power, "Unto us a Child is born," repeated, again and again, in sweet whispered accents, playing upon the thought; the shepherds having kept watch over their flocks by night in the fields, and having heard the revelation voices of the angels say it—"For unto us a Child is born;" and then rolls in the grand thunder, "And His name shall be called Wonderful;" and then, you return back to the sweet silvery accents, "For unto us a Child is born;" and the thought is, that the Wise Men are there offering their gifts; and then roll in, again, the grand, overwhelming words, "And His name shall be called Wonderful;" and yet again that for which we waited, the tender, silvery whisperings, "Unto us a Child is born;" until it seems as if flocks, and herds, and fields, shepherds, and wise men, all united with the family of Jesus, beneath the song-singing through the heavens in the clear starry night, "Unto us a Child is born, and His name shall be called Wonderful." Those who have listened to this chorus, may form some idea of the way in which a great Welsh preacher—and Williams of Wern as a special illustration—would run his thought, and its corresponding expression, up and down, through various tones of feeling, and with every one awaken, on some varying accent, a fresh interpretation, and expression. Perhaps, the nearest approach we have heard, in England, to the peculiar gifts of this preacher, has been in the happiest moods of the beloved, and greatly honoured Thomas Jones, once minister of Bedford Chapel, London.

CHAPTER VI.
CONTEMPORARIES—JOHN ELIAS.

Fire and Smoke—Elias's Pure Flame—Notes in the Pulpit—Carrying Fire in Paper—Elias's Power in Apostrophe—Anecdote of the Flax-dresser—A Singular First Appearance in the Pulpit—A Rough Time in Wales—The Burning of the Ravens' Nests—A Hideous Custom put down—The Great Fair of Rhuddlan—The Ten Cannon of Sinai—Action in Oratory—The Tremendous Character of his Preaching—Lives in an Atmosphere of Prayer—Singular Dispersion on a Racecourse—A Remarkable Sermon, Shall the Prey be taken from the Mighty?—Anecdote of a Noble Earl—Death and Funeral.

WE have already implied that Welsh preaching has had many varieties, and very various influences too. Even the very excitements produced by these famous men, whose names we are recording, varied considerably; but one characteristic certainly seemed to attend them—the influence was real, and very undoubted. When Rowland Hill was in Wales, and witnessed some of the strong agitations resulting from great sermons, he said, he "liked the fire, but he did not like the smoke." It was, like so many of the sayings of the excellent old humorist, prettily, and wittily said. But it may, also, be remarked, that it is, usually, impossible to have real fire without smoke; and it has further been well said, that the stories of the results of such preaching make us feel that, could we only get the fire, we need not object to a little of the smoke.

We are introducing to our readers, now, in John Elias, one who, certainly, does not seem to have surrounded the clear flames of his eloquence with unnatural excitement. If the effects of his oratory seem to rival all that we have heard of the astonishing power of George Whitefield, the material of his sermons, the severity of their tone of thought, and the fearfulness of their remorseless logic, remind us of Jonathan Edwards. He had read extensively, especially in theology; and, it has been truly said, his mind was a storehouse, large, lofty, and rich. Like his great coadjutors, he prepared for the pulpit with amazing care, and patience, but apparently never verbally—only seeing his ideas clearly, and revolving them over and over until, like fuel in the furnace, they flamed. He tells us how, having done his part, by earnest, and patient study, he trusted to God to give to his prepared mind its fitting expression, and speech. Of course, like the rest, he disclaimed all paper in the pulpit. An eminent brother minister, Thomas Jones, of Denbigh, was coming to London to preach what was considered the great annual sermon of the London Missionary Society, at Surrey Chapel. In his own country, Mr. Jones preached always extempore; but, being in company with Matthew

Wilkes, and John Elias, he inquired of old Matthew whether, for such an occasion, he did not think that he had better write his sermon.

"Well, for *such* an occasion," said Matthew, "perhaps it would be better to write your discourse; but, at any rate, let us have plenty of fire in it."

"But," said John Elias, "he cannot carry fire in paper!"

"Never mind," said Matthew; "paper will do very well to light the fire with!"

Mr. Wilkes' witty rejoinder seems to give the entire value to notes, and writing in the pulpit; but, no doubt, Elias expressed his conviction, and the conviction of all these men, that you cannot carry fire in paper. But we have before said that it was by no means wild-fire. One of the great poets of Wales imagined a conversation going on between the soul and the body of Elias, before they both went up together in the pulpit, when the soul said to the body, "Now, you must be a sacrifice for an hour. You must bear all my fire, and endure all my exertion, however intense it may be." And another writer says of him that, while some preachers remind us of Pharaoh's chariots, that drove heavily, Elias reminded us, rather, of that text, "He maketh His angels spirits, and His ministers a flame of fire."

Whatever is to be said of the peculiarities of other great Welsh preachers, it seems to be admitted, on all hands, that John Elias was the Demosthenes of the group. Let no reader smile, however high his regard for the classic orator. The stories told of the effects of the preaching of John Elias, greatly resemble those of the great Grecian orator, who, at the close of his tremendous orations, found the people utterly oblivious to all the beauty, and strength of his discourses—utterly indisposed to admire, or criticise, but only conducted to that point of vehement indignation, and passionate action, which had been, all along, the purpose of the speaker, exclaiming, "Let us march against Philip!"

If profound passionate conviction, persuasion altogether insensible of anything besides its own emotions, be the chief attribute of the gifted orator, John Elias must stand, we will not say matchless, but, from all that we have heard of him, unsurpassed. We have no means of testing this by any published sermons; scraps and fragments we have, and traditions of the man, and his soul-piercing eloquence, float about over Wales; but we apprehend it was an order of eloquence which would not submit itself to either penmanship, or paper, either to the reporter, or the printing-press.

How extravagant some things seem when quietly read, unaccompanied by the passion, and excitement which the preacher has either apprehended, or produced! The reader remembers very well—for who does not?—Whitefield's vehement apostrophe, "Stop, Gabriel!" Who could deliberately write it down to utter it? and what an affectation of emotion it seems to read it! But that was not the effect produced on David Hume, who heard it; and we may be very sure that man,—the most acute, profound, cold philosopher, and correct writer, had no friendly feelings either to Whitefield, or Gabriel— to the message which the preacher had to give, or the archangel to carry. A quiet, ordinary, domestic state of feeling scarcely knows how to make allowances for an inflamed orator, his whole nature heaving beneath the passion produced by some great, and subduing vision, an audience in his hands, as a river of water, prepared to move whithersoever he will. Thus Elias, when he was handling some weighty subject, would suddenly say, "Stop! silence!" (*Disymwth*! *Gosteg*!) "What are they saying in Heaven on the subject?" His hearers testify that, in such moments, he almost brought them within the precincts of the glory. The effect was thrilling. And, dealing with alarming truths, he would exclaim, "Stop! silence! What do they say in hell on this subject?"

The man who can do these things must be no hearsay man, or such questionable excursions of speech would be likely to provoke laughter, and contempt, rather than overwhelming awe. The effect of this preacher was unutterable. It is said that upon such occasions, had the people heard these things from the invisible world, as he expatiated on the things most likely to be uttered, either in Heaven or hell, upon the subject, they could scarcely have been more alarmed.

His biographer, Mr. Morgan, Vicar of Syston, in Leicestershire, tells how he heard him preaching once to a crowd in the open air, on "the Last Day," representing the wicked as "tares gathered into bundles," and cast into the everlasting burnings. There was a certain flax-dresser, who, in a daring and audacious way, chose to go on with his work in an open room opposite to where Elias was preaching from the platform; but, as the preacher grew more and more earnest, and the flames more flashing, the terrible fire more and more intense in its vehemence, the man was obliged to leave his work, and run into a yard behind his house, to get out of the reach of the cruel flames, and the awful peals of the thunder of the preacher's subduing voice. "But the awful language of that Elias followed me there also," said the panic-stricken sinner.

There was a preacher of Caernarvon, one Richardson, a preacher of peculiar tenderness, and sweetness, who made his hearers weep beneath the lovely message he generally carried. On one occasion, while Elias was pouring forth his vehement, and dreadful words, painting the next world in very living, and fearful colours, his audience all panic-stricken, and carried along as if they were on the confines of the darkness, and the gates opening to receive them, a man, in the agony of his excitement, cried out, "Oh, I wish I could hear Mr. Richardson, of Caernarvon, just for five minutes!" No anecdote could better illustrate the peculiar gifts, and powers of both men.

John Elias was a native of Caernarvonshire. His parents were people in very humble circumstances, but greatly respected. His paternal grandfather lived with them. He was a member of the Church of England. His influence over the mind of Elias appears to have been especially good; and it is, perhaps, owing to this influence that, although he became a minister, and the eminent pride of the Calvinistic Methodist body, he, throughout his life, retained a strong affection for the services, and even the institution, of the Church of England. Through his grandfather, he acquired, what was not usual in that day, the rudiments of education very early, and as a young child, could read very well and impressively. Thus, when quite a child, they went together to hear some well-known Methodist preacher. The time for the service had long passed, and the preacher did not arrive. The old gentleman became impatient, and said to his little grandson, "It's a pity the people should be idling like this; go up into the pulpit, John, and read a chapter to them;" and, suiting the action to the word, he pushed the child up into the pulpit, and shut the door after him. With much diffidence, he began to read portions of the Sermon on the Mount, until, venturing to withdraw his eye from the Bible, and look aside, lo! to his great dismay, there was the preacher quietly waiting outside the pulpit door. He gently closed the book, and slipped down the pulpit stairs. This was his first appearance in the pulpit. Little could any one dream that, in after years, he was to be so eminent a master in it.

But he was only twenty years of age when he began to preach, indeed; and it is said that, from the first, people saw that a prophet of God had risen amongst them. There was a popular preacher, with a very Welsh name, David Cadwalladr, who went to hear him; and, after the sermon, he said, "God help that lad to speak the truth, for he'll make the people believe,— he'll make the people believe whatever he says!" From the first, John Elias appears to have been singularly like his two namesakes, John the Baptist, and Elias the prophet. He had in him a very tender nature; but he was a severe man, and he had a very severe theology. He believed that sin held, in itself, very tremendous, and fearful consequences, and he dealt with sin, and sinners, in a very daring, and even dreadful manner.

He appeared in a rough time, when there were, in the neighbourhood, rough, cruel, and revolting customs. Thus, on Whitsunday in each year, a great concourse of people used to assemble together to burn the ravens' nests. These birds bred in a high and precipitous rock, called Y *gadair* (that is, "the chair"). The birds were supposed to prey on young poultry, etc., and the people thought it necessary to destroy them; but they always did so on the Sabbath, and it became quite a wild festival occasion; and the manner of their destruction was most savage, and revolting. The nests were beyond their reach; but they suspended a fiery fagot by a chain. This was let down to set the nests on fire; and the young birds were roasted alive. At every blaze which was seen below, triumphant shouts rose from the brutal crowd, rending the air. When the savages had put the birds to death, they usually turned on each other; and the day's amusement closed in fights, wounds, bruises, and broken bones. One of the first of Elias's achievements was the daring feat of invading this savage assembly, by proclaiming, in their very midst, the wrath of God against unrighteousness, and Sabbath-breaking. Perhaps, to us, the idea of preaching in such a scene seems like the attempting to still a storm by the waving of a feather; but we may also feel that here was a scene in which that terrible eloquence, which was a chief power of Elias, was well bestowed. Certainly, it appears chiefly due to Elias that the hideous custom was put down, and put to an end for ever.

It was no recreative play, no rippling out of mild, meditative, innocent young sermons, these first efforts of young Elias. For instance, there was a great fair which was wont to be held at Rhuddlan, in Denbighshire. It was always held on the Lord's Day. Thither, into the midst of the fair, went the young man. He took his stand on the steps of the New Inn, the noise and business of the fair going on all around him. His friends had earnestly tried to dissuade, and entreated him not to venture into the midst of so wild, and dangerous a scene. Farmers were there, to hire labourers; crowds of rough labourers were there. It was the great market-day for scythes, and reaping-hooks. In the booths all round him were the sounds of harps, and fiddles; it was a wild scene of dissipation. There stood the solemn young man, thoughtful, grave, and compassionate. Of course, he commenced with a very solemn prayer; praying so that almost every order of person on the ground felt himself arrested, and brought, in a solemn way, before God. Singular effects, it is said, seemed to follow the prayer itself. Then he took for his text the fourth commandment; but he said he had come to open upon them "the whole ten cannon of Sinai." The effects could hardly have been more tremendous had the congregation really stood at the foot of the mountain that "might not be touched." In any case, Elias was an awful preacher; and we may be sure that upon this occasion he did not keep his terrors in reserve.

One man, who had just purchased a sickle, was so alarmed at the tremendous denunciations against Sabbath-breakers, that he imagined that the arm which held the sickle was paralysed; he let it fall on the ground. He could not take his eye from the preacher; and he feared to stoop to pick it up with the other hand, lest that should be paralysed also. It ought, also, to be said this man became an entirely changed character, and lived, to an advanced age, a consistent Christian. The great crowd was panic-stricken. The fair was never after held on the Lord's Day. Some person said to Elias, afterwards, that the fair was an old custom, and it would recover itself, notwithstanding his extraordinary sermon. Elias, in his dreadful manner, replied, "If any one will give the least encouragement to the revival of that fair, he will be accursed before the Holy Trinity, in the name of the Father, the Son, and the Holy Ghost!" A dreadfully earnest sort of man this. We are not vindicating his speeches, only giving an account of them.

Mr. Jones, the Rector of Nevern, one of the most eminent of the Welsh bards, says, "For one to throw his arms about, is not action; to make this, or that gesture, is not action. Action is seen in the eye, in the curling of the lip, in the frowning of the nose—in every muscle of the speaker." Mentioning these remarks to Dr. Pugh, when speaking of Elias, he said he "never saw an orator that could be compared to him. Every muscle was in action, and every movement that he made was not only graceful, but it spoke. As an orator," said Dr. Pugh, "I considered him fully equal to Demosthenes!"

It was tremendous preaching. It met the state of society—the needs of the times. What is there in a sermon?—what is there in preaching? some have flippantly inquired. We have seen that the preaching of Elias effected social revolutions; it destroyed bad customs, and improved manners. He lived in this work; it consumed him. Those who knew him, applied to him the words of Scripture: "The zeal of Thine house hath eaten me up." In estimating him, and his work, it ought never to be forgotten, that, as has always been the case with such men, he lived in a life of wondrous prayerfulness, and spiritual elevation. He was called to preach a great Association sermon at Pwlheli. In the whole neighbourhood the state of religion was very low, and distressingly discouraging to pious minds; and it had been so for many years. Elias felt that his visit must be an occasion with him. It may almost be said of that day, that "Elias prayed, and the heavens gave rain." He went. He took his text, "Let God arise, and let His enemies be scattered!" It was an astonishing time. While the preacher drove along with his tremendous power, multitudes of the people fell to the ground. Calm stood the man, his words rushing from him like flames of fire. There were added to the Churches of that immediate neighbourhood, Mr. Elias's clerical biographer tells us, in consequence of the powerful impetus of that sermon, two thousand five hundred members.

The good man lived in an atmosphere of prayer. The stories which gather about such men, sometimes seem to partake of the nature of exaggerations; but, on the other hand, it ought to be recollected that all anecdotes and popular impressions arise from some well-known characteristic to which they are the correspondents. There was a poor woman, a neighbour's wife. She was very ill, and her case pressed very much upon the mind of Elias in family prayer. But one morning he said to his wife, "I have somehow missed Elizabeth in my prayer this morning; I think she cannot be alive." The words had scarcely passed from his lips when the husband was at the door, to tell him of his wife's departure.

There is a singular circumstance mentioned of some horse-races, a great disturbance to the best interests of the neighbourhood; on the day of the great race, Elias's spirit was very much moved, and he prayed most passionately and earnestly that the Lord would do something to put a stop to them. His prayer was so remarkable, that someone said, "Ahab must prepare his chariot, and get away." The sky became so dark shortly after, that the gas was lighted in some of the shops of the town. At eleven o'clock the rain began to pour in torrents, and continued until five o'clock in the afternoon of the next day. The multitudes on the race-ground dispersed in half-an-hour, and did not reassemble that year; and what seemed more remarkable was, that the rainfall was confined to that vicinity. It is our duty to mention these things. An adequate impression could not be conveyed of the place this man held in popular estimation without them. And his eminence as a preacher was astonishing; wherever he went, whatever day of the week, or whatever hour of the day, no matter what the time or the season, business was laid aside, shops were closed, and the crowds gathered to hear him. Sometimes, when it was arranged for him to preach in a chapel, and more convenient that he should do so, a window was taken out, and there he stood, preaching to the crowded place within, and, at the same time, to the multitudes gathered outside. Mr. Morgan, late vicar of Christ Church, in Bradford, gives an account of one of these sermons. There was a great panorama exhibiting at the same time. Elias took the idea of moving succession—the panorama of all the miracles wrought by Christ. It is easy to see how, from such lips, a succession of wonderful pictures would pass before the eye, of living miracles of Divine working,—a panorama of wonderful cures. Mr. Morgan says, "I was very ill at the time, but that striking sermon animated me, and I have often stirred the cold English with the account of it."

We have said that no sermons are preserved; Elias himself regretted, in his advanced life, that some, which had been of a peculiar interest to him, had gone from him. Fragments there are, but they are from the lips of hearers. Many of these fragments still present, in a very impressive manner, his rousing, and piercing, and singularly original style; his peculiar mode of dealing at will, for his purposes of illustration, with the things of earth, heaven, and hell.

Take one illustration, from the text, "*Shall the prey be taken from the mighty, or the lawful captive be delivered?*" "*Satan!*" he exclaimed, "what do you say? Shall the prey be taken from the mighty? 'No, never. I will increase the darkness of their minds; I will harden more the hardness of their hearts; I will make more powerful the lusts in their souls; I will increase the strength of their chains; I will bind them hand and foot, and make my chains stronger; the captives shall never be delivered. Ministers! I despise ministers! Puny efforts theirs!' '*Gabriel*!' exclaimed the preacher, 'messenger of the Most High God: shall the prey be taken from the mighty?' 'Ah! I do not know. I have been hovering over this assembly. They have been hearing the Word of God. I did expect to see some chains broken, some prisoners set free; but the opportunity is nearly over; the multitudes are just upon the point of separating; there are no signs of any being converted. I go back from this to the heavenly world, but I have no messages to carry to make joy in the presence of the angels.'" There were crowds of preachers present. Elias turned to them. "'What think you? You are *ministers* of the living God. Shall the prey be taken from the mighty?' 'Ah! who hath believed our report? and to whom is the arm of the Lord revealed? We have laboured in vain, and spent our strength for nought; and it seems the Lord's arm is not stretched out. Oh, there seems very little hope of the captives being delivered!' '*Zion*! Church of Christ! answer me, Shall the prey be taken from the mighty? What do you say?' And Zion said, 'My God hath forgotten me; I am left alone, and am childless. And my enemies say, This is Zion, whom no man seeketh after.' Oh, I am afraid the prey will not be taken from the mighty—the captive will not be delivered. *Praying Christians*, what do you think? 'O Lord, Thou knowest. High is Thy hand, and strong is Thy right hand. Oh that Thou wouldst rend the heavens, and come down! Let the sighing of the prisoner come before Thee. According to the greatness of Thy power, preserve Thou them that are appointed to die. I am nearly wearying in praying, and yet I have a hope that the year of jubilee is at hand.'" Then, at this point, Elias assumed another, higher, and his most serious manner, as if about to speak to the Almighty; and, in quite another tone, he said, "What is the mind of the Lord respecting these captives? Shall the prey be taken from the mighty?" Then he exclaimed, "'Thus saith the Lord, Even the captives of the mighty shall be taken away, and the prey of the terrible shall be delivered.' Ah!" he exclaimed, "there is no doubt about the mind and will of the Lord—no room for doubt, and hesitation. 'The ransomed of the Lord shall return, and come to Zion with songs and everlasting joy upon their heads.'"

This is the fragment of a sermon preached when Elias was about thirty years of age. Of course it can give but a very slender idea, but perhaps it shows something of the manner of the master. His imagination was very brilliant, but more chastened, and subdued, than that of many. His eloquence, like all of the highest order, was simple, and he trusted rather to a fitting word, than to a large furniture of speech. It is said that, to his friends, every sermon appeared to be a complete masterpiece of elocution, a nicely-compacted, and well-fitted oration.

Among the great Welsh preachers, David Davies, and Williams of Wern were, like Rowlands of Llangeitho, comparatively fixtures. Of course, they appeared on great Association occasions. But John Elias, and Christmas Evans itinerated far, and wide. Unlike as they were in the build of their minds, and the character of their eloquence, they had a great, and mutual, regard, and affection for each other; and it is told how, when either preached, the other was seen with anxious interest drinking in, with the crowd, the words of his famous brother. Theirs are, no doubt, the two darling names most known to the religious national heart of Wales. To John Elias it is impossible to render such a mede of justice, or to give of his powers even so comprehensive a picture, as is attempted, even in this volume, of Christmas Evans.

Something like an illustration of the man may be gathered from an anecdote of the formation of one of the first Bible Societies in North Wales. It was a very great occasion. A noble Earl, the Lord Lieutenant of the county, was to take the chair; but when he heard that John Elias was expected to be the principal speaker, he very earnestly implored that he might be kept back, as "a ranter, a Methodist, and a Dissenter, who could do no good to the meeting." The position of Elias was such that, upon such an occasion, no one could have dared to do that; so the noble Lord introduced him, but with certain hints that "brevity, and seriousness would be desirable." The idea of recommending seriousness to John Elias, certainly, seems a very needless commendation; but when Elias spoke,—partly in English, and partly in Welsh,—especially when, in stirring Welsh, he referred to the constitution of England, and the repose of the country, as illustrating the value of the Bible to society, and some other such remarks,—of course with all the orator's piercing grandeur of expression,—the chairman, seeing the inflamed state of the people, and himself not well knowing what was said, would have the words translated to him. He was so carried away by the dignified bearing of the great orator, that he would have a special introduction to him at the close of the meeting. A day or two after, a special messenger came to invite him to visit, and spend some time at the house of the Earl. This, however, was respectfully declined, for reasons, no doubt, satisfactory to Elias, and which would satisfy the peer also, that the preacher had no desire to use his great popularity for his own personal influence, and aggrandisement.

After a life of eminent usefulness, he died, in 1841, at the age of sixty-eight. His funeral was a mighty procession, of about ten thousand persons. They had to travel, a distance of some miles, to the beautiful little churchyard of Llanfaes, a secluded, and peaceful spot,—a scene of natural romance, and beauty, the site of an old Franciscan monastery, about fourteen miles from Llangefni, the village where Elias died. The day of the funeral was, throughout the whole district, as still as a Sabbath. As it passed by Beaumaris, the procession saw the flags of the vessels in the port lowered half-mast high; and as they passed through Beaumaris town, and Bangor city, all the shops were closed, and all the blinds drawn before the windows. Every kind of denomination, including the Church of England, joined in marks of respect, and justified, more distinctly than could always be done, the propriety of the text of the funeral oration: "Know ye not that a prince and a great man has fallen?" Of him it might truly be said, *"Behold I will make thee a new sharp threshing instrument, having teeth: thou shalt thresh the mountains, and beat them small, and shalt make the hills like chaff."*

CHAPTER VII.
CONTEMPORARIES—DAVIES OF SWANSEA.

Traditions of his Extraordinary Eloquence—Childhood—Unites in Church Fellowship with Christmas Evans, and with him preaches his First Sermon—The Church of Castell Hywel—Settles in the Ministry at Frefach—The Anonymous Preacher—Settles in Swansea—Swansea a Hundred Years Since—Mr. Davies reforms the Neighbourhood—Anecdotes of the Power of his Personal Character—How he Dealt with some Young Offenders—Anecdote of a Captain—The Gentle Character of his Eloquence—The Human Voice a Great Organ—The Power of the "Vox Humana" Stop—A Great Hymn Writer—His Last Sermon.

WE shall, in the next chapter, mention several names of men, mightily influential as Welsh preachers in their own country, and to most English readers utterly unknown. Perhaps the most conspicuous of these lesser known men is, however, David Davies, of Swansea. Dr. Thomas Rees, in every sense a thoroughly competent authority, speaks of him as one of the most powerful pulpit orators in his own, or any other, age; and he quotes the words of a well-known Welsh writer, a minister, who says of David Davies: "In his best days, he was one of the chief of the great Welsh preachers." This writer continues: "I may be deemed too partial to my own denomination in making such an observation. What, it may be asked, shall be thought of John Elias, Christmas Evans, and others? In point of flowing eloquence, Davies was superior to every one of them, although, with regard to his matter, and the energy, and deep feeling with which he treated his subjects, Elias, in his best days, excelled him." As to this question of feeling, however, the writer of these pages was talking, some time since, with Dr. Rees himself, about this same David Davies, when the Doctor said: "What the old people tell you about him is wonderful. It was in his voice—he could not help himself; without any effort, five minutes after he began to speak, the whole congregation would be bathed in tears."

This great, and admirable man was born in the obscure little village of Llangeler, in Carmarthenshire, in June, 1763. His parents, although respectable, not being in affluent circumstances, could give him very few advantages of education. Thus it happened that, eminent as he became as a preacher, as one of the most effective hymn-writers in his language, and as a Biblical commentator, he was entirely a self-made man. However, as is so often the case in such instances, his earnest eagerness in the acquisition of knowledge was manifest when he was yet very young; and he was under the influence of very strong religious impressions at a very early age.

Even when he was quite a child, he would always stand up, and gravely ask a blessing on his meals; and it is said that there was something so impressive, and grave, in the manner of the child, that some careless frequenters of the house always took off their hats, and behaved with grave decorum until the short prayer was ended. His parents were not religious persons, and, therefore, it is yet more remarkable that one day, while he was still in his earliest years, his father heard him fervently in prayer for them behind a hedge. It is not wonderful to learn that he was greatly affected by it. It does not seem that this depth of religious life accompanied him all the way through his boyhood, and his youth; but a very early marriage—in most instances, so grave, and fatal a mistake—would appear to have been the occasion of the restoration of his religious convictions. He was but twenty when he married Jane Evans, a respectable, and lovely young woman of his own neighbourhood; and now his religious life began in real earnest.

It is surely very remarkable, as we have already seen, that he, and Christmas Evans were admitted into Church fellowship on the same evening,—the Church to which we have already referred,—beneath the pastorate of the eminent scholar, and bard, David Davies, of Castell Hywel. The singularity did not stop here. Christmas Evans, and the young Davies, preached their first sermon in the same little cottage, in the parish of Llangeler, within a week of each other. The two youths were destined to be the most eminent lights of their different denominations, in their own country, in that age; but neither of them continued long in connection with the Church at Castell Hywel; and as they joined at the same time, so about the same time they left.

David Davies, their pastor, was a great man, and an eminent preacher, but he was an Arian, and the Church members were chiefly of the same school of thought; and the convictions of both youths were altogether of too deep, and matured an order, to be satisfied by the Arian view of the person, and work of Christ. Moreover, they both, by the advice of friends, were looking to the work of the Ministry, for which they must have early shown their fitness; and, as we have noticed in the case of Christmas Evans, there was a rule in the Church at Castell Hywel, that no one should be permitted to preach who had not received an academical training.

This, in addition to their dissatisfaction with services devoted chiefly to the frigid statements of speculative points of doctrine, or the illustration of worldly politics, soon operated to move the young men into other fields. Evans, as we know, united himself with the Baptists; Davies found a congenial ministration at Pencadair, under the direction of a noted evangelical teacher of those parts, the Rev. William Perkins. There his deepest religious convictions became informed, and strengthened. Davies was always a man of emotion; it was his great strength when he became a preacher; and his biographer very pleasingly states the relation of his after-work to this moment of his life, when he says that, "Beneath the teaching of Mr. Perkins, a delightful change came over his feelings; he could now see, in the revealed testimony concerning the work finished by our Divine Surety, and Redeemer, enough to give confidence of approach 'into the holiest,' to every one who believes the report of it, as made known to all alike in the Scriptures. We may justly say, 'Blessed are their eyes who see' this; who see that God is now 'reconciling the world unto Himself, not imputing unto men their trespasses.' They, indeed, see the heavens opened, and the angels of God ascending, and descending upon the Son of Man. They see that fulfilled which was set forth of old in vision to Jacob, the restoration of intercourse between earth and heaven through a mediator; and, in the discovery of it, they walk joyfully in the way of peace, and in the gracious presence of their reconciled Father."

It was after this period that the first sermon was preached, in the cottage to which we have alluded. "The humble beginning of both Davies, and Evans, naturally reminds us," says Davies' biographer, "of the progress of an oak from the acorn to the full-grown tree, or that of a streamlet issuing from an obscure valley among the mountains, and swelling, by degrees, into a broad, and majestic river." David Davies soon became well known in his neighbourhood as a mighty evangelist. Having grounded his own convictions, and even then possessed of a copious eloquence, it is not wonderful to read that dead Churches rose into newness of life, and became, in the course of time, flourishing societies. He was ordained as a co-pastor with the Rev. John Lewis, at Trefach. The chapel became too small, and a new one was built, which received the name of Saron. He became a blessing to Neuaddlwyd, and Gwernogle; his words ran, like flames of fire, through the whole district. It is said that his active spirit, and fervent style of preaching, gave a new tone to the ministry of the Independents throughout the whole Principality. Hearers, who have been unaccustomed to the penetrating, the quietly passionate emotionalness of the great Welsh preachers, can scarcely form an idea of the way in which their at once happy, and invincible words would set a congregation on fire.

The beloved, and revered William Rees, of Liverpool, in his memoir of his father, gives an illustration of this, in connection with a sermon preached by Mr. Davies; and it furnishes a striking proof of the force of his eloquence. The elder Rees speaks of one meeting in particular, which he attended at Denbigh, at the annual gathering of the Independents. A minister from South Wales preached at the service with unusual power, and eloquence. Among the auditors, there was a venerable man, named William Lewis, who possessed a voice loud, and clear as a trumpet, and who was, at that time, a celebrated preacher among the Calvinistic Methodists. The southern minister, in full sail, with the power of the "*hwyl*" strong upon him, and the whole congregation, of course, in full sympathy, all breathless, and waiting for the next word, came to a point in his sermon where he repeated, says Mr. Rees, in his most pathetic tones, the verse of a hymn, which can only be very poorly conveyed in translation:—

> "Streams from the rock, and bread from heaven,
> Were, by their God, to Israel given;
> While Sinai's terrors blazed around,
> And thunders shook the solid ground,
> No harm befell His people there,
> Sustained with all a Father's care,
> Perversely sinful though they were."

The drift of the passage was to show that the believer in Christ is just as safe amidst terrors from within, and without. The sentiment touched the electric chord in the hearts of the multitude. Old William Lewis could bear it no longer. Up he started, unable to conceal his feelings. "Oh, yes! oh, yes!" he exclaimed; "blessed be His name! God supported His people amidst all the terrors of Sinai, sinful, and rebellious though they were. That was the most dreadful spot in which men could ever be placed; yet, even there, God preserved His people unharmed. Oh, yes! and there He sustained me, too, a poor, helpless sinner, once exposed to the doom of His law, and trembling before Him!" No sooner had the old man uttered these words, than a flame seemed instantaneously to spread through the whole congregation, which broke forth into exclamations of joy, and praise. But the preacher, who had kindled this wonderful fire, and who could do such things! For some time, Mr. Rees was unable to find out who it was; and it was the younger Rees, long the venerable minister in Liverpool, who discovered afterwards, from one of his father's old companions, that it was David Davies, from the south,—he who came to be called, in his more mature years, "The great Revivalist of Swansea."

For, after labouring until the year 1802 in the more obscure regions we have mentioned, where, however, his congregations were immense, and his influence great over the whole Principality, he was invited by the Churches of Mynyddbach, and Sketty—in fact, parts of Swansea—to become their pastor; and on this spot his life received its consummation, and crown.

When Mr. Davies entered the town, it was a remarkably wicked spot; the colliers were more like barbarians than the inhabitants of a civilized country. Gangs of drunken ruffians prowled through its streets, and the suburbs in different directions, ready to assault, and ill-treat any persons who ventured near them. They were accustomed to attack the houses as they passed, throwing stones at the doors, and windows, and could scarcely open their mouths without uttering the most horrid oaths, and blasphemies. It seems almost strange, to our apprehensions now, that the presence of a preacher should effect a change in a neighbourhood; yet nothing is more certain, than the fact that immense social reformations were effected by ministers of the Gospel, both in England, and in Wales.

Mr. Davies had not long entered Swansea before the whole neighbourhood underwent a speedy, and remarkable change. He had a very full, and magnificent voice; a voice of amazing compass, flexibility, and tenderness; a voice with which, according to all accounts, he could do anything—which could roll out a kind of musical thunder in the open air, over great multitudes, or sink to the softest intonations, and whispers, for small cottage congregations. It was well calculated to arrest a rude multitude. And so it came about that Mynyddbach became as celebrated for the work of David Davies, as the far-famed Llangeitho for the great work, and reformation of David Rowlands. The people poured in from the country round to hear him. Then, although very tender, and genial, his manner was so solemn, and he had so intense a power of realizing, to others, the deep, and weighty truths he taught, that he became a terror to evil-doers.

It is mentioned that numbers of butchers from the neighbourhood of Cwmamman, and Llangenie, were in the habit of attending Swansea market on Saturdays. Some of them, after selling the meat which they had brought, were accustomed to frequent the public-houses, and to remain there drinking, and carousing until the Sunday morning. It is a well-known, and amusing circumstance, that, in the course of a little time, when proceeding homewards on their ponies, if they caught a glimpse of Mr. Davies coming in an opposite direction, they hastily turned round, and trotted off, until they could find a bystreet, or lane, to avoid his reproving glances, or warnings, which had the twofold advantage of pertinency and serious wit, conveyed in tones sufficiently stentorian to reach their ears. And there was a man, proverbially notorious for his profane swearing, who plied a ferry-boat between Swansea, and Foxhole; whenever he perceived Mr. Davies approaching, he took care to give a caution to any who might be using improper expressions: "Don't swear, Mr. Davies is coming!"

And there is another story, which shows what manner of man this Davies was. One Saturday night, a band of drunken young men, and boys, threw a quantity of stones against his door, according to their usual mode of dealing with other houses. While they were busy at their work of mischief, he suddenly opened the door, rushed out, and secured two or three of the culprits, who were compelled to give him the names of all their companions. He then told them that he should expect every one of them to be at his house on a day which he mentioned. Accordingly, the whole party came at the appointed hour, but attended by their mothers, who were exceedingly afraid lest the offending lads should be sent to prison in a body. Instead of threatening to take them before the magistrates, Mr. Davies told them to kneel down with him; and having offered up an earnest prayer, and affectionately warned them of the consequences of their evil ways, he dismissed them, requesting, however, that they would all attend at Ebenezer Chapel on the following Sunday. They were, of course, glad to comply with his terms, and to be let off so easily. In after years, several of them became members of his Church, and maintained through life a consistent Christian profession. "And one of them," said Dr. Rees, when writing the story of his great predecessor, "is an old grey-headed disciple, still living."

Such anecdotes as these show how far the character of the man aided, and sustained the mighty power of the minister. Our old friend, the venerable William Davies, of Fishguard, says: "I well remember Mr. Davies of Swansea's repeated preaching tours through Pembrokeshire, and can never forget the emotions, and deep feelings which his matchless eloquence produced on his crowded congregations everywhere; he had a penetrating mind, a lively imagination, and a clear, distinctive utterance; he had a remarkable command of his voice, with such a flow of eloquence, and in the most melodious intonations, that his enraptured audience would almost leap for joy."

Instances are not wanting, either in the ancient, or modern history of the pulpit, of large audiences rising from their seats, and standing as if all spellbound, while the preacher was pursuing his theme, and, to the close of his discourse, subdued beneath the deepening impression, and rolling flow of words. Perhaps the reader, also, will remember, if he have ever been aware of such scenes, that it is not so much glowing splendour of expression, or the weight of original ideas, still less vehement action, which achieves these results, as a certain marvellous, and melodious fitness of words, even in the representation of common things.

But to return to Mr. Davies. Davies of Fishguard, aforementioned, gives an illustration of his preaching: "The captain of a vessel was a member of my Church at Fishguard, but he always attended Ebenezer, when his vessel was lying at Swansea. One day, he asked another captain, 'Will you go with me next Sunday, to hear Mr. Davies? I am sure he will make you weep.' 'Make *me* weep?' said the other, with a loud oath. 'Ah! there's not a preacher in this world can make *me* weep.' However, he promised to go. They took their seats in the front of the gallery. The irreligious captain, for awhile, stared in the preacher's face, with a defiant air, as if determined to disregard what he might say; but when the master of the assembly began to grow warm, the rough sailor hung down his head, and before long, he was weeping like a child." Here was an illustration of the great power of this man to move, and influence the affections.

As compared with other great Welsh preachers, Davies must be spoken of as, in an eminent manner, a singer, a prophet of song, and the swell, and cadences of his voice were like the many voices, which blend to make up one complete concert. He was not only a master of the deep bass notes, but he had a rich soprano kind of power, too; for we read that "when he raised his voice to a higher pitch than ordinary, it increased in melody, and power, and its effects were thrilling in the extreme; there were no jarring notes—all was the music of eloquence throughout." This must not be thought wonderful—it is natural; all men cannot be thus, nor all preachers, however good, and great. There are a few noble organs in the world. The organ itself, however considered, is a wonderful instrument, but there are some built with such extraordinary art that they are capable of producing transcendent effects beyond most other instruments. Davies, the preacher, was one of these amazing organs, in a human frame; but the power of melody was still within his own soul, and it was the wonderful score which he was able to read, and which he compelled his voice to follow, which yet produced these amazing effects.

Surely, it is not more wonderful, that the human voice should have its great, and extraordinary exceptions, than that most wonderful piece of mechanism and art, an organ. We have the organs of Berne, Haarlem, and the Sistine Chapel—such are great exceptions in those powers which art exercises over the kingdom of sound; their building, their architecture, has made them singular, and set them apart as great instruments. But even in these, who does not remember the power of the *vox humana* stop? We apprehend that few who have heard it in the organs of Berne, or Fribourg, will sympathise with Dr. Burney's irreverent, and ridiculous condemnation of it, in his "History of Music," as the "cracked voice of an old woman of ninety, or Punch singing through a comb." Far from this, the hearer waits with intense anxiety, almost goes to hear this note, and realizes in it, what has been said so truly, that music, as it murmurs through the ear, is the nurse of the soul. But all organs have not the *vox humana* stop, nor all preachers either. The human voice, like the organ, is a mighty instrument, but it is the soul which informs the instrument with this singular power, so that within its breast all the passions seem to reign in turn. Singular, that we have thought so much of the great organs of the Continent, and have listened with such intensity to the great singers, and have failed to apply the reflection that the greatest preachers must be, in some measure, a combination of both.

Davies was one of those preachers, without whose presence the annual gatherings, in which the Welsh especially delighted, would have been incomplete. On such occasions, he was usually the last of the preachers—the one waited for. As the service proceeded, it naturally happened that some weariness fell over the assembly; numbers of people might be seen in different parts, sitting, or reclining, on the grass; but as soon as David Davies appeared on the platform, there was a gathering in of all the people, pressing forward from all parts of the field, eager to catch every word which fell from the lips of the speaker. When a great singer appears at a concert, who of all the audience would lose a single bar of the melody? He gave out his own hymn in a voice that reached, without effort, to the utmost limits of the assembled multitude, though he spoke in a quiet, natural tone, without any exertion. He read his text deliberately, but in accents sufficiently loud to be heard with ease by ten thousand people. What is any great singer, without distinctness of enunciation? And distinct enunciation has always been one of the strong points of the great Welsh preachers. Hence, from this reason, he was always impressive, and he seldom preached without using some Scriptural story, which he made to live, through his accent, in the hearts of the people; illustrative similes, and not too many of them; striking thoughts, beneath the pressure of which his manner became more and more impressive, until, at each period, his hearers were overpoweringly affected. Every account of him speaks of his wonderfully impressive voice; and all this gained additional force from his dignified bearing, and appearance, which took captive, and carried away, not only more refined intelligences, but even coarsest natures, while the preacher never approached, for a moment, the verge of vulgarity. Contemporary preachers bore testimony that when the skilful singer had closed his strain, the people could not leave the spot, but remained for a long time after, weeping, and praising.

We have said, already, that Mr. Davies was one of the Welsh hymn-writers; eighty of his hymns are said to be among the best in the Welsh language. He was a strong man, of robust constitution, but, it may be said, he died young; before he had reached his fiftieth year, his excessive labours had told visibly on his health, and for many months before his death, he was strongly impressed with the idea that the time of his departure was at hand. He died in the year 1816. The first Sabbath of that year, he preached a very impressive sermon, from the text, "Thus saith the Lord, This year thou shalt die."

His last sermon was preached about three weeks before he died, when he also administered the ordinance of the Lord's Supper, and gave the right hand of fellowship to thirteen persons, on their admission into the Church. He spoke only a few words during the service, and in those, in faltering accents, told his people he did not expect to be seen amongst them any more. And, indeed, there was every indication, by his weakness, that his words would be fulfilled. Every cheek was bedewed with tears. The hearts of many were ready to burst with grief; for this man's affections were so great, that he produced, naturally, that grief which we feel when the holders of our great affections seem to be parted from us.

He went home from this meeting to die. The struggle was not long protracted. On the morning of December 26th, 1816, he breathed his last. On the day of the funeral, a large concourse, from the town, and neighbourhood, followed his remains to the grave. These lie in a vault, which now occupies a space in the centre of the new chapel, reared on the site of that in which he ministered so affectionately; and over the pulpit, a chaste, and beautiful mural marble tablet memorialises, and very conspicuously bears the name of David Davies. Of him, also, it might be said: *"The Lord God hath given me the tongue of the learned, that I should know how to speak a word in season to him that is weary."*

CHAPTER VIII.
THE PREACHERS OF WILD WALES.

Rees Pritchard, and "The Welshman's Candle"—A Singular Conversion—The Intoxicated Goat—The Vicar's Memory—"God's better than All"—Howell Harris—Daniel Rowlands at Llangeitho—Philip Pugh—The Obscure Nonconformist—Llangeitho—Charles of Bala—His Various Works of Christian Usefulness—The Ancient Preachers of Wild Wales characterised—Thomas Rhys Davies—Impressive Paragraphs from his Sermons—Evan Jones, an Intimate Friend of Christmas Evans—Shenkin of Penhydd—A Singular Mode of Illustrating a Subject—Is the Light in the Eye?—Ebenezer Morris—High Integrity—Homage of Magistrates paid to his Worth—"Beneath"—Ebenezer Morris at Wotton-under-Edge—His Father, David Morris—Rough-and-ready Preachers—Thomas Hughes—Catechised by a Vicar—Catching the Congregation by Guile—Sammy Breeze—A Singular Sermon in Bristol in the Old Time—A Cloud of Forgotten Worthies—Dr. William Richards—His Definition of Doctrine—Davies of Castell Hywel, the Pastor of Christmas Evans, and of Davies of Swansea—Some Account of Welsh Preaching in Wild Wales, in Relation to the Welsh Proverbs, Ancient Triads, Metaphysics, and Poetry—Remarks on the Welsh Language and the Welsh Mind—Its Secluded and Clannish Character.

AMONGST the characteristic names of Wales, remarkable in that department to which we shall devote this chapter, whoever may be passed by, the name of Rees Pritchard, the ancient Vicar of Llandovery, ought not to go unmentioned. We suppose no book, ever published in Wales, has met the acceptance and circulation of "Canwyll-y-Cymry," or "The Welshman's Candle." Since the day of its publication, it has gone through perfectly countless editions; and there was a time, not long since, when there was scarcely a family in Wales, of any intelligence, which did not possess a copy.

Its author was born in the parish of which he became the vicar, so far back as 1575. He was educated at Oxford. His early life was more remarkable for dissipation of every kind, than for any pursuits compatible with his sacred profession. He was, especially, an inveterate drunkard; the worst of his parishioners were scandalised by his example, and said, "Bad as we may be, we are not half so bad as the parson!" The story of his conversion is known to many, who are not acquainted with his life, and work, and the eminence to which he attained; and it certainly illustrates how very strange have been some of the means of man's salvation, and how foolish things have confounded the wise. As George Borrow says in his "Wild Wales," in his account of Pritchard, "God, however, who is aware of what every man is capable, had reserved Rees Pritchard for great, and noble things, and brought about his conversion in a very remarkable manner."

He was in the habit of spending much of his time in the public-house, from which he was, usually, trundled home in a wheelbarrow, in a state of utter insensibility. The people of the house had a large he-goat, which went in, and out, and mingled with the guests. One day, Pritchard called the goat to him, and offered it some ale, and the creature, so far from refusing it, drank it greedily, and soon after fell down in a state of intoxication, and lay quivering, to the great delight of Pritchard, and his companions, who, however, were horrified at this conduct in one, who was appointed to be their example, and teacher. Shortly after, as usual, Pritchard himself was trundled home, utterly intoxicated. He was at home, and ill, the whole of the next day; but on the day following, he went down to the public-house, and called for his pipe, and tankard. The goat came into the room, and again he held the tankard to the creature's mouth; but it turned away its head in disgust, hurried away, and would come near him no more. This startled the man. "My God!" he said, "is this poor dumb creature wiser than I?" He pursued, in his mind, the train of feeling awakened by conscience; he shrank, with disgust, from himself. "But, thank God!" he said, "I am yet alive, and it is not too late to mend. The goat has taught me a lesson; I will become a new man." Smashing his pipe, he left his tankard untasted, and hastened home. He, indeed, commenced a new career. He became, and continued for thirty years, a great, and effective preacher; "preaching," says Mr. Borrow, "the inestimable efficacy of Christ's blood-shedding."

Those poetical pieces which he wrote at intervals, and which are called "The Welshman's Candle," appear only to have been gathered into a volume, and published, after his death. The room in which he lived, and wrote, appears to be still standing; and Mr. Borrow says: "Of all the old houses in Llandovery, the old Vicarage is, by far, the most worthy of attention, irrespective of the wonderful monument of God's providence, and grace, who once inhabited it;" and the old vicar's memory is as fresh in Llandovery, to-day, as ever it was. While Mr. Borrow was looking at the house, a respectable-looking farmer came up, and was about to pass; "but observing me," he says, "and how I was employed, he stopped, and looked now at me, and now at the antique house. Presently he said, 'A fine old place, sir, is it not? But do you know who lived there?' Wishing to know what the man would say, provided he thought I was ignorant as to the ancient inmate, I turned a face of inquiry upon him, whereupon he advanced towards me, two or three steps, and placing his face so close to mine, that his nose nearly touched my cheek, he said, in a kind of piercing whisper, '*The Vicar*!' then drawing his face back, he looked me full in the eyes, as if to observe the effect of his intelligence, gave me two or three nods, as if to say, 'He did indeed,' and departed. *The* Vicar of Llandovery had then been dead nearly two hundred years. Truly the man in whom piety, and genius, are blended, is immortal upon earth!" "The Welshman's Candle" is a set of homely, and very rememberable verses, putting us, as far as we are able to judge, in mind of our Thomas Tusser.

Mr. Borrow gives us a very pleasant taste in the following literal, vigorous translation, which we may presume to be his own:—

"GOD'S BETTER THAN ALL."

"God's better than heaven, or aught therein;
Than the earth, or aught we there can win;
Better than the world, or its wealth to me—
God's better than all that is, or can be.

"Better than father, than mother, than nurse;
Better than riches, oft proving a curse;
Better than Martha, or Mary even—
Better, by far, is the God of heaven.

"If God for thy portion thou hast ta'en,
There's Christ to support thee in every pain;
The world to respect thee thou wilt gain;
To fear thee, the fiend, and all his train.

"Of the best of portions, thou choice didst make,
When thou the high God to thyself didst take;
A portion, which none from thy grasp can rend,
Whilst the sun, and the moon on their course shall wend.

"When the sun grows dark, and the moon turns red;
When the stars shall drop, and millions dread;
When the earth shall vanish, with its pomp, in fire,
Thy portion shall still remain entire.

"Then let not thy heart, though distressed, complain;
A hold on thy portion firm maintain.
Thou didst choose the best portion, again I say;
Resign it not till thy dying day!"

But the age of preachers in Wales, to which the following pages will more immediately refer, commences with those two great men, who were indeed the Whitfield, and the Wesley of Wales—Howell Harris of Trevecca, and Daniel Rowlands of Llangeitho. It is remarkable that these two men, born to be such inestimable, and priceless blessings to their country, were born within a year of each other—Harris at Trevecca, in 1714, Rowlands at Pantybeidy, in Cardiganshire, in 1713. As to Harris, he is spoken of as the most successful preacher that ever ascended a pulpit, or platform in Wales; and yet nothing is more certain, than that he neither aimed to preach, nor will his sermons, so far as any knowledge can be obtained of them, stand the test of any kind of criticism. This only is certain, their unquestioned, and greatly pre-eminent usefulness.

He did not deliver composed sermons, but unpremeditated addresses, on sin, and its tremendous consequences; on death, and the judgment, and the world to come. It is said, "His words fell like balls of fire, on the careless, and impenitent multitudes." Himself destined for a clergyman of the Church of England, an Oxford man, and with a fair promise of success in the Church—since before he left Oxford, he had a benefice offered him—he repeatedly applied, in vain, for ordination. Throughout his life, he continued ardently attached to the services of the Church of England.

It was, unhappily, from that Church, in Wales, he encountered his most vehement opposition, and cruel persecution. He, however, roused the whole country,—within the Church of England, and without,—from its state of apathy, and impiety; while we quite agree with his biographer, who says: "Any attempt to account philosophically for the remarkable effects which everywhere attended the preaching of Howell Harris, would be nothing better than an irreverent trifling with a solemn subject. All that can be said, with propriety, is, that he was an extraordinary instrument, raised by Providence, at an extraordinary time, to accomplish an extraordinary work."

But Llangeitho, and its vicar, seem to demand a more lengthened notice, as coming more distinctly within the region of the palpable, and apprehensible. Daniel Rowlands was a clergyman, and the son of a clergyman. At twenty-two years of age, he was appointed perpetual curate, or incumbent, of the united parishes of Nantcwnlle and Llangeitho, at a salary of ten pounds a year. He never received any higher preferment in the Church on earth, although so eminent a blessing to his country. He must have been some such man as our William Grimshaw, of Haworth. When he entered upon his curacy, he was quite an unconverted young man, given to occasional fits of intoxication, and in the summer he left his pulpit, to take his part, with his parishioners, in the sports, and games in the neighbouring fields, or on the village green.

But, in the immediate neighbourhood of his own hamlet, ministered a good and consistent Nonconformist, Philip Pugh, a learned, lovable, and lowly man; and, in the smaller round of his sphere, a successful preacher. Daniel Rowlands appears to have been converted under a sermon of the eminent Rev. Griffith Jones of Llanddouror, at Llanddewibrefi; but it was to Philip Pugh that he was led for that instruction, and influence, which instrumentally helped to develop his character. It would seem that Rowlands was a man bound to be in earnest; but conversion set on fire a new genius in the man. He developed, hitherto undiscovered, great preaching power, and his church became crowded. Still, for the first five years of his new course of life, he did not know that more glorious and beautiful Gospel which he preached through all the years following.

He was a tremendous alarmist; the dangers of sin, and the terrors of the eternal judgments, were his topics; and his hearers shrank, and recoiled, while they were fascinated to listen. Again, the venerable Nonconformist stepped in; Philip Pugh pointed out his defect. "My dear sir," said he, "preach the Gospel—preach the Gospel to the people. Give them the balm of Gilead; show the blood of Christ; apply it to their spiritual wounds; show the necessity of faith in a crucified Redeemer." "I am afraid," said Rowlands, "that I have not all that faith myself, in its full vigour, and exercise." "Preach on it," said Mr. Pugh; "preach on it, until you feel it in that way,—it will come. If you go on preaching in the way you have been doing, you will kill half the people in the country. You thunder out the curses of the law, and preach in such a terrific manner, that nobody can stand before you. Preach the Gospel!" And again the young clergyman followed the advice of his patriarchal friend, and unnumbered thousands in Wales had occasion, through long following years, to bless God for it.

Does not the reader call up a very beautiful picture of these two, in that old and obscure Welsh hamlet, nearly a hundred and fifty years since?—the conversation of such an one as Paul, the aged, with his young son, Timothy; and if anything were needed to increase our sense of admiration of the young clergyman, it would be that he did not disdain to receive lessons from old age, and an old age covered with the indignities attaching to an outlawed Nonconformist. In Wales, there were very many men like Philip Pugh; we may incidentally mention the names of several in the course of these pages— names well worthy of the commendation in Johnson's perfect lines:

> "Their virtues walked their narrow round,
>   Nor made a pause, nor left a void;
> And sure the Eternal Master found
>   Their single talent well employed.
>
> "And still they fill affection's eye,
>   Obscurely wise, and coarsely kind;
> And let not arrogance deny
>   Its praise to merit unrefined."

Then there opened a great career before Rowlands, and Llangeitho became as a shrine in evangelical Wales. He received invitations to preach in every neighbourhood of the Principality; many churches were opened to him, and where they were not, he took freely, and cheerfully, to the chapels, or the fields. His words, and accents were of that marvellous kind we have identified with Welsh preaching. Later on, and in other times, people said, he found his successor in Davies of Swansea; and the highest honour they could give to Swansea, in Davies' day, was that "it was another Llangeitho."

Rowlands had the power of the thunder, and the dew; he pressed an extraordinary vitality into words, which had often been heard before, so that once, while reading the Church Service, in his own church, he gave such a dreadful tenderness to the words, "By thine agony, and bloody sweat!" that the service was almost stopped, and the people broke forth into a passion of feeling. Christmas Evans says: "While Rowlands was preaching, the fashion of his countenance became altered; his voice became as if inspired; the worldly, dead, and careless spirit was cast out by his presence. The people, as it were, drew near to the cloud, towards Christ, and Moses, and Elijah. Eternity, with its realities, rushed upon their vision. These mighty influences were felt, more or less, for fifty years. Thousands gathered at Llangeitho for communion every month, and they came there from every county in Wales."

Such power there is in human words when divinely wielded; such was the spiritual power of Daniel Rowlands. Well does one writer say, the story of Llangeitho, well written, would read like a chapter in religious romance. It is very doubtful whether we have the record of any other man who drew such numbers to the immediate circle of his ministry, as Rowlands. He did not itinerate so largely as most of the great Welsh preachers. In an obscure spot in the interior of Cardiganshire, in an age of bad roads, and in a neighbourhood where the roads were especially bad, he addressed his immense concourses of people. His monthly communion was sometimes attended by as many as three thousand communicants, of whom, often, many were clergymen. Upwards of a hundred ministers ascribe to him the means of their conversion. Thus, in his day, it was a place of pilgrimages; and even now, there are not a few who turn aside, to stand, with wonder, upon the spot where Rowlands exercised his marvellous ministry.

The four great Welsh preachers, Christmas Evans, John Elias, Williams of Wern, and Davies of Swansea, on whose pulpit powers, and method, we have more distinctly dilated, may be styled the tetrarchs of the pulpit of Wild Wales of these later times. Their eminence was single, and singular. Their immense powers unquestioned: rivals, never, apparently, by their own selection, the great Welsh religious mind only rivalled them with each other. After them it might be said, "Great was the company of preachers,"—great, not merely in number, carrying also influence, and usefulness of another kind; perhaps even superior to those honoured names.

How, for instance, can we do sufficient honour to the labours of CHARLES OF BALA? This truly apostolic man was born at Llanvihangel, in 1755. While yet a boy, he managed to introduce family worship into his father's house; but it was in his eighteenth year that he heard the great Daniel Rowlands preach, and he says: "From that day I found a new heaven, and a new earth, to enjoy; the change experienced by a blind man, on receiving his sight, is not greater than that which I felt on that day." In his twentieth year he went to Oxford, and received Deacon's orders, and was appointed to a curacy in Somersetshire; he took his degree at his University, but he could never obtain priest's orders; in every instance objection was made to what was called his Methodism.

The doors of the Establishment were thus closed against him, and he was compelled to cast in his lot with the Welsh Methodists, in 1785. Before this, he had preached for Daniel Rowlands in his far-famed church at Llangeitho, and the great old patriarch simply uttered a prophecy about him when he said, "Mr. Charles is the gift of God to North Wales." He was an eminent preacher, but it was rather in other ways that he became illustrious, in the great religious labours of his country. Moving about to preach, from place to place, his heart became painfully impressed, and distressed, by the great ignorance of the people everywhere, and that such multitudes were unable to read the Word of God; so he determined on the establishment of schools upon a singular principle.

It was two or three years before he commenced his more settled labours in Wales, that Robert Raikes had originated the Sunday-school idea in Gloucester. Thomas Charles was the first to seize upon the idea, and introduce it into his own country. Charles had an organizing, and administrative, mind; he fixed upon innumerable places, where he settled schoolmasters, for periods of from six to nine, and twelve months, to teach the people to read, giving them the initial elements, and rudiments, of education, and then removing these masters to another locality.

So he filled the country with schools—Sabbath, and night-schools. He visited the schools himself, periodically, catechizing the children publicly; and in the course of his lifetime, he had the satisfaction of seeing the aspect of things entirely changed. He used no figure of speech, when, towards the close of his life, he said, "The desert blossoms as the rose, and the dry land has become streams of water." To these purposes of his heart he was able to devote whatever money he received from the work of the ministry; he testifies affectionately that "the wants of my own family were provided for by the industry of my dear wife;" and he received some help by donations from England. He found, everywhere, a dearth of Bibles, and it is curious to read that, although the Church of England would not receive him as one of her ministers, when his work became established, the Society for Promoting

Christian Knowledge made him, after considerable reluctance, a grant of no less than ten thousand Welsh Bibles. After this, he went to London, for the purpose of establishing a Society to supply Wales with the Holy Scriptures. It was at a meeting of the Religious Tract Society, which was called together for that purpose, that it was resolved to establish the British and Foreign Bible Society; and before that society had been established ten years, it had supplied Wales with a hundred thousand copies of the Word of God.

Other men were great preachers, but Thomas Charles was, in the truest sense of the word, a bishop, an overseer,—travelling far, and wide, preaching, catechizing, administrating, placing and removing labourers. All his works, and words, his inward, and his outward life, show the active, high-toned saintliness, and enthusiastic holiness, of the man. There is, perhaps, no other to whom Wales is so largely indebted for the giving direction, organization, and usefulness to all religious labour, as to him. His modesty transcended his gifts, and his activity. John Campbell, of Kingsland, himself noted in all the great, and good works of that time, relates that at a meeting, at Lady Anne Erskine's, at which Mr. Charles was requested to state the circumstances which had made little Bala a kind of spiritual metropolis of the Principality of Wales, "he spoke for about an hour, and never once mentioned himself, although he was the chief instrument, and actor, in the whole movements which had made the place so eminent."

This good man, John Campbell, afterwards wrote to Mr. Charles's biographer: "I never was at Bala but once, which was not long after his removal to the regions of immortality; and such was my veneration for his character, and labours, that, in approaching it, I felt as if I was about coming in sight of Sinai, or Jerusalem, or treading on classical ground. The events of his life, I believe, are viewed with more interest by the glorified than the battles of Actium, or Waterloo."

But, as a preacher, he was unlike those men, whose words moved upon the wheels of thunder, and who seemed to deal with the lightnings of imagination, and eloquence. As we read his words, they seem to flow with refreshing sweetness. He was waited for, and followed everywhere, but his utterances had nothing of the startling powers we have seen; we should think he preached, rather, to those who knew, by experience, what it is to grow in grace. There is a glowing light of holiness about his words—a deep, sweet, experimental reality. Of course, being a Welshman, his thoughts were pithily expressed. They were a sort of spiritual proverbs, in which he turned over, again and again, some idea, until it became like the triads of his country's literature; and dilating upon an idea, the various aspects of it became like distinct facets, setting forth some pleasant ray.

Such was Thomas Charles. Wales lost him at the age of sixty—a short life, if we number it by years; a long life, if we consider all he accomplished in it; and, to this day, his name is one of the most revered throughout the Principality.

It is impossible to do the justice even of mentioning the names of many of those men, who "served their generation" so well, "according to the will of God, and then fell asleep." And it is as necessary, as it is interesting, to notice how the various men, moved by the Spirit of God, found Him leading, and guiding them in the path of labour, their instincts chose.

In the history of preaching, we believe there is no more curious chapter than this, of these strange preachers in Wales. They have an idiosyncrasy as entirely, and peculiarly, their own, as is that of the country in which they carried on their ministrations. The preaching friars of the times we call the dark, or middle ages, are very remarkable, from the occasional glimpses we are able to obtain of them. Very remarkable the band of men, evoked by the rise of Methodism in England,—those who spread out all over the land, treading the paths indicated by the voice, and finger of Whitfield, or Wesley. Very entertaining are the stories of the preachers of the backwoods of America, the sappers, and miners, who cleared a way for the planting of the Word among the wild forests of the Far West.

These Welsh preachers were unlike any of them,—they had a character altogether their own. A great many of them were men of eminent genius, glowing with feeling, and fancy; never having known college training, or culture, they were very often men who had, somehow, attained a singular variety of knowledge, lore, and learning, which, perhaps, would be despised as unscientific, and unclassified, by the schools, but which was not the less curious, and, to the Celtic mind, enchanting.

They all lived, and fared hard; all their thoughts, and fancies were high. If they marched before us now, the nineteenth century would, very likely, regard them as a set of very rough tykes. Perhaps the nineteenth century would regard Elijah, Amos, and Nahum, and sundry other equally respectable persons, in much the same manner. Rude, and rough in gait, and attire, the rudeness, and the roughness would, perhaps, be forgotten by us, if we could interpret the torrent, and the wail of their speech, and be, for a short time, beneath the power of the visions, of which they were the rapt seers, and unveilers. We wonder that no enthusiastic Welshman has used an English pen to pourtray the lives, and portraits of a number of these Welsh worthies; to us, several of them—notably, John Elias, and Christmas Evans—seem to realize the idea of the Ancient Mariner,—

> "I pass like night from land to land,
> I have strange power of speech;

> The moment that his face I see,
> I know the man that must hear me—
>   To him my tale I teach."

For instance, how many people in England ever heard the name of THOMAS RHYS DAVIES, an extraordinary man? And he left an extraordinary diary behind him, for he seems to have been a very methodical man; and his diary shows that he preached during his lifetime at least 13,145 times, and this diary contains a distinct record of the time, place, and text; and it is said that there is scarcely a river, brook, or tarn, from Conway to Llansanan, from Llanrwst to Newbridge, from the sea at Llandudno, to the waters of the Berwyn mountains, in whose waves he had not baptized.

In fact, he was, perhaps, in his own particular, and peculiar line, second to none of the great Welsh preachers; only, it is said that his power was inexplicable, and yet that it stood the severest tests of popularity. His sermons are said to have been exceedingly simple, and very rememberable; they sprang out of a rare personal charm; he was himself; but, perhaps, if he resembled one of his great brethren, it would be Williams of Wern. His style was sharp, pointed, axiomatic, but antithetic, never prodigal of words, his sermons were short; but he was able to avail himself of any passing circumstance in the congregation, and to turn it to good account. Once, when a congregation seemed to be even more than usually disposed to cough, he said, "Cough away, my friends, it will not disturb me in the least; it will rather help me than not, for if you are coughing, I shall be sure that you are awake."

He had that rare gift in the preacher, perfect self-possession, the grand preliminary to mastery over a congregation, an entire mastery over himself. All great Welsh preachers, however they may sometimes dilate, and expand truths into great paintings, and prolonged descriptions, excel in the pithy, and proverb-uttering power; but Thomas Rhys Davies was remarkable in this. Here are a few illustrations:—

> "Ignorance is the devil's college."

> "There are only three passages in the Bible which declare what God is, although there are thousands which speak about Him. God is a Spirit, God is Light, and God is Love."

> "Pharaoh fought ten great battles with God, and did not gain one."

> "The way through the Red Sea was safe enough for Israel, but not for Pharaoh; he had no business to go that way, it

was a private road, that God had opened up for His own family."

"Let the oldest believer remember that Satan is older."

"Christ is the Bishop, not of titles, but of souls."

"Moses was learned, but slow of speech; it was well that he was so, or, perhaps, he would not have found time to write the law. Aaron had the gift of speech, and it does not appear that he had any other gift."

"If you have no pleasure in your religion, make haste to change it."

"Judas is much blamed for betraying Christ for three pounds; many, in our day, betray Him a hundred times for three pence."

"Pharaoh commanded that Moses should be drowned; in after days, Pharaoh was paid back in his own coin."

"Many have a brother's face, but Christ has a brother's heart."

Such was Thomas Rhys Davies; like Christmas Evans, journeying from North through South Wales, he was taken ill in the same house in which Christmas Evans died. Conscious of his approaching death, he begged that he might die in the same bed; this was not possible, but he was buried in the same grave.

Then there was EVAN JONES; he had been a *protégé* of Christmas Evans; Christmas Evans appears to have brought him forward, giving his verdict on his suitability as to the ministry. Christmas Evans was able to appreciate the young man, for he seems to have possessed really brilliant powers; in his country, and in his land's language, he attained to the distinction of a bard; and it is said that his poetry rose to an elevation of wild, and daring grandeur. As a preacher, he does not appear to have studied to be popular, or to seek to adapt his sermons to the multitude; he probably moved through cloudy grandeurs, from whence, however, he sometimes descended, with an odd quaintness, which, if always surprising, was sometimes reprehensible. Once, he was expatiating, glowingly, on the felicities of the heavenly state, in that tone, and strain which most preachers love, occasionally, to indulge, and which most hearers certainly, occasionally, enjoy; he was giving many descriptive delineations of heavenly blessedness, and incidentally said, "There they neither marry, nor are given in marriage." There was sitting beneath him a fervent brother, who, probably, not knowing what he said, sounded forth a hearty "Amen!" Evan heard it, looked the man full in the face, and said, "Ah, you've had enough of it, have you?"

This man was, perhaps, in his later years, the most intimate friend of Christmas Evans. Christmas poured his brilliant imagination, couched in his grand, although informal, rhetoric over the multitudes; Evan Jones frequently soared into fields whither, only here and there, an eye could follow his flight; but when the two friends were alone, their spirits could mingle pleasantly, for their minds were cast very much in the same mould; and when Christmas Evans died, it was this friend who published in Welsh one of the most graceful tributes to his memory.

In the history of the preaching, and preachers of a hundred years since, we meet, of course, with many instances of men, who possessed considerable power, but allied with much illiterate roughness; still, the power made itself very manifest—a power of illustrating truth, and making it clearly apprehended. Such a preacher must SHENKIN OF PENHYDD have been, rough, and rude farmer as he was, blending, as was not at all uncommon then, and even in our own far more recent knowledge, the occupations of a farmer, and the ordained minister. Shenkin has left a very living reputation behind him; indeed, from some of the accounts we have read of him, we should regard him as quite a type of the rude, yet very effective, Welsh orator.

Whatever the Welsh preacher had to say, however abstract, it had to be committed to an illustration, to make it palpable, and plain. In those early times, a very large room, or barn, in which were several hundreds of people, would, perhaps, have only one solitary candle, feebly glimmering over the gloom. It was in such circumstances, or such a scene, that Shenkin was once preaching on Christ as the Light of the world. In the course of his sermon, he came to show that the world was not its own light, and announced to his hearers what, perhaps, might startle some of them, that "light was not in the eye." It seemed as if he had no sooner said this, than he felt it to be a matter that required illustration. As he warmed with his subject, going round, and round to make his meaning plain, but all the time seeming to fear that he was not doing much towards it with his rustic congregation, he suddenly turned to the solitary candle, and blew it out, leaving his congregation in utter darkness. "There," he exclaimed, triumphantly, to his invisible congregation, "what do you say to that? Is the light in the eye?" This, of course, settled the matter in the minds of the most obtuse; but it was still a serious matter to have to relight, in a lonely little chapel, an extinguished candle.

He was a singular creature, this Shenkin. Not many Welsh preachers have a greater variety of odd stories told than he, of his doings, and sayings. He had a very downright, and straightforward method of speech. Thus, he would say, "There are many who complain that they can scarcely remember anything they hear. Have done with your lying!" he exclaimed. "I'll be bound to say you remember well what you sold your old white horse for at Llandaff fair three years ago. Six or seven pounds, was it? Certainly that has not escaped your memory. You can remember anything but the Gospel." And many of his images were much more of the rough-and-ready, than of the classical, order. "Humility," he once said, "is as beautiful an ornament as a cow's tail; but it grows, like the cow's tail, downwards."

Wales was covered with men like this. Every district possessed them, and many of them have found their memorial in some little volume, although, in most instances, they only survive in the breath of popular remembrance, and tradition.

One of the mightiest of these sons of thunder, who has left behind him a name, and fame, scarcely inferior to the great ones on whom we have more lengthily dwelt, was EBENEZER MORRIS. He was a fine, free, cheerful spirit; his character sparkled with every Christian virtue,—a man of rare gifts, and grace. With a severe sense of what was just in the relations of life, and what constituted the principles of a strong theology, keeping his unblemished course beneath the dominion of a peaceful conscience, he enjoyed, more than many, the social fireside chat, with congenial friends. Although a pastor, and a preacher of wide fame, he was also a farmer; for he was one of an order of men, of whom it has been said, that good people were so impressed with the privilege conferred by preaching the gospel, that their hearers were careful not to deprive them of the full enjoyment of it, by remunerating their labours too abundantly.

Ebenezer Morris held a farm, and the farmer seems to have been worthy of the preacher. A story is told of him that, wanting to buy a cow, and going down to the fair, he found one for sale which he thought would suit him, and he bought it at the price named by its owner. Some days after, Mr. Morris found that the price of cattle had gone up considerably, and meeting the previous owner of the cow, he said, "Look here, I find you gave me too great a bargain the other day; the cow is worth more than I purchased her for,—here is another guinea; now I think we shall be about right."

There are several stories told, in the life of this good, and great man, showing that he could not take an unfair advantage, that he was above everything mean, unfair, and selfish, and that guineas, and farms weighed nothing with him in the balance against righteousness, and truth. His influence over his whole country was immense; so much so, that a magistrate addressed him once in public, saying, "We are under great obligations to you, Mr. Morris, for keeping the country in order, and preserving peace among the people; you are worth more than any dozen of us." On one occasion he was subpœnaed, to attend before a court of justice, to give evidence in a disputed case. As the book was handed to him, that he might take the oath, the presiding magistrate said, "No! no! take it away; there is no necessity that Mr. Morris should swear at all; his word is enough."

His appearance in preaching, his entire presence, is described as most majestic, and commanding: his voice was very loud, and it is said, a word from his mouth would roll over the people like a mighty wave. "Look at that window," said an aged deacon, in North Wales, to a minister, who had come to preach at the chapel to which the former belonged, "look at that window! It was there that Ebenezer Morris stood, when he preached his great sermon from the words, 'The way of life is above to the wise, that he may depart from hell beneath,' and when we all turned pale while we were listening to him." "Ah!" said the minister, "do you remember any portion of that sermon?" "Remember!" said the old deacon; "remember, my good man? I should think I do, and shall remember for ever. Why, there was no flesh here that could stand before it!" "What did he say?" said the minister. "Say! my good man," replied the deacon; "say? Why, he was saying, 'Beneath, beneath, beneath! Oh, my people, hell is beneath, beneath, *beneath*!' until it seemed as if the end of the world had come upon us all in the chapel, and outside!"

When Theophilus Jones was selected as Rowland Hill's co-pastor at Wooton-under-Edge, Ebenezer Morris came to preach on his induction. In that place, the audience was not likely to be a very sleepy one, but this preacher roused them beyond their usual mark, and strange stories are told of the sermon, while old Rowland sat behind the preacher, ejaculating the whole of the time; and many times after, when Mr. Hill found the people heavy, and inattentive, he was in the habit of saying, "We must have the fat minister from Wales here, to rouse you up again!" We know his likeness very well, and can almost realize his grand, solemn manner, in his black velvet cap, which made him look like a bishop, and gave much more impressiveness to his aspect, than any mitre could have done.

This Ebenezer Morris was the son of a man eminent in his own day, David Morris, of whom it was said, that he scarcely ever preached a sermon which was not the means of the conversion of men, and in his evangelistic tours he usually preached two, or three times a day. There is a sermon, still spoken of, preached at Rippont Bridge, Anglesea. The idea came to him whilst he was preaching, that many of the people before him might surely be lost, and he burst forth into a loud dolorous wail, every line of his countenance in sympathy with his agonizing cry, in Welsh, which no translation can render, "O bobl y golled fawr! y golled fawr!" The English is, "O ye people of the great loss! the great loss!" It seems slight enough to us, but it is said that the people not only moved before his words, like reeds in a storm, but to this day they speak in Anglesea of David Morris's sermon of "The Great Loss."

The great authority for the most interesting stories of the religious life in Wales, is the "History of Welsh Methodism," by the late Rev. John Hughes, of Liverpool; unfortunately, we believe it only exists in Welsh, in three volumes, amounting to nearly two thousand pages; but "Welsh Calvinistic Methodism; a Historical Sketch," by the Rev. William Williams, appears to be principally a very entertaining digest, and condensation, of many of the most noticeable particulars from the larger work. There have certainly appeared, from time to time, many most interesting, and faithful men in the ministry of the Gospel in Wales, quite beyond the possibility of distinct mention; some of them were very poor, and lowly in life, and circumstances. Such was THOMAS HUGHES. He is described as a man of small talent, and slender knowledge, but of great holiness, and with an intense faith that many of his neighbours were in a very bad condition, and that it was his duty to try to speak words to them, whereby they might be saved. He used to stand under the old walls of Conway, and numbers gathered around him to listen; until at last he excited the anger of the vicar, who caused him to be arrested, and brought into his presence, when the following conversation took place:—

Vicar. "You ought to be a learned man, to go about, and to be able to answer deep questions."

Hughes. "What questions, sir?"

Vicar. "Here they are—those which were asked me by the Lord Bishop. Let's see whether you will be able to answer them. Where was St. Paul born?"

Hughes. "In Tarsus."

Vicar. "Hem! I see that you know something about it. Well, can you tell me who took charge of the Virgin Mary after our blessed Redeemer was crucified?"

Hughes. "John."

Vicar. "Well, once again. Who wrote the Book of Revelation? Answer that if you can."

Hughes. "John the Apostle."

Vicar. "Ho! you seem to know a good deal, after all."

Hughes. "Perhaps, sir, you will allow me to ask you one or two questions?"

Vicar. "Oh yes; only they must be religious questions."

Hughes. "What is holiness? and how can a sinner be justified before God?"

Vicar. "Ho! we have no business to bother ourselves with such things, and you have no business to put such questions to a man in my position; go out of my sight, this minute." And to the men who had brought him, "Take care that you do not bring such people into my presence any more."

Hughes was a simple, earnest, believing man, with a good deal of Welsh cuteness. After this interview with the vicar, he was permitted to pursue his exhortations at Conway in peace. But there is a place between Conway, and Llandudno, called Towyn Ferry; it was a very ignorant little nook, and the people were steeped in unbelief, and sin; thither Hughes determined to go, but his person was not known there. The news, however, was circulated abroad, that there was to be a sermon, and religious service. When he arrived, he found things did not appear very pleasant; there were heaps of stones prepared for the preacher's reception, when he should make his appearance, or commence his work. Hughes had nothing clerical in his manner, or garb, any more than any one in the crowd, and no one suspected him to be the man, as he threw himself down on the grass, and entered familiarly into conversation with the people about him. After a time, when their patience began to fail, he stood up, and said, "Well, lads, there is no sign of any one coming; perhaps the man has heard that you are going to stone him; let one of us get up, and stand on that heap of stones, and talk, and the rest sing. Won't that be first-rate?"

"Capital," said a bully, who seemed to be the recognised leader of the crowd. "You go on the heap, and preach to us."

"Very well," said Hughes, "I'm willing to try; but mind you, I shall make some blunders, so you must be civil, and not laugh at me."

"I'll make 'em civil," said the bully. "Look here, lads, whoever laughs, I'll put one of these stones into his head!"

"Stop you!" said Hughes; "the first thing we have to do, is to pray, isn't it?"

"Ay, ay!" said the bully, "and I'll be clerk. I'll stand before you, and you shall use my shoulder for the pulpit."

So prayer was offered, short, and simple, but in real earnest; and at its close, a good many favourable words were uttered. Some volunteered the remark that, "It was every bit as good as a parson." Hughes proceeded to give out a text, but the bully shouted,—

"Hold on, you fool! we've got to sing first."

"Ay, ay!" said Hughes, "I forgot that."

So they sang a Welsh hymn, after a fashion, and then came the text, and the sermon, which was short, and simple too, listened to very attentively; and the singular part of the story is, that the bully, and clerk, left the ground with the preacher, quieted, and changed, and subsequently he became a converted man. The regeneration of Wales, through its villages, and lone remote districts, is full of anecdotes like this,—stories of persecution, and the faithful earnestness of simple men, who felt in them a strong desire to do good, and fulfilled their desire, becoming humble, but real blessings to their neighbourhoods.

Only in a history of the Welsh pulpit—and that would be a volume of no slight dimensions—would it be possible to recapitulate the names of the men who exercised, in their day, considerable influence over the scattered thousands of the Principality. They constitute a very varied race, and were characterized by freshness, and reality, taking, of course, the peculiar mental complexion of the preacher: some calm, and still, but waving about their words like quiet lightnings; some vehement, overwhelming, passionate; some remarkable for their daring excursions of imagination; some abounding in wit, and humour. One of the most remarkable of these last, one who ought not to go unmentioned in such an enumeration, was SAMUEL BREEZE. This was the man who first introduced "The Churchyard World" to Dr. Raffles,— of whom it was said, that if you heard one of his sermons, you heard three preachers, so various were not only the methods of his sermons, but even the tone of his voice. He is said to have produced extraordinary effects. Christmas Evans said of him, that "his eyes were like a flame of fire, and his voice like a martial strain, calling men to arms."

The writer of this volume, in a work on the "Vocation of the Preacher," mentions a curious instance, which he gives from the unpublished reminiscences of a dear departed friend—the Rev. John Pyer, late of Devonport—who was present when the incident happened, in Bristol, perhaps nearly eighty years since. Sammy Breeze, as he was familiarly called by the multitudes who delighted in his ministry, came, periodically, from the mountains of Cardiganshire, or the neighbourhood of Aberystwith, to Bristol, where he spoke with more than tolerable efficiency in English. Mr. Pyer, then a youth, was in the chapel, when, as was not unusual, two ministers, Sammy Breeze and another, were to preach. The other took the first place, a young man with some tints of academical training, and some of the livid lights of a then only incipient rationalism in his mind. He took for his text, "He that believeth shall be saved, and he that believeth not shall be damned;" but he condoned the heavy condemnation, and, in an affected manner, shaded off the darkness of the doom of unbelief, very much in the style of the preacher in Cowper's satire, who never mentioned hell to ears polite. The young man, also, grew sentimental, and "begged pardon" of an audience, rather more polite than usual, for the sad statement made in the text. "But, indeed," said he, "he that believeth shall be saved, and he that believeth not—indeed, I regret to say, I beg your pardon for uttering the terrible truth, but, indeed, he shall be sentenced to a place which here I dare not mention."

Then rose Sammy Breeze. He began: "I shall take the same text, to-night, which you have just heard. Our young friend has been fery fine to-night, he has told you some fery polite things. I am not fery fine, and I am not polite, but I will preach a little bit of truth to you, which is this: 'He that believeth shall be saved, and he that believeth not shall be damned,' *and I begs no pardons.*" He continued, "I do look round on this chapel, and I do see people all fery learned and in-tel-lect-u-al. You do read books, and you do study studies, and fery likely you do think that you can mend God's Book, and are fery sure you can mend me. You have great—what you call thoughts, and poetries; but I will tell you one little word, and you must not try to mend that; but if you do, it will be all the same; it is this, look you: 'He that believeth shall be saved, and he that believeth not shall be damned, *and I begs no pardons.* And then I do look round your chapel, and I do see you are a foine people, well-dressed people, well-to-do people. I do see that you are fery rich, and you have got your moneys, and are getting fery proud; but I tell you, it does not matter at all; for I must tell you the truth, and the truth is, 'He that believeth shall be saved, and he that believeth not shall be damned,' *and I begs no pardons.* And now," continued the preacher, "you will say to me, 'What do you mean by talking to us in this way? Who are you, sir?' And now I will tell you. I am Sammy Preeze. I have come from the mountains of Cardiganshire, on my Master's business, and His message I must deliver. If you will never hear me again, I shall not matter much, but while you shall hear me, you shall hear me, and this is His word in me, and in me to you: 'He that believeth shall be saved, and he that believeth not shall be damned,' *and I begs no pardons.*"

It was a strange scene; but as he went on, in quaint, but terribly earnest strain, anger passed into awe, and mute astonishment into rapt attention. No one, who heard the words, could ever again hear them unheeded, nor think lightly of the doom of the unbelieving. The anecdote is worth being laid to heart, in these days, when there is too often a reserve in declaring the whole counsel of God.

After service, in the vestry, the deacons were in great anger with the blunt preacher; and one, a well-known religious man in Bristol, exclaimed, "Mr. Breeze, you have strangely forgotten yourself to-night, sir. We did not expect that you would have behaved in this way. We have always been very glad to see you in our pulpit, but your sermon to-night, sir, has been most insolent, shameful!" He wound up a pretty sharp condemnation by saying, "In short, I don't understand you!"

"Ho! ho!" exclaimed Sammy. "You say you do not understand me? Eh! look you then, I will tell you; I do understand you! Up in our mountains, we have one man there, we do call him exciseman; he comes along to our shops and stores, and says, 'What have you here? Anything contraband here?' And if it is all right, the good man says, 'Step in, Mr. Exciseman, come in, look you.' He is all fair, open, and above-board. But if he has anything secreted there, he does draw back surprised, and he makes a fine face, and says, 'Sir, I do not understand you.' Now, you do tell me that you don't understand me, but I do understand you, gentlemen, I do; and I do fear you have something contraband here; and I will say good-night to you; but I must tell you one little word; that is: 'He that believeth shall be saved, and he that believeth not shall be damned,' *and I begs no pardons.*"

But, with these simple illustrations, we have not exhausted the number of noticeable names. In connection with every name as it occurs, some interesting anecdote meets the memory. There was Robert Lloyd, the shoemaker, and Thomas the turner, and Robert Roberts, of whom, from the stories before us, we do not find it difficult to believe, that he had the power to describe things in such a vivid, and graphic manner, as to make his hearers feel as if the scenes were passing before their eyes. Then there were David Evans of Aberayron, and Ebenezer Richard of Tregaron, and William Morris of St. David's, whose every sermon was said to be a string of sparkling gems; John Jones of Talysarn, and his brother, David Jones; John Hughes; the seraphic Henry Rees, and Thomas Philips, and many another name, concerning whom an illustration might be furnished, of their powers of wit, wisdom, or eloquence. England, itself, has been indebted, in many a circle, to eminent Welsh preachers, who have stimulated thought, created the sphere of holy usefulness, moved over the minds of cultivated members with the freshness of a mountain wind, or a mountain stream. It would be invidious to mention their names—many are yet living; and some, who have not long quitted the Church on earth, have still left behind them the fragrance of loved, and honoured names, and exalted, and earnest labours.

Few of our readers, we may suppose, can be unacquainted with the name, and memory of "The Man of Ross," so famous through the verses of Pope. Ross is a well-known little town in Monmouthshire, on the banks of the Wye, on the borders of Wales. There, in the parish church, in the pew in which John Kyrle, the Man of Ross, sat, more than a hundred years since, a curious sight may be seen: two elm-trees rise, and spread out their arms, and flourish within the church; especially during the spring, and summer months, they form a singular adornment to the sacred edifice. The tradition is, that they are suckers from a tree planted by the "Man of Ross," outside the church; but it was cut down by a certain rector, because it excluded the light; the consequence was that they forced their way inside, where they had continued to grow, and flourish. As we have looked upon the singular sight of those trees, in the Man of Ross's pew, we have often thought of those who, in Wales, planted in the house of the Lord, flourish in sacred, and sainted memories, in the courts of our God. Although all that was mortal of them has passed away, they still bring forth fruit, and flourish in the grateful recollections of the country, they were permitted to bless, and adorn.

Yes, it is very singular to think of many of these men of Wild Wales. Even those who were counted heretical, were more than extraordinary men; they were, perhaps, men who, in our day, would seem rather remarkable for their orthodoxy of sentiment. Rhys Stephen, in an extended note in his Memoirs of Christmas Evans, refers to the influence of discussions, in the Principality, raised by the Rev. WILLIAM RICHARDS, LL.D. A large portion of the ministerial life of this distinguished man, was passed in England; he was educated for the ministry at the Baptist Academy in Bristol, for some time co-pastor with Dr. Ash, author of the Dictionary, and then became the minister of the Baptist Church at Lynn, in Norfolk, where he remained for twenty years. He always continued, however, in every sense of the word, a Welshman, and, notwithstanding his English pastorates, his residences in Wales were frequent and long.

He was born at Pen-hydd, in Pembrokeshire, in 1749. He published a Welsh-English dictionary, and his services to Welsh literature were eminent. But he was regarded as a heretic; his temperament, singular as it seems in a Welshman, was almost purely philosophic, and neither imaginative, nor emotional; he disliked the great annual religious gatherings of his countrymen, and called them fairs, and the preachers, upon these occasions, he sometimes described in epithets, which were not complimentary. Naturally, his brethren paid him back; they called him a heretic,—which is also an exceedingly convenient, and not unusual method of revenge. Dr. Richards's influence, however, in Wales, at the beginning of this century, appears to have been very great; the charges against him, he does not appear to have been very mindful to disprove, and it is exceedingly likely that a different, or more guarded mode of expression, was the height of his offending. Who can fathom, or delineate, all the fine shades and divergencies of the Arian controversy?—men whose perfect soundness, in evangelical doctrine, was utterly undisputed, talked with Dr. Richards, and said, that they could not discover that he held opinions different from their own. In a letter, dated December 7th, 1804, when grave charges had been urged against him, and all the religious mischiefs throughout the Principality ascribed to him, he writes as follows, to a friend:—

> "I think I may safely say, that no great change, of any kind, has taken place in my sentiments since I knew you. You must know, surely, that I did not use to be an *Athanasian*, or

even a *Waterlandian*. Such views of the Deity always appeared to me too *Tritheistical*. I have been used to think, and do so still, that there is a particular meaning in such words as these of the Apostle's, 'To us there is but one God, the Father;' but I never could say, or think, with the Socinians, that Jesus Christ is no more than *a man*, like ourselves. I believe, indeed, that He is a Man; but I, also, believe that He is 'Emmanuel, God with us'—that he is 'the form of God'—'the image of the invisible God'—an object of Divine worship, so that we should 'honour the Son as we honour the Father'—'that all the fulness of the Godhead dwells in Him bodily,' or substantially. In short, I believe everything of the dignity, and glory of Christ's character, that does not *divide* the Deity, or land in *Tritheism*."

Again, to another correspondent: "I believe, also, in the doctrine of the atonement, or sacrifice, of Christ, in the virtue of His blood, and in the prevalence of His mediation."

Something of the same order of man, so far as sentiment, and knowledge are indications, but possessed of more wit, imagination, and emotion, was DAVIES, of CASTELL HYWEL, the first pastor of Christmas Evans, and of Daniel Davies, of Swansea. He was, in his day, a man of many-sided reputation, but of suspicious doctrinal relations. He was so eminent a classical scholar, and so many of the Welsh clergy had received their education from him, that when Dr. Horsley was appointed Bishop of St. David's, he expressed, in his usual passionate manner, his irritation that the most distinguished tutor in South Wales was a Nonconformist, and gave out that he would not ordain any of Mr. Davies' pupils. Davies was a great bard; and Welshmen who know both languages, say that his translation of Gray's "Elegy" is, in force, and pathos, superior to the original. This will scarcely seem strange, if the deep pathos of the Welsh language be taken into account. His epitaph on Dr. Priestley—satirizing, of course, the materialism of Priestley—illustrates, at once, his humour, and versification:

> "Here lies at rest, in oaken chest,
>   Together packed most nicely,
> The bones, and brains, flesh, blood, and veins,
>   And *soul* of Dr. Priestley!"

As an illustration of his readiness of wit, a story is told, how one of the most noted of the Welsh bards one day met him, while the rain was streaming down upon him. Umbrellas, probably, were scarce. He was covered with layers of straw, fastened round with ropes of the same material; in fact, thatched all over. To him his brother bard exclaimed:

> "Oh, bard and teacher, famed afar,
>   Such sight I never saw!
> It ill becomes a house like yours
>   To have a roof of straw."

To which Davies instantly replied:

> "The rain is falling fast, my friend;
>   You know not what you say,
> A roof of straw, methinks, doth well
>   Beseem a wall of clay."

Such was Christmas Evans's first "guide, philosopher, and friend."

And if we refer to certain characteristics of the Welsh language, which make it eminently fine furniture for preaching-power, to these may be added, what we have not so particularly dwelt on, but which does follow, as a part of the same remark—the singular proverbial power of the Welsh language. In reading great Welsh sermons, and listening to Welsh preachers, we have often felt how much the spirit of their own triads, and the manner of old Catwg the Wise, and other such sententious bards, falls into their modern method. Welsh proverbs are the delightful recreations of the archæologists of the old Welsh language. Here, while we write these lines, we have piles of these proverbial utterances before us; short, compact sayings, wherever they come from, but which have been repeated on, from generation to generation. The Bardic triads, for instance, relating to language, selected by Mr. Owen Pugh,—how admirable they are for any preacher! They may stand as the characteristics of their most eminent men.

"The three indispensables of language—purity, copiousness, and aptness; the three supports of language—order, strength, and harmony; the three uses of language—to relate, to describe, to excite; the correct qualities of language,—correct construction, correct etymology, and correct pronunciation; three marks of the purity of language—the intelligible, the pleasurable, the credible; three things that constitute just description—just selection of words, just construction of language, and just comparison; three things appertaining to just selection—the best language, the best order, and the best object." It must be admitted, we think, that, in these old triads, there is much of the compact wisdom of a primeval people, with whom books were few, and thoughts were fresh, and constant. There seemed to be a singular propensity, in the old mind of Wales, to throw everything into the form of a trinity of expression, or to bind up words, as far as possible, in short, sententious utterances. Catwg's "Essay on Metaphysics" is a very brief, and concise one, but it illustrates that rapid running-up-the-ladder kind of style, which has always been the delight of the Welsh poet or teacher.

> "In every person there is a soul. In every soul there is intelligence. In every intelligence there is thought. In every thought there is either good, or evil. In every evil there is death; in every good there is life. In every life there is God; and there is no God but He than whom there can be none better. There is nothing that cannot have its better, save the best of all. There is no best of all except love. There is no love but God. God is love!"

Illustrations of this kind fill volumes. It is not for us here to say how much of the admirable, or the imitable there may be in the method. It was the method of the old Welsh mind; it was the method into which many of the best preachers fell, not because they, perhaps, knew so much of the words of the bards, as because it represented the mind of the race. Take a few of the Welsh proverbs.

> "He that is intent upon going, will do no good before he departs."

> "Every one has his neighbour for a mirror."

> "The water is shallowest where it bubbles."

> "A lie is the quickest traveller."

> "Fame outlives riches."

> "He that is unlucky at sea, will be unlucky on land."

> "There is always time for meat, and for prayer."

> "He mows the meadow with shears."

> "Calumny comes from envy."

> "Every bird loves its own voice."

> "The life of a man is not at the disposal of his enemy."

> "He that loves the young, must love their sports."

> "Prudence is unmarried without patience."

> "He that is the head, should become the bridge."

> "Three things come unawares upon a man: sleep, sin, and old age."

But it is not only that this sententious characteristic of the Welsh language makes it a vehicle for the transparent expression of sentiment; even our translations cannot altogether disguise the pathetic tones of the language, and bursts of feeling. The following verse of an old Welsh prayer, which, a

Quarterly Reviewer tells us, used to form, with the Creed and Ten Commandments, part of the peasant's daily devotion, illustrates this:—

> "Mother, O mother! tell me, art thou weeping?"
>   The infant Saviour asked, on Mary's breast.
> "Child of th' Eternal, nay; I am but sleeping,
>   Though vexed by many a thought of dark unrest."
> "Say, at what vision is thy courage failing?"
>   "I see a crown of thorns, and bitter pain;
> And thee, dread Child, upon the cross of wailing,
>   All heaven aghast, at rude mankind's disdain."

It is singular that Mr. Borrow found, on an old tombstone, an epitaph, which most of our readers will remember, as very like that famous one Sir Walter Scott gives us, from an old tomb, in a note to "The Lay of the Last Minstrel." The following is a translation:—

> "Thou earth, from earth, reflect, with anxious mind,
> That earth to earth must quickly be consigned;
> And earth in earth must lie entranced, enthralled,
> Till earth from earth to judgment shall be called."

The following lines also struck Mr. Borrow as remarkably beautiful, of which he gives us this translation. They are an inscription in a garden:—

> "In a garden the first of our race was deceived;
> In a garden the promise of grace was received;
> In a garden was Jesus betrayed to His doom;
> In a garden His body was laid in the tomb."

Such verses are very illustrative of the alliterative character of the Welsh mind.

But Wales, in its way—and no classical reader must smile at the assertion—was once quite as much the land of song as Italy. Among the amusements of the people was the singing of "Pennilion," a sort of epigrammatic poem, and of an improvisatorial character, testing the readiness of rural wit. With this exercise there came to be associated, in later days, a sort of rude mystery, or comedy, performed in very much the same manner as the old monkish mysteries of the dark ages. These furnished an opportunity for satirizing any of the unpopular characters of the village, or the Principality. Such mental characteristics, showing that there was a living mind in the country, must be remembered, when we attempt to estimate the power which extraordinary preachers soon attained, over the minds of their countrymen. Then, no doubt, although there might be exceptions, and a Welshman prove that he could be as stupid as anybody else, in general there was a keen love, and admiration of nature. The names of places show this. Mr. Borrow illustrates both characters in an anecdote. He met an old man, and his son, at the foot of the great mountain, called Tap-Nyth-yr Eryri.

"Does not that mean," said Mr. Borrow, "the top nest of the eagles?"

"Ha!" said the old man, "I see you understand Welsh."

"A little. Are there eagles there now?"

"Oh, no! no eagle now; eagle left Tap-Nyth."

"Is that young man your son?" said Mr. Borrow, after a little pause.

"Yes, he my son."

"Has he any English?"

"No, he no English, but he plenty of Welsh; that is, if he see reason." He spoke to the young man, in Welsh, asking him if he had ever been up to the Tap-Nyth; but he made no answer.

"He no care for your question," said the old man; "ask him price of pig."

"I asked the young fellow the price of hogs," says Mr. Borrow, "whereupon his face brightened up, and he not only answered my question, but told me that he had a fat hog to sell."

"Ha, ha!" said the old man, "he plenty of Welsh now, for he see reason; to other question he no Welsh at all, no more than English, for he see no reason. What business he on Tap-Nyth, with eagle? His business down below in sty with pig. Ah! he look lump, but he no fool. Know more about pig than you, or I, or anyone, 'twixt here and Machunleth."

It has been said, that the inhabitants of a mountainous country cannot be insensible to religion, and whether, or not this is universally true, it is, certainly, true of Wales. The magnificent scenery seems to create a pensive awe upon the spirit. Often the pedestrian, passing along a piece of unsuggestive road, suddenly finds that the stupendous mountains have sloped down, to valleys of the wildest, and most picturesque beauty, valley opening into valley, in some instances; in others, as in the vale of Glamorgan, stretching along, for many miles, in plenteous fruitfulness, and beauty, illuminated by some river like the Tivy, the Towy, or the Llugg, some of these rivers sparkling, and flashing with the glittering *gleisiad*, as an old Welsh song sings it—

> "*Glan yw'r gleisiad yn y llyn,*
> Full fair the *gleisiad* in the flood
> Which sparkles 'neath the summer's sun."

The *gleisiad* is the salmon. We have dwelt on the word here, for the purpose of calling the reader's attention to its beautiful expressiveness. It seems to convey the whole idea of the fish—its silvery splendour, gleaming, and glancing through the lynn.

It seems rather in the nature of the Welsh mind, to take instantly a pensive, and sombre idea of things. A traveller, walking beneath a fine row of elms, expressed his admiration of them to a Welsh companion. "Ay, sir," said the man; "they'll make fine chests for the dead!" It was very nationally characteristic, and hence, perhaps, it is that the owl (the *dylluan*) among birds, has received some of the most famous traditions of the Welsh language. Mr. Borrow thought there was no cry so wild, as the cry of the *dylluan*—"unlike any other sound in nature," he says, "a cry, which no combination of letters can give the slightest idea of;" and, surely, that Welsh name far better realizes it, than the *tu whit tu whoo* of our Shakespeare.

Certainly, it is not in a page, or two, that we can give anything like an adequate idea of that compacted poetry, which meets us in Wales, whether we think of the varied scenery of the country, of the nervous, and descriptive language, or of its race of people, so imaginative, and speculative.

It ought to be mentioned, also, as quite as distinctly characteristic, that there is an intense clannishness prevalent throughout the Principality. Communication between the people has no doubt somewhat modified this; but, usually, an Englishman resident in Wales, and especially in the more sequestered regions, has seldom found himself in very comfortable circumstances. The Welsh have a suspicion that there are precious secrets in their land, and language, of which the English are desirous to avail themselves. And, perhaps, there is some extenuation in the recollection that we, as their conquerors, have seldom given them reason to think well of us.

CHAPTER IX.
CHRISTMAS EVANS CONTINUED—HIS MINISTRY AT CAERPHILLY.

Caerphilly and its Associations—"Christmas Evans is come!"—A Housekeeper—His Characteristic Second Marriage—A Great Sermon, The Trial of the Witnesses—The Tall Soldier—Extracts from Sermons—The Bible a Stone with Seven Eyes—"Their Works do Follow them"—A Second Covenant with God—Friends at Cardiff—J. P. Davies—Reads Pye Smith's "Scripture Testimony to the Messiah"—Beattie on Truth—The Edwards Family—Requested to Publish a Volume of Sermons, and his Serious Thoughts upon the Subject.

It was in the year 1826 that Christmas Evans, now sixty-two years of age, left Anglesea, accepting an invitation to the Baptist Church at Tonyvelin, in Caerphilly. His ministry at Anglesea had been long, affectionate, and very successful; but, dear as Anglesea was to him, he had to leave it, and he left it, as we have seen, under circumstances not honourable to the neighbouring ministers, or the churches of which he had been the patriarchal pastor. Little doubt can there be, that even he suffered from the jealousy of inferior minds, and characters; so old as he was, so venerable, and such a household name as his had become, throughout all Wales, it might have been thought that he would not have been permitted to depart. He left the dust of his beloved wife, the long companion of his Cildwrn cottage, behind him, and commenced his tedious journey to his new home. He had about two hundred miles to travel, and the travelling was not easy; travelling in Wales was altogether unrelated to the more comfortable, and commodious modes of conveyance in England, even in that day; and now he would have to cross a dangerous ferry, and now to mount a rugged, and toilsome hill, to wind slowly along by the foot of some gigantic mountain, to wend through a long, winding valley, or across an extensive plain. As the old man passed along, he says he experienced great tenderness of mind, and the presence of Christ by his side. A long, solitary journey! he says, he was enabled to entrust the care of his ministry to Jesus Christ, with the confidence that He would deliver him from all his afflictions; he says, "I again made a covenant with God which I never wrote."

Caerphilly would seem a very singular spot in which to settle one of the most remarkable men, if not the most remarkable, in the pulpit of his country, and his time,—beyond all question, the most distinguished in his own denomination, there, and then. Even now, probably, very few of our readers have ever heard of Caerphilly; it is nearly forty years since the writer of the present pages was there, and there, in a Welsh cottage, heard from the lips of an old Welsh dame the most graphic outlines he has ever heard, or read, of some of the sermons of Christmas Evans. Since that day, we suppose Caerphilly may have grown nearer to the dignity of a little town, sharing some of the honours which have so lavishly fallen upon its great, and prosperous neighbour, Cardiff.

Caerphilly, however insignificant, as it lies in its mountain valley, a poor little village when Christmas Evans was there, has its own eminent claims to renown: tradition says—and, in this instance, tradition is, probably, correct—that it was once the seat of a large town. There, certainly, still stands the vast ruins of Caerphilly Castle, once the largest in all Great Britain next to Windsor, and still the most extensive ruin; here was the retreat of the ill-fated Edward II.; here was that great siege, during which the King escaped in the depth of a dark, and stormy night, in the disguise of a Welsh peasant, flying to the parish of Llangonoyd, twenty miles to the west, where he hired himself at a farm, which, it is said, is still pointed out, or the spot where once it stood, the site made memorable, through all these ages, by so singular a circumstance. This was the siege in which that grand, and massive tower was rent, and which still so singularly leans, and hangs there,—the leaning tower of Caerphilly, as wonderful an object as the leaning tower of Pisa, a wonder in Wales which few have visited.

After this period, it was occupied by Glendower; gradually, however, it became only famous for the rapacity of its lords, the Spencers, who plundered their vassals, and the inhabitants of the region in general, so that from this circumstance arose a Welsh proverb, "It is gone to Caerphilly,"—signifying, says Malkin, that a thing is irrecoverably lost, and used on occasions when an Englishman, not very nice, and select in his language, would say, "It is gone to the devil." Gloomy ideas were associated for long ages with Caerphilly, as the seat of horror, and rapacity; it had an awful tower for prisoners, its ruinous walls were of wondrous thickness, and it was set amidst desolate marshes.

And this was the spot to which Christmas Evans was consigned for some of the closing years of his life; but, perhaps, our readers can have no idea of the immense excitement his transit thither caused to the good people of the village, and its neighbourhood. Our readers will remember, what we have already said, that a small village by no means implied a small congregation. His arrival at Caerphilly was looked upon as an event in the history of the region round about; for until he was actually there, it was believed that his heart would fail him at last, and that he would never be able to leave Anglesea.

It is said that all denominations, and all conditions of people, caught up, and propagated the report, "CHRISTMAS EVANS IS COME!" "*Are you sure of* it?" "YES, *quite sure of it; he preached at Caerphilly last Sunday*! I know a friend who was there." These poor scattered villagers, how foolish, to us, seems their enthusiasm, and frantic joy, because they had their country's great preaching bard in their midst; almost as foolish as those insane Florentines, who burst into tears and acclamations as they greeted one of the great pictures of Cimabue, and reverently thronged round it in a kind of triumphal procession. What makes it more remarkable, is that they should love a man as poor, as he was old. If they could revere him as, wearied and dusty, he came along after his tedious two hundred miles' journey, spent, and exhausted, what an affluence of affection they would have poured forth had he rode into Caerphilly, as the old satirist has it, in a coach, and six!

Well, he was settled in the chapel-house, and a housekeeper was provided for him. In domestic matters, however, he did not seem to get on very well. North, and South Wales appeared different to him, and he said to a friend, he must get a servant from the north. It was suggested to him, that he might do better than that, that he had better marry again, and the name of an excellent woman was mentioned, who would have been probably not unwilling; and she had wealth, so that he might have bettered his entire worldly circumstances by the alliance, and have made himself pleasantly independent of churches, and deacons, and county associations; and when it was first suggested to him, he seemed to think for a moment, and then broke out into a cheerful laugh. "Ho! ho!" he said, "I tell you, brother, it is my firm opinion that I am never to have any property in the soil of this world, until I have a grave;" and he would talk no more on the subject, but he took a good brother minister of the neighbourhood into his counsel, Mr. Davies, of Argoed, and he persuaded him to take his horse, and to go for him to Anglesea, and to bring back with him the old, and faithful servant of himself, and his departed wife, Mary Evans; and, in a short time, he married her, and she paid him every tribute of untiring, and devoted affection, to the last moment of his life. A really foolish man, you see, this Christmas Evans, and, as many no doubt said, old as he was, he might have done so much better for himself. It is not uninteresting to notice a circumstance, which Mr. Rhys Stephen discovered, that Christmas Evans was married the second time in the same parish of Eglwysilian, in Glamorganshire, the church in which George Whitefield was married: the parish register contains both their names.

And what will our readers think, when they find that those who knew Christmas Evans, both at this, and previous periods of his history, declare that his preaching now surpassed that of any previous period? Certainly, his ministry was gloriously successful at Caerphilly. Caerphilly, the village in the valley, became like a city set upon a hill; every Sabbath, multitudes might be seen, wending their way across the surrounding hills, in all directions. The homes of the neighbourhood rang, and re-echoed with Christmas Evans's sermons; his morning sermon, especially, would be the subject of conversation, in hundreds of homes, many miles away, that evening. The old dame with whom we drank our cup of tea, in her pleasant cottage at Caerphilly, near forty years since, talked, with tears, of those old days. She said, "We used to reckon things as they happened, by Christmas Evans's sermons; people used to say, 'It must have happened then, because that was the time when Christmas Evans preached The Wedding Ring,' or The Seven Eyes, or some other sermon which had been quite a book-mark in the memory."

No doubt, many grand sermons belong to the Caerphilly period: there is one which reads, to us, like an especial triumph; it was preached some time after he settled in the south; the subject was, "God manifest in the flesh, justified in the spirit." The grand drama in this sermon was the examination of the evidences of Christ's resurrection:—

"THE TRIAL OF THE WITNESSES.

> "The enemies of Christ, after His death, applied for a military guard to watch at His tomb, and this application for a military guard was rested on the fact, that the 'impostor' had said, in His lifetime, that He would rise again on the third day. Without a doubt, had they found His body in the grave, when the time had transpired, they would have torn it from the sepulchre, exhibited it through the streets of Jerusalem, where Jesus had preached, where He had been despitefully used, and scourged; they would have shouted forth with triumph, 'This is the body of the impostor!' But He had left the grave, that morning, too early for them. The soldiers came back to the city, and they went to the leaders of the people who had employed them, and the leaders exclaimed, 'Here is the watch! What is the matter? What is that dread settled in their faces? Come in here, and we charge you to tell the truth.' 'You have no need to charge us, for the fright, the terror of it, is still upon us.' 'How? What has happened at the grave? Did His disciples come, and take Him away?' 'They! no; but if they had, our spears would have sufficed for them.' 'Well, but how was it? What has taken place?' 'Well, see; while we were on the watch, and early, in the dawn of the morning, a great earthquake, like to that one that took place on Friday afternoon, *when He died*, and we all fell powerless to the ground; and we saw angels, bright, like the lightning; we were not able to bear the sight; we looked down at once; we

endeavoured, again, to raise our eyes, and we beheld One coming out of the grave, but He passed by the first angel we saw, who now was sitting on the removed stone; but He who came out of the grave! we never saw one like unto Him before,—truly He was like unto the Son of God.' 'What, then, became of the angel?' 'Oh, a legion of them came down, and one of them, very fair, like a young man, entered the grave, and sat where the head of Jesus had lain; and, immediately, another, also, very fair, and beautiful, sat where His feet had rested.' 'And did the angels say nothing to you?' 'No, but they looked with eyes of lightning.' 'Saw you not His friends, the women?' 'Oh, yes; they came there, but He had left the tomb before their arrival.' 'Talked the angels to the women?' 'Yes; they seemed to be of one family, and very well acquainted with one another.' 'Do you remember anything of the conversation?' 'Yes; they said, "Fear you not! let the Pharisees, and Darkness fear to-day! You seek Jesus! He is not here, for He is risen indeed; He is alive, and lives for ever. He has gone before you to Galilee." We heard one angel say, "Come, see the place where the Lord lay." Another angel spoke to a woman called Mary, and said, "Why weepest *thou*, while thy Lord is risen indeed, and is alive, so near unto thee? *let His enemies weep to-day!*"' 'WHAT!' exclaimed the leader of those priests, and of the council, who had asked for the guard,—'What! how say you? *Close that door!* You, *tall* soldier, approach: was it not you who pierced His side?' 'Yes, it was I; but all that these soldiers have said is all true; oh, alas! it is all true! He must have been the Son of God.' The Pharisees lost their cause, on the day of their appeal; they gave the soldiers money, to say that His disciples had stolen the body while they slept! *If they were asleep, how did they know in what manner He had left the grave?* They, however, suffered themselves to be suborned, and for money lied, and, to this hour, the kingdom of Satan hangs upon that lie!"

This sermon produced a profound impression. We have said, to render the sermons of Christmas Evans in print, or by description, is impossible,—as impossible as to paint tones, and accents, or the varying expressions which pass over eye, and face, and lip. He was entreated to publish this sermon, but he could only write out something like an outline of it, and when it appeared in print, those who had been enraptured with it, in its delivery, declared that it was not the same sermon; so he was entreated to preach the sermon again. He made a humorous remark, on the strangeness of a man preaching his own printed sermon; still, he complied. His accomplished biographer, Rhys Stephen, heard it then, and says of it, "While I have the faintest trace of memory, as to sermons I have heard, this must always be pre-eminent, and distinct; in its oratorical eminence, it stands alone, even among his great achievements. One of the most striking parts of the sermon, was in the examination of the Roman guard, the report of the soldiers to the authorities." Mr. Stephens continues, "We heard them talk, had a clear perception of the difference of the tone, and more especially, when one of the chief priests, in an anxious, agonizing whisper, said, '*Shut the door!*' And then, 'You, tall soldier, approach: was it not you who pierced His side?' 'Yes, it was I.' When Christmas Evans simulated the chief priest, and singled out the tall soldier, and the conversation went on between the two, such a combined triumph of sanctified fancy, and perfect oratory, I never expect to witness again." We may, also, say, that it illustrates wherein, very greatly, lay the preacher's power,—seizing some little circumstance, and, by its homeliness, or aptness, giving reality, and vivacity to the whole picture.

It must be said, his are very great sermons; the present writer is almost disposed to be bold enough to describe them, as the grandest Gospel sermons of the last hundred years. Not one, or two, but several, are especially noble. One of these we have, already, given: the splendid embodiment, and personification of the twenty-second Psalm, *The Hind of the Morning*, from the singular, and most significant designation, or title of the Psalm itself.

Another sermon which, probably, belongs to this period is

"THE BIBLE REGARDED AS A STONE WITH SEVEN EYES,"

evidently from Zech. iii. 9, "*Upon one stone shall be seven eyes.*"

It was, in fact, a review of

"*The Internal Evidences which prove the Gospel to be of God.*

> "God's perfections are, in some sort, to be seen in all He has done, and in all He has spoken. He imprints some indication of His character, on everything that His hand forms, and that His mouth utters, so that there might be a sufficient difference between the work, and the speech of God, and those of man. The Bible is the Book of books, a book breathed out of heaven. It was easy enough for John to determine, when he saw the Lamb, with the seven horns, and the seven eyes, in the midst of the throne, that the Godhead was there, and that such a Lamb was not to be found amongst creatures. When one saw a stone, with seven eyes, before Zerubbabel, it was not difficult to

conclude that it was a stone from some unusual mine. In looking at the page of the starry sky, the work of the fingers of the Everlasting Power is traced in the sun, and moon, and stars; all proclaim His name, and tell His glory. I am very thankful for books written by man, but it is God's book that sheds the light of the life everlasting on all other books. I cannot often read it, hear it, or reflect upon it, but I see—

"1. *Eternity*, like a great fiery Eye, looking at me from the everlasting, and the infinite distance, unfolding mysteries, and opening before me the doors, windows, and chambers, in the (otherwise) unknown, and awful state! This Eye leads me to the source, and cause of all things, and places me in the presence, and sight of the Almighty, who has in Him something that would destroy me for ever, and yet something that spares, and animates me; pressing me down, and at the same time, saying, 'Fear not;' something that melts me into penitence, and, at once, causes me to rejoice in the faith, inspiring me with the fear of joy; something that creates a wish in me, to conceal myself from Him, and then a stronger wish, to stay, for ever, in the light of His countenance.

"2. *Omniscience* looks at me, also, like a Divine Eye, out of every chapter, verse, doctrine, and ordinance of the Gospel, and searches me through and through. The attempt at concealment from it is utterly vain. To this Eye, darkness is as the light. It has descried, correctly, into the deepest abysses of my spirit; and it has truthfully drawn my likeness before I received God's grace; having received it; and the future is, also, transparent before it. There is something in the scanning of this Eye, that obliges me to confess, against myself, my sins unto the Lord; and to cry out for a new heart, and a right spirit; for the Author of the Book knows all.

"3. When I yield to pensive reflections, under a sense of sin, and when I see the tops of dark mountains of disease, and trouble at the terrors of the grave, I see in the Bible *Infinite Goodness*, fairer than the Shekinah of old, looking at me, out of eternity; it is like the smile of the Eternal King, from His throne of mercy. Divine love, merits of Christ, riches of grace, they are all here, and they assure me, and I listen to the still, small voice, that follows in its train, until I feel myself lifted up, out of the cave of despair, by the dark mountain; and I stand on my feet, and I hope, and hear the proclamation of the great mystery—'Behold, I come, as it is written in the roll of the Book. If I must die, I am willing to die; for I come to seek, and to save that which is lost.'

"4. *Holiness, righteousness*, and *purity* look at me, out of the midst of the Book, like the fires of Sinai to Israel, or the I AM, out of the burning bush; causing me to fear, and tremble, while I am yet desirous of looking at the radiant glory, because it is attempered with mercy. I take my shoes from off my feet, and approach on my knees, to see this great sight. I cannot live, in sin, in this presence,—still it does not slay me. The Eternal Power is here, and, with one hand, it conceals me, in the shadow of redeeming mercy, and, with the other, it points out the glory of the great, and wondrous truth, that God is, at once, a just God, and justifier of him that believeth in Jesus. Where Thy glory rests, O my God, there let me have my abode!

"5. I also see *Infinite might* radiating from the doctrine of the Book, like God's own Eye, having the energy of a sharp, two-edged sword. Without asking permission of me, it proves itself 'quick and powerful, and pierces even to the dividing asunder of the soul, and spirit, and of the joints, and marrow;' it opens the private recesses of my heart, and becomes a discerner, and judge of its thoughts, and intents. When Lord Rochester, the great wit, and unbeliever of his day, read Isa. liii. 5, 'He was wounded for our transgressions,' etc., Divine energies entered his spirit, and did so thoroughly pierce, and pervade it, that his infidelity died within him, and he gladly received the faith, and hope that are in Christ. The power of the Gospel visited Matthew, at the receipt of custom, the woman at the well of Samaria, the malefactor on the cross, the converts on the day of Pentecost, Paul by the way, and the jailer at Philippi; in them all was exerted this resistless might of grace, the '*Let there be*' of the original creation, which none can withstand.

"6. When I am weak, and *distressed*, and *alone*, and none to receive my tale of sorrow, none to express a word of fellow-feeling, or of care for me, in the living oracles of the Gospel I see Divine wisdom, and loving-kindness, looking at me tenderly, compassionately, through the openings of my prison, and I feel that He, who dresses the lily of the field, and numbers the sparrows, is near me, numbering the hairs of my head, listening to my cries; and in all the treasure of grace, and power, that was able to say to the lost one, at the very door of the pit, 'To-day shalt thou be with me in Paradise,' fearing no hindrances that might intervene, between Golgotha and heaven, He is the same gracious Redeemer, and Preserver to every one, that believes in His name. Who will teach me the way of wisdom? who will guide me to her dwelling-place? It was in the Gospel that wisdom came to reside near me, and here she teaches the most untoward, convinces the most hard-hearted, reforms the most licentious, and makes the simple wise unto salvation.

"7. *I am sometimes filled with questions of anxious import.* Art thou from heaven, O Gospel? Thou hast caused me to hope: Art thou a rock? The reply: Dost thou not see, in my face, the true character of God, and of the Eternal Power Incarnate? Dost thou not discern, in Jesus, the image of the invisible God, which, unlike the first Adam, the second Adam has preserved untarnished? and dost thou not feel, in looking at it, thyself gradually changed into the same image, even as by the Spirit of the Lord? In looking at God's image in the creature, the vision had no transforming power, but left 'the wise men' of the ancient world where it found them, destitute of true knowledge, and happiness, without hope, and without God in the world; but here the vision transforms into the glorious likeness of the sublime object, even Christ.

"*The character of God*, given in the Gospel, is complete, and perfect, worthy of the most blessed One, and there is no perfect portraiture given of Him but in the Gospel. Mohammed's God is *unchaste*; Homer gave his Jupiter *revenge*; Voltaire deified *mockery*; Insurrection and War were the gods of Paine;—but the character of the God of the Gospel is awful in truth, and lovely in goodness. In Isa. vi., the vision of the Divine glory caused the six-winged cherubs to conceal their faces; but in Rev. iv., the six-winged living things employ five wings to fly, and only one to veil their faces, while they are full of eyes behind, and before, looking forth unveiled. All the worshippers under the

Gospel, look with open face—without a veil, and on an unveiled object."

We have here, evidently, only the rudiments of a sermon, but a very fine one, a very suggestive one. To most minds, the Bible has, probably, been, as Thomas Carlyle, or Jean Paul, would express it, "an eyeless socket, without the eye." Christmas Evans was expressing, in this very suggestive sermon, the thoughts of some men whose words, and works he had probably never met with; as George Herbert says it—

"In ev'ry thing
Thy words do find me out."

"Beyond any other book," says Samuel Taylor Coleridge, "the Bible *finds* me;" while John Keble, in the "Christian Year,"—probably written about the same time, when Christmas Evans was preparing his sermon,—was employing the very same image in some of his most impressive words:—

"*Eye of God's Word*! where'er we turn,
  Ever upon us! thy keen gaze
Can all the depths of sin discern,
  Unravel every bosom's maze:

"Who, that has felt thy glance of dread
  Thrill through his heart's remotest cells,
About his path, about his bed,
  Can doubt what Spirit in thee dwells?"

In the following extract, we have a more sustained passage, very fresh, and noble:—

"THEIR WORKS DO FOLLOW THEM.

"In this world, every man receives according to his faith; in the world to come, every man shall receive according to his works. 'Blessed are the dead who die in the Lord, for they rest from their labours, and their works do follow them.' Their works do not go *before* them, to divide the river of Jordan, and open the gates of heaven. This is done by their faith. But their works are left behind, as if done up in a packet, on this side of the river. John saw the great white throne, descending for judgment, the Son of man sitting thereon, and all nations gathered before Him. He is dividing the righteous from the wicked, as the shepherd divideth the sheep from the goats. The wicked are set on the left hand—'Depart from me, ye accursed, into everlasting fire, prepared for the devil and his angels!' But the righteous are placed on the right hand, to hear the joyful welcome—'Come, ye blessed of my Father, inherit the kingdom prepared for you from the foundation of the world!' The books are opened, and Mercy presents the packets that were left on the other side of Jordan. They are all opened, and the books are read, wherein all their acts of benevolence are recorded. Justice examines the several packets, and answers—'All right. Here they are. Thus it is written—"I was hungry, and ye gave Me meat; I was thirsty, and ye gave Me drink; I was a stranger, and ye took me in; I was naked, and ye clothed Me; I was in prison, and ye came unto Me!"' The righteous look upon each other, with wonder, and answer—'Those packets must belong to others. We know nothing of all that. We recollect the wormwood, and the gall. We recollect the strait gate, the narrow way, and the slough of despond. We recollect the heavy burden, that pressed so hard upon us, and how it fell from our shoulders, at the sight of the cross. We recollect the time, when the eyes of our minds were opened, to behold the evil of sin, the depravity of our hearts, and the excellency of our Redeemer. We recollect the time when our stubborn wills were subdued, in the day of His power, so that we were enabled both to will, and to do, of His good pleasure. We recollect the time, when we obtained hope in the merit of Christ, and felt the efficacy of His blood, applied to our hearts by the Holy Spirit. And we shall never forget the time, when we first experienced the love of God, shed abroad in our hearts. Oh, how sweetly, and powerfully it constrained us to love Him, His cause, and His ordinances! How we panted after communion, and fellowship with Him, as the hart panteth after the waterbrooks! All this, and a thousand other things, are as fresh in our memory as ever. But we recollect nothing of those bundles of good works. Where was it? Lord, when saw we Thee hungry, and fed Thee; or thirsty, and gave Thee drink; or a stranger, and took Thee in; or naked, and clothed Thee? We have no more recollection, than the dead, of ever having visited Thee in prison, or ministered to Thee in sickness. Surely, those bundles cannot belong to us.' Mercy replies—'Yes, verily, they belong to you; for your names are upon them; and, besides, they have not been out of my hands since you left them on the stormy banks of Jordan.' And the King answers—'Verily, I say unto you,

> Inasmuch as ye have done it unto one of the least of these My brethren, ye have done it unto Me.'

> "If the righteous do not know their own good works; if they do not recognize, in the sheaves which they reap at the resurrection, the seed which they have sown, in tears, on earth,—they, certainly, cannot make these things the foundation of their hopes of heaven. Christ is their sole dependence, for acceptance with God, in time, and in eternity. Christ, crucified, is the great object of their faith, and the centre of their affections; and, while their love to Him prompts them to live soberly, and righteously, and godly, in this present evil world, they cordially exclaim, 'Not unto us, not unto us, but to Thy name, O Lord, give glory.'"

In leaving Anglesea behind him, the sufferings, and contradictions he had known there, did not quench his enthusiastic holiness, and fervent ardour. We are assured of this when we read his

"SECOND COVENANT WITH GOD.

> "While returning from a place called Tongwynlâs, over Caerphilly Mountain, the spirit of prayer descended, very copiously, upon me. I wept for some hours, and heartily supplicated Jesus Christ, for the blessings here following. I found, at this time, a particular nearness to Christ, as if He were close by me, and my mind was filled with strong confidence that He attended to my requests, for the sake of the merits of His own name. This decided me in favour of Cardiff.

> "I. Grant me the great favour of being led by Thee, according to Thy will—by the directions of Thy providence, and Word, and this disposing of my own mind, by Thy Spirit, for the sake of Thine infinitely precious blood. Amen.—C. E.

> "II. Grant, if I am to leave Caerphilly, that the gale (of the Spirit's influence), and religious revival I had there, may follow me to Cardiff, for the sake of Thy great name. Amen.—C. E.

> "III. Grant Thy blessing upon bitter things, to brighten, and quicken me, more and more, and not to depress, and make me more lifeless. Amen.—C. E.

"IV. Suffer me not to be trodden under the proud feet of members, or deacons, for the sake of Thy goodness. Amen.—C. E.

"V. Grant me the invaluable favour of being, in Thy hand, the means of calling sinners unto Thyself, and of edifying Thy saints, wherever Thou wilt send me, for the sake of Thy name. Amen.—C. E.

"VI. If I am to stay at Caerphilly, give me some tokens, as to Gideon of old, by removing the things that discourage me, and are in the way of the prosperity of religion, in that church. Amen.—C. E.

"VII. Grant, Lord of glory, and Head of Thy Church, that the Ark of the cause which is Thine, in Anglesea, and Caerphilly, may be sustained from falling into the hands of the Philistines. Do not reject it. Aid it speedily, and lift up the light of Thy countenance upon it; and by Thy Spirit, Word, and providence, so operate, as to carry things forward in the churches, and neighbourhoods, in such a manner as will produce changes in officers, and measures, that will accomplish a thorough improvement, in the great cause, for the establishment of which, in the world, Thou hast died,—and by scattering those that delight in war, and closing the mouths of those that occasion confusion. Amen.—C. E.

"VIII. Grant me way-tokens, by the time I begin my journey to Liverpool, and from thence to Anglesea, if it is Thy will that I should go thither this year. Amen.—C. E.

"IX. Oh, grant me succour, beneath the shadow of the sympathy that is in Thee, towards them who are tempted, and the unbounded power there is in Thee, to be the relief of such. Amen.—C. E.

"X. Accept of my thanksgiving, a hundred millions of times, that Thou hast not hitherto cast me from Thine hand, as a darkened star, or a vessel in which there is no pleasure; and suffer not my life to be extended beyond my usefulness. Thanks that Thou hast not given me a prey to the teeth of any. Blessed be Thy name. Amen.—C. E.

"XI. For the sake of Thine infinite merit, do not cast me, Thy servant, under the feet of pride, and injustice, of *worldly* greatness, riches, and selfish oppression of any men, but hide me in the secret of Thy tabernacle, from the strife of tongues. Amen.—C. E.

"XII. Help me to wait silently, and patiently upon Thee, for the fulfilment of these things, and not become enraged, angry, and speak unadvisedly with my lips, like Moses, the servant of the Lord. Sustain my heart from sinking, to wait for fresh strength from Zion. Amen.—C. E.

"XIII. Help me to wait upon Thee, for the necessaries of life; let Thy mercy, and goodness follow me, while I live; and, as it hath pleased Thee to honour me greatly, by the blessing Thou hast vouchsafed upon the ministry through me, as an humble instrument, at Caerphilly, after the great storm had beaten upon me in Anglesea, like Job, grant that this honour may continue to follow me the remainder of my days, as Thou didst unto Thy servant Job. Amen.—C. E.

"XIV. Let this covenant abide, like the covenant of salt, until I come to Thee, in the world of eternal light. I entreat aid to resign myself to Thee, and to Thy will. I beseech Thee, take my heart, and inscribe upon it a deep reverence of Thyself, with an inscription, that time, and eternity cannot efface. Oh, let the remainder of my sermons be taken, by Thee, from my lips; and those which I write, let them be unto Thee for a praise. Unto Thee I dedicate them. If there should be anything, in them, conducive to Thy glory, and to the service of Thy kingdom, do Thou preserve it, and reveal it unto men; else, let it die, like the drops of a bucket in the midst of the scorching heat of Africa. Oh, grant that there may be a drop of that water, which Thou, alone, canst impart, and which springs up to eternal life, running through all my sermons. In this covenant, which, probably, is the last that will be written between me and Thee, on the earth, I commit myself, my wife, and the churches amongst whom I have preached, to the protection of Thy grace, and the care of Thy covenant. Amen.—C. E.

"XV. Let this covenant continue, when I am in sickness, or in health, or in any other circumstance; for Thou hast overcome the world, fulfilled the law, finished justifying righteousness, and hast swallowed up death, in victory, and all power, in heaven and earth, is in Thy hand. For the sake of Thy most precious blood, and perfect righteousness, note this covenant, with Thine own blood, in the court of the memorials of forgiving mercy: attach unto it Thy name, in which I believe; and here I, this day, set my unworthy name unto it, with my mortal hand. Amen.—CHRISTMAS EVANS. Dated Cardiff, April 24th, 1829."

This document, found among his papers, after death, contains many affecting words, which give an insight to painful experiences, and sufferings. The standard set by Christmas Evans, was very high; his expectations from the Christian profession were such as to give, to his ideas of the pastoral office, perhaps somewhat of a stern aspect; nor can we forget that all his life had been passed in a very severe school. He was, perhaps, disposed to insist somewhat strenuously upon Church discipline. No doubt, his years at Caerphilly were among the happiest, and most unvexed in Church relations; his ministerial power, and success were very great; still, as the covenant we have just recited hints, there were probabilities of removal to Cardiff.

The appearance of Christmas Evans in Caerphilly was regarded, as we have seen, as something like an advent, and, to him, it was, for a short time, a haven of pleasant rest. There were some eminent ministers, men of considerable knowledge, and real power, residing in the neighbourhood, with whom he appears to have had most pleasant intercourse; among others, a Mr. J. P. Davies, in his way a mighty theologian, and clear, and ready expositor; he was laid by, for some months, under medical care, at Caerphilly, but was able to attend the ministry of the old preacher every Sabbath, and became one of his most intimate friends; they met almost daily, and the younger man was astonished by the elder's insatiable thirst for knowledge, and equally astonished by the extensive, and varied, stores of information he had accumulated, in his busy, and incessantly toilsome career. He acknowledged, afterwards, with delight, the variety of lights he had received, both as to the construction of a text, or the clearer definition of a principle, from his aged friend. As to the preaching, he said it gave him quite a new impression of the order of the preacher's mind: he expected flashes of eloquence, brilliant pictures,—of these he had long heard,—but what astonished him, was the fulness, and variety of matter, Sabbath after Sabbath. Mr. Davies only returned home to die; but he delighted his people, when he returned, by repeatedly describing the comfort, and light he had received, from the company of the matured, the aged, and noble man.

The society he enjoyed was, probably, more cultivated, small as was the village, than that by which he had been surrounded in Anglesea; from all the inhabitants, and from the neighbourhood, he received marks of great respect; it was, probably, felt, generally, that, by some singular turn of affairs, a great man, a national man, a man of the Principality, had settled in their midst. And he always after, and when he had left, remembered this brief period of his life with deep gratitude. He was more able to borrow books: here, for the first time, he read a work, which was regarded as a mighty book in that day, Dr. Pye Smith's "Scripture Testimony to the Messiah;" he read it with intense eagerness, incorporating many of its valuable criticisms into his sermons, and, especially, making them the subjects of ordinary conversation. Rhys Stephen says, "I remember listening to him with wonder, when, in conversation with Mr. Saunders, of Merthyr, he gave the substance of Dr. Pye Smith's criticism on John xvii. 3. And I distinctly remember, that when Mr. Evans said, 'Mr. Saunders, you will observe that, on these grounds, the knowledge of Jesus Christ, here mentioned, is the same knowledge as that of the only true God, and that the knowledge of the former is as necessary to salvation, as the knowledge of the latter—indeed, they are one, and the same thing,' 'Yes, yes,' was the reply; 'capital, very excellent. I never heard that interpretation before.' I was then a youth, and was not astonished by the interpretation, which, of course, was new to me, so much as by the admissions of the aged men that it was new to them." At any rate, it illustrates the avidity with which this mind still pursued the rays of light, from book to book, from conversation to conversation.

On another occasion, he met a young minister at Llantrissant, and, after a meeting in the morning, he inquired of the young man what he was then reading; the reply was, that he was going slowly through Beattie on Truth a second time. Christmas Evans immediately replied, "You must come to see me before you return to Swansea, and give me the substance of Beattie: was he not the man that replied to David Hume, eh?" The young man said he had the book in his pocket, and that he would cheerfully give it him, but the print was very small. He, with still greater eagerness, said, "I can manage that. I will take of it, with many thanks." It was a pleasure to give it him, and he pocketed it with as much pleasure as ever a school-boy did the first prize, at the end of the session. In three days after, the young man called upon him, at his own house, and spent a couple of hours with him; but he says he could get no farther, in conversation, than upon Beattie,—he was thoroughly absorbed in the argument with Hume, and his school of scepticism, and unbelief. Yet he was now sixty-five years of age; his one eye was very weak, though seeing well enough, without a glass, at the proper distance; and he was, otherwise, full of bodily infirmities; but his love of reading was unabated, as was, also, his earnest curiosity to know what was passing on in the world of thought.

And among his friends, at this period, we notice some members of the Edwards family,—David Edwards, of Beaupre, or, as it is commonly pronounced, Bewper, in Glamorganshire; and Evan Edwards, of Caerphilly, the son, and grandson of one of the most remarkable men modern Wales has produced, William Edwards, in his day a mighty engineer. Until his time, the Rialto, in Venice, was esteemed the largest arch in Europe, but he threw an arch over the Taff forty-two feet wider, and thus, for a long time, it held its reputation of being the largest arch in the world. A wonderful man was William Edwards, entirely self-made, not only a great engineer, but a successful farmer, and an ordained Independent minister. He was wealthy, of course, but he insisted upon receiving a good income from his church, although he distributed every farthing among the poor of his own neighbourhood, and added, considerably, to the sum he distributed, from his own property. The successor to Mr. Edwards, as the pastor of the Independent Church of Y-Groeswen, was the Rev. Griffith Hughes, a person of about the same age as Christmas Evans, also, although a polished gentleman, a self-taught man, a wit, a man of considerable reading, and information, and widely advanced in his religious opinions; although, professedly, a Calvinist, beyond the narrow, and technical Calvinism of his time, and even beyond the Fullerism, or doctrines of Andrew Fuller, which had been charged on Christmas Evans, as a crime, by his enemies in Anglesea.

It was about this time that he was earnestly entreated to prepare a volume of sermons for publication, and it seemed to be in connection with this, and with some fears, and discouragements which still troubled his mind, that he made the following entry, discovered among his papers after his death:—

> "Order things so, O Lord, that they may not prove a hindrance, and a discouragement to me, and an obstacle to the progress of Thy cause. Thy power is infinite, and Thy wisdom infallible. Stand between me, and all strife, that no evil effect may fall upon me. I flee under the shadow of Thy wings to hide myself, as the chickens do under the wings of the hen. Let nothing corrupt, and extinguish my gifts, my zeal, my prosperity; let nothing hinder the Church.
>
> "I have been earnestly requested, by many of my brethren in the ministry, to prepare some of my sermons for the press. In Anglesea, I had no leisure for such work, although I once commenced it, and wrote out five for the purpose. I let the work rest for two years, at Caerphilly; but, here, my mind has been moved towards it anew; and now I come to Thee, O Lord, who art the Head of the Church, and the chief Prophet and Teacher of the Church, to consult Thee, whether I shall proceed with the work, or not. Is it a part of my duty, or a foolish device of my own? I beseech, for Thy name's sake, Thy gracious guidance herein. Permit me

not to labour, with my weak eyesight, at a work that Thou wilt not deign to bless, but that shall be buried in oblivion,—unless it may please Thee (for Thou hast the keys of the house of David), in Thy providence, to prepare my way to publish the work, without danger to myself, of debt, and disgrace; and unless it may please Thee, the great Shepherd of the sheep, to guide me, to give forth the true Gospel, not only without error, but with the savour, and unction that pervade the works of Bunyan, and the hymns of William Williams; and, also, may they prove for the edification of Thy Church, and the conversion of sinners! If Thou wilt condescend to take the work under Thy care, help me to accomplish the design.

"In reading the 91st Psalm, I perceive that he who dwelleth in the secret place of the Most High, shall abide under the shadow of the Almighty; and that is so safe a place, and so impenetrable a protection, that the arrow that flieth by day, and the pestilence that walketh in darkness, with the sting of the serpent, the asp, and the viper, cannot hurt or injure him who hath made it his refuge. It is by faith, I hope, that I have gathered together all my jewels, and placed them under the shadow of safety that is in God. I have given my name anew to Christ, my body, my talents, my facility in preaching,—my name, and character as a man, a Christian, and as a preacher of the Gospel; my time, the remainder of my preaching services, my success, my wife, and all my friends, and helpers in the cause of the Lord, for whom I earnestly pray that they may be blessed in Anglesea, Caernarvonshire, Caerphilly, Cardiff, and all the churches in Wales, many of which have helped me in my day."

CHAPTER X.
CAERNARVON AND LAST DAYS.

Leading a Forlorn Hope again—More Chapel Debts—A Present of a Gig—Jack, *bach*!—The One-eyed Man of Anglesea once more—The Old Man's Reflections in his Journal—Characteristic Letters on Church Discipline—Threescore Years and Twelve—Starts on his Last Journey to liquidate a Chapel Debt—An Affecting Appeal to the Churches—Laid up at Tredegar—Conversations—In Swansea—This is my Last Sermon—Dying—Last Words—"Good-bye! Drive on!"

The last field of the great, good man's pastorate was Caernarvon; thither he removed when about sixty-seven years of age. It might be thought, that after such a hard, and exhausting life of travel, and toil, some plan might have been devised, by which his last days should be passed in restfulness, and peace; but it was not to be so: throughout his life, his had been up-hill work, no path of roses, no easy way; and, indeed, we usually know that such spheres are reserved for men who can carry nothing with them but the weight of dignified dulness. Of every sphere, from his first settlement at Lleyn, we read, that the cause was in a prostrate condition; and so, here, Christmas Evans appears to have been invited to take the charge of the Caernarvon church because it consisted of about thirty members, chiefly of the lowest class, of course quarrelling, and disunited. The dissolution of the church was advised. There was a fairly respectable place of worship, but it was £800 in debt, apparently, to us, in these days, not a very large sum, but a sum of considerable importance in Wales, and especially in that day.

So the question was discussed at a ministerial association, and some brother minister present, delivered himself of a confirmatory dream he had had on the subject, and the matter was practically settled, when a young minister spoke up, in the conference, and said to the venerable man, "Yes, you had better go to Caernarvon: it is not likely your talents would suit, but you might do excellently well at Caernarvon." The impudent speech astounded all the ministers present, except the unfortunate utterer of it. They knew not what to say. After a pause, the brethren all struck utterly dumb, Christmas Evans opened his one large eye upon his adviser, and, with some indignation, he said, "Ay, where hast thou come from? How long is it since thou didst chip thy shell?" Well, it was the very word: no one else could have, in so summary a manner, crunched up the thin egg-shell of pretentious conceit.

There was a real desire, on the part of the trustees of Caernarvon, and of English friends in Liverpool, that he should return to the north; and some gentlemen facilitated his return by giving him a gig, so that he might travel at his ease, and in his own way. This was not a very great donation, but it added, materially, to his comfort: he was able to travel pleasantly, and conveniently with Mrs. Evans. His horse, Jack, had been his companion for twenty years, but the pair were very fond of one another. Jack knew, from a distance, the tones of his master's voice; and Christmas, on their journeys, would hold long conversations with Jack. The horse opened his ears the moment his master began to speak, made a kind of neighing, when the rider said, as he often did, "Jack, *bach*, we have only to cross one low mountain again, and there will be capital oats, excellent water, and a warm stable," etc.

So he bade farewell to Cardiff in 1832, and upon the following Sunday, after his farewell there, he appears to have commenced his new ministry. It seems pathetic to us, to think of the old man, but we have no idea that he had any such pity, or sympathy for himself. Who can doubt, either, that he favoured, and hailed the opportunity of the return to the north? and Caernarvon, and Anglesea were almost one: he had but to cross the Menai Straits to be again in Anglesea—Anglesea, the scene of so many trials, and triumphs, where he had planted so many churches, sustained so many spiritual conflicts, and enjoyed, in his Cildwrn cottage, no doubt, years of much domestic happiness. It seems to us he ought never to have left Anglesea; but he regarded his exile to Caerphilly as a mission, that was to terminate, if success should crown it. And so he was back again in the old neighbourhood, and it appears, that the announcement of his return created universal delight, and joy, and strong excitement. He had been absent for about seven years, and the people, on account of his advanced age, when leaving them, expected to see him bowed with infirmity, and his preaching power, they supposed, would rather affectingly remind them of what he had been.

Shortly after his entrance upon the work of Caernarvon, a public occasion presented itself for his appearance in Anglesea. The whole neighbourhood flocked out, to see the patriarch. As he appeared on the platform, or preaching-place, in the open-air,—for no chapel could have contained the multitude,—the people said, "Why, he does not seem at all older! he looks more like a man of forty-five, than sixty-five, or sixty-six." And his preaching was just the same, or, possibly, even richer, and greater: it was his own old self, their own old Christmas Evans; the same rich, and excursive fancy, the same energetic, and fiery delivery. The appearance of such a man, under such circumstances,—one who has worn well, borne the burden and heat of the day, and taken his part "on the high places of the field,"—is a mighty awakening, and heart-healing time for old believers, who find their love to each other renewed in the rekindled love to the old pastor, and father in Christ. Old memories very tenderly touch reciprocating hearts. The old words, and the old voice, awaken old emotions, which now have become new. But, then, it is only a minister with a heart, who can touch this well-spring of feeling: starched respectability will not do it, eminent collegiate learning will not do it, rolling rhetorical periods will not do it. It is only the great hearts who can open these sluices of feeling, these fountains of emotion, in which the past, and the present mingle together, as the hearers drink refreshing streams from the fountains of recollection.

While in Caernarvon, he penned in his journal the following pious reflections:—

> "I have been thinking of the great goodness of the Lord unto me, throughout my unworthy ministry; and now, in my old age, I see the work prospering wonderfully in my hand, so that there is reason to think that I am, in some degree, a blessing to the Church, when I might have been a burden to it, or rather a curse, by which one might have been induced to wish me laid in the earth, that I might no longer prevent the progress of the work. Thanks be to God, that it is not so! though I deserve no better, yet I am in the land of mercy. This is unto me, according to the manner of God unto His people. My path in the valley, the dangers, and the precipices of destruction upon which I have stood, rush into my thoughts, and also the sinking of many in death, and the downfall of others by immorality, and their burial in Kibroth-Hattaavah, the graves of inordinate desire; together with the withering, the feebleness, and the unfruitfulness of some, through the influence of a secret departure from God, and of walking in the hidden paths, that lead to apostasy."

And here we may most appropriately insert a very characteristic letter, which shows the exceedingly stringent ideas which Christmas Evans entertained with regard to Church membership,—strait ideas, which, we suppose, would be scarcely tolerable now:—

"LETTER TO A BROTHER MINISTER ON CHURCH DISCIPLINE.

> "BELOVED BROTHER,—I write to you, August 5th, 1836, in the seventieth year of my age, and in the fiftieth of my ministry, after conversing much with ministerial brethren, earnestly desiring to see our Associational Union brought into action, by representatives of the churches, with a view to promote a determination,—1. To bear each other's burden more efficiently, in the denomination to which we belong. I lament the deficiency in this point, and ardently wish to see it effectually remedied. 2. To watch over and promote a holy conversation among all the members, and all the preachers, in a more efficient manner, to prevent

persons of unbecoming conversation from obtaining privileges, in any church, when they have been excluded in another; for that would occasion blots, and blemishes to appear on the bright countenance of the ministry. The Associational Union, in which all the churches of the same faith, and order join, should be a defence of the independence of the churches, through their representatives: it should also operate as a sort of check upon independency, lest it should become opposed to the general good, and frustrate the co-operation of the whole body. *That they may all be one*, is the motto.

"Respecting Church discipline. We cannot be certain that we are doing right, by administering the same punishment to all offenders, even for the same offence; for the general character weighs heavily, in the balance of discipline. Also, a distinction should be made between the seducer, and the seduced; and between being overcome, or falling into sin, and living habitually in sin, and following it, as a slave following his master. The denial of Peter, from weakness, and without previous deliberation, was very different from the betrayal of Judas, and his intentional selling of Christ. The different characters of Saul, king of Israel, and that of David, required different treatment, in discipline, on account of their offences. The Lord's discipline upon Saul was that of a rod of iron, but upon David, the correcting rod of a Father, for his good, that he might be a partaker of His holiness.

"There are two things, brother, which we ought to avoid in the exercise of discipline: 1, we should avoid too great severity on the one part; and, 2, too much leniency on the other part. Wisdom is necessary here to distinguish the different characters,—those who require severity, and those who claim tenderness: the two are to be found blended in the principle of evangelical discipline. A difference is to be made betwixt some, who may have been companions in the same crime; snatching some of them as brands from the burning. The ground of the distinction lies in the different amount of guilt, which subsists between the seducer, and seduced.

"I have witnessed danger, and have sustained some harm myself, and seen harm done in churches, by exercising tenderness towards some persons, in the vain hope of their reformation. Receiving verbal testimony, or mere fluent acknowledgments, from their lips, without waiting for fruit, in action, also; some having been often accused; and as often turning to the refuges frequented by them. I never exercised tenderness towards such as these, without being repaid by them afterwards, if they had opportunity: Shimei-like, they would curse me, after I had shed the best oil of tenderness on their heads. There are some in the Christian Church like Jezebel; and there are some in our congregations like Joab, the son of Zeruiah, that you can scarce discipline them without rending the kingdom, until they become ripe for judgment; for they hardly ever repent, more than did Joab and Shimei: they are ultimately suddenly broken, without any danger to the Church from their fall.

"I perceive that the Scriptures make a difference between one that falls into sin, and one wallowing in it; between one overtaken by a party of marauders, and dragged into the camp, and made drunk at supper, and one, like Judas, going to the party, and being secretly one of them, having pistols as they had: such are hypocrites. I have many times been the advocate of the fallen, and in a variety of instances have observed this operating beneficially for the Church. Sometimes I have found those who had been spared upon their own verbal contrition, blessing God for His long forbearance of them, and also their spiritual brethren, who had in a manner set their bones; as the Scripture hath it, 'Restore such an one in the spirit of meekness.'

"We should be careful that discretion, and love, be in exercise, though in strife, and contention it be not always an easy matter to do this. When the beasts of dissension get loose from the caravan, Satan sometimes drives them through the streets of Zion, that they may enter the houses of the inhabitants; and like the lioness that escaped from the keepers at Shrewsbury, and attacked the foremost horse in the carriage, so contentions frequently attack the leaders, in order to stop the carriage of the ministry as it travels on, in the labours of the pulpit. In the midst of the noise of strife, the man of God must raise his voice to heaven for courage, and tenderness, so that the oil of Christ's love to the souls of men may be found in the oil-flagon of reproof, which is poured on the head; for if anger, and revenge enter in, they will drop, like the spider in Germany, into the pot, and that will prevent the salutary effect of the oil, because the poison of wrath is mixed with it. The righteousness of God cannot be fulfilled in this manner in the discipline. Oh, brother! who is sufficient for these things, without constant help from heaven? How awful is this place! This is the house of God, and the gate of heaven; and here is a ladder, by which we may climb up for help, and a school, in which we may learn how to conduct ourselves in the house of God.

"You cannot but be conscious, brother, of the great difficulty there is not to speak unadvisedly with our lips, as did Moses, whilst drawing water for the rebellious Israelites. The rebellion of the people had embittered his spirit, so that his obduracy stood like a cloud between the people, and the tenderness of the Lord, when He was showing mercy upon them by giving them water. Moses upbraided their rebellion instead of showing mercy, as the dispensation of God now required; a dispensation which contained in it a secret intimation of the great mercy to be shown by the death of Christ on the cross. Their strife was the cause of embittering the spirit of Moses, yet he should have possessed his soul in patience.

"There are two things, brother, which you should observe. First, you will be called upon to attend to causes of contention; and you will find persons so hardened, that you will not be able to obtain weapons, in all the armoury of God's Word, that will terrify them, and make them afraid of entering their old haunts. Such are persons without faith, and without the fear of God, and the love of Christ influencing their minds; and though you warn them of the consequences of their contentions, that they are likely to deprive them of the privileges of the house of God, and thus forfeit the promised land, yet they stand unmoved, nothing terrified, for they value the flesh-pots of Egypt, and their livelihood there, more than the manna, and the land of promise. You cannot frighten them by speaking of the danger, and loss of the immunities of the Church below, or that above. Esau-like, they will sell their birthright, as Christian professors, for a mess of pottage. A man who has no money is not afraid to meet with robbers in the wood; but he who has gold to lose will be cautious, and watchful, lest he should be robbed of his property. On a night of great storm, when ships are broken to pieces, and sinking, a person who has no share in any of them will not tremble, or feel any concern on their account. Thus there are some men, concerning whom it is impossible to make them dread going out among the rapacious beasts of backslidings, and no storms can keep them in fear. Their spirit is one with the marauders, and they have no care, for they have nothing to lose in the tempests that blow upon the cause of the religion of Christ. These are the tares, or the children of the wicked one, in the Church.

"Secondly, for your own encouragement, brother, I remark that you will have to attend to the exercise of discipline, and to treat with persons that may be alarmed, and made to tremble at the Word of God, and not rush on presumptuously in their evil course. These are professors, who possess white garments, and the gold of faith, and eye-salve from the unction of the Holy One. These individuals are rich in faith. They are afraid of revolutions, and upsettings of the constitutional order of the new covenant, for they have funds invested in the stocks of God's kingdom. They are afraid that any storm, or rock of offence should come in the way of the Gospel ship, for their treasure is on board it, and they have an interest in it. They dread the thought of walking unwatchfully, and licentiously, lest they should be robbed of their riches, and forfeit the fellowship of God in prayer, lose the light of His countenance, and His peace in the means of grace, and lest they should be deprived of their confidence in the merits of Christ, and a good conscience. They have denied themselves, and have pulled out the right eye, lest they should not be acceptable before God. They dread harbouring in their bosoms the old guilt and former doubts. They are cautious not to give a night's lodging to such miscreants as anger, revenge, lust, and things which are of the earth; for they know that these are robbers, and if they have any indulgence they will steal away the *title-deeds* of assurance to the inheritance. They are well aware, also, that they will sustain the loss of a pure conscience, which has been purged by the blood of Christ, and which, as a golden chest, is a preserver of our confidence, immovable unto the end. It is possible, brother, to manage, and discipline such professors. They have something to lose, consequently they will not flee from their refuge, lest they should be destroyed. *Keep that which thou hast.* David lost for a season the enjoyment of the above blessings; but he was cleansed with hyssop, had his spirit renewed, and his riches were restored to him by faith's view of the Messiah, for which he vowed to sing aloud for ever, and ever. He prayed, after this, to be delivered from presumptuous sins, lest he should be imprisoned a second time by a party so wicked, and detestable. May the spiritual gift be kindled in you, brother. Grace be with you, for ever, and ever.

"Affectionately,
"CHRISTMAS EVANS.

"*Caernarvon, August 5th*, 1836."

But it was hard work in Caernarvon. The debt upon the chapel was a perpetually-recurring trouble. We have said when he went there eight hundred pounds was the burden, and that the people were very poor. Of this eight hundred, four hundred seems to have been collected by a Mr. John Edwards, who used, as his introduction, in asking for contributions, the specimen of Welsh eloquence to which we have referred (The Graveyard World); so that Christmas Evans may, really, be regarded as the liquidator of the debt to that extent. The time came when the whole remaining sum had to be paid. What could be done? Over seventy years of age, the old man started forth, on a tour through the south, to attempt to raise the sum. In April, 1838, when he had been four years in Caernarvon, he set off with his wife, and a young preacher, the Rev. John Hughes. Before he set out, he wrote a circular to his brethren, which was published in the *Welsh Magazine*. It is scarcely possible, we think, to read it, remembering who wrote it, and the circumstances under which it was written, without tears of feeling:—

"DEAR BRETHREN,—We have received notice to pay up three hundred pounds. The term of the lease of life has expired in my case, even threescore and ten years, and I am very much afflicted. I have purposed to sacrifice myself to this object, though I am afraid I shall die on the journey" (he did die on his journey); "and I fear I shall not succeed in my errand for Christ. We have no source to which we can now repair, but our own denomination in Wales, and brethren, and friends of other communities, that may sympathize with us. Oh, brethren, pray, with me, for protection on the journey—for strength, and health this *once*, on occasion of my bidding farewell to you all! pray for the light of the Lord's countenance upon me in preaching;

pray for His own glory, and that His key may open the hearts of the people, to contribute towards His cause in its present exigency. Oh, help us, brethren!—when you see the old brother, after having been fifty-three years in the ministry, now, instead of being in the grave with his colleagues, or resting at home with three of them who are yet alive—brethren Lewis of Llanwenarth, Davies of Velin Voel, and Thomas of Aberduar,—when you see him coming, with the furrows of death in his countenance, the flowers of the grave on his head, and his whole constitution gradually dissolving; having laboured fifty years in the ministry in the Baptist denomination. He comes to you with hundreds of prayers, bubbling, as it were, from the fountain of his heart, and with a mixture of fear, and confidence. Oh, do not frown upon him!—he is afraid of your frowns. Smile upon him, by contributing to his cause, this once for all. If you frown upon me, ministers and deacons, by intimating an *irregular case*, I am afraid I shall sink into the grave before returning home. This is my last sacrifice for the Redeemer's cause."

Naturally, wherever he passed along, he was received by all the churches, and throughout every county, with more than cordiality—with great joy. He was very successful in raising money for the purpose which urged him forth from home: perhaps his popularity was never so great as now. Mr. Cross, one of his biographers, says, that wherever he preached, the place was thronged at an early hour, and, frequently, multitudes remained outside, unable to obtain admittance. He reached Monmouthshire, and preached before the County Association; and it is said, that the sermon evinced all his vigour of intellect, and splendour of genius, and as perfect a command over the feelings of the great audience as ever. One of his great images here was his description of the Gospel, on the day of Pentecost, as a great electrical machine, Christ turning the handle, Peter placing the chain in contact with the people, and the Holy Ghost descending like a stream of ethereal fire, and melting the hearts of three thousand at once. His text was, "By grace ye are saved."

But the effort was too much for him, and he was laid up for a week at the house of Mr. Thomas Griffith, a kind host, who, with his whole family, attempted, in every way, to minister to his comfort, and, with affectionate assiduity, sought to restore him. On the whole, he appears to have been full of vivacity that week, and, during the intervals of pain, cheered, and charmed his friends. He had, one day, come downstairs, and Mr. James, the son-in-law of his host, was helping him up again. He had only got a few steps, when he said buoyantly, "Mr. James, I dare say if I thought the French were behind me with their bayonets, I should be able to get upstairs without your help." With the word he took his arm from Mr. James's shoulder, and briskly ran up the flight of steps, laughing at his feat.

His conversation was, however, usually brightly religious. "This is the Gospel," he said once in the course of talk—"This is the Gospel: 'He that believeth shall be saved.' Now, in order to the truth of this declaration, every believer must be saved. If, in the last day, the great enemy find one single soul not saved, who ever believed the Gospel, he would take that soul up, present that soul to the Judge, and to the immense assembly, and say, 'The Gospel is not true.' He would take that lost believer through all the regions of pandemonium, and exhibit him in triumph to the devils, and the damned." "But," said his host, "that shall never be, Mr. Evans." "No," said he, planting the forefinger of his right hand on his knee, as was his wont, and exclaiming, in a tone of triumphant congratulation, "*Never*! *never*! *never*!"

Leaving the house of Mr. Griffith, of Tredegar, he proceeded on his way, preaching at Caerphilly, Cardiff, Cowbridge, Bridgend, and Neath, and he reached Swansea on Saturday, July 14th. The next day, Sunday, he preached twice—preached like a seraph, says one of his memorialists: in the morning his subject was the Prodigal Son; the evening, "I am not ashamed of the Gospel of Christ." He was the guest of Daniel Davies, the pastor of the Welsh Baptist Church in the town, the blind preacher, as he was called, a man of great celebrity, and unquestioned power. He was to be the last host of his greater brother, or rather father, in the ministry. On the Monday evening, he went out to tea, with a friend who was always glad to greet him, Mr. David Walters; and on the same evening he preached, in English, in Mount Pleasant Chapel: his text was, "Beginning at Jerusalem." He was very feeble,—perhaps we need scarcely wonder at that, after the two services of the day before. He always felt a difficulty when preaching in English, and, upon this occasion, he seemed much tried; gleams, and flashes of his ordinary brilliancy there were, as in the following:—

"Beginning at Jerusalem! Why at Jerusalem? The Apostles were to begin there, because its inhabitants had been witness to the life, and death of Christ; there He had preached, wrought miracles, been crucified, and rose again. Here, on the very spot of His deepest degradation, He was also to be exalted: He had been crucified as a malefactor, He was now to be elevated in the same place as a King; here were accorded to Him the first-fruits of His resurrection." This was the strain of the sermon:—"'At Jerusalem, Lord?' 'Yes.' 'Why, Lord, these are the men who crucified Thee; we are not to preach it to *them*?' 'Yes, preach it to all.' 'To the man who plaited the crown of thorns, and placed it on Thy Head?' 'Yes; tell him that from My degradation he may obtain a crown of glory.' 'Suppose we meet the very man that nailed Thy hands and feet to the cross, the very man that pierced

Thy side, that spat in Thy face?' 'Preach the Gospel to them all: tell them all that I am the Saviour; that all are welcome to participate in the blessings of My salvation; I am the same Lord over all, and rich unto all that call on Me.'" Such were some of the most characteristic passages. As he was coming down the pulpit stairs, he said, loud enough to be heard by many present, "*This is my last sermon!*"

And it was even so. He was taken very ill during the night; the next day he was worse, the next day worse still, and then medical assistance was called in. But on the Thursday, he got up, and walked for some time in the garden. It seems doubtful whether he thought that his end was so near, although he had a dream, in one of the early evenings in the week, in which he seemed to come up to a great river, which he did not then cross, so that he scarcely thought his work or life might be over even yet.

But on Thursday night he was worse again, and on Friday morning, at two o'clock, he said to his friends, Mr. Davies, Mr. Hughes, and others round his bed, "I am leaving you. I have laboured in the sanctuary fifty-three years, and this is my comfort, that I have never laboured without blood in the basin,"—the ruling power of imagination strong in him to the close, evidently meaning that he had never failed to preach Christ and Him crucified. A few more remarks of the same character: "Preach Christ to the people, brethren. Look at me: in myself I am nothing but ruin, but in Christ I am heaven, and salvation." He repeated a verse from a favourite Welsh hymn, and then, as if he had done with earth, he waved his hand, and exclaimed, "GOOD-BYE! DRIVE ON!"

It seems another instance of the labour of life pervading by its master-idea the hour of death. For how many years the "one-eyed man" of Anglesea had gone to, and fro on his humble nag! As we have seen, lately his friends had given him a gig, that he might be more at ease in his Master's service; still he had his old horse, companion of his many journeys. While he was dying, the old mountain days of travel came over his memory—"GOOD-BYE!" said he. "DRIVE ON!" He turned over, and seemed to sleep. He slept indeed. His friends tried to rouse him, but the angelic postman had obeyed the order,—the chariot had passed over the everlasting hills. So he died, July 19th, 1838, in the seventy-third year of his age, and fifty-fourth of his ministry.

His funeral took place four days after his death, in the burying-ground attached to the Welsh Baptist Chapel, in Swansea. It is said there never was such a funeral in Swansea, such a concourse, and crowd of mourners, weeping their way to the grave, and following, as it had been their father. Fountains of sorrow were everywhere unsealed throughout the Principality, in Anglesea especially, where he had passed the greater portion of his life; indeed, throughout the Principality, there was scarcely a pulpit, of the order to which he belonged, which was not draped in black; and it was evident that all felt "a prince and a great man had fallen in Israel."

CHAPTER XI.
SUMMARY OF GENERAL CHARACTERISTICS OF CHRISTMAS EVANS, AS A MAN AND A PREACHER.

A Central Figure in the Religious Life of Wales—In a Singular Degree a Self-made Man—His Words on the Value of Industry—His Honest Simplicity—Power of Sarcasm Repressed—Affectionate Forgiveableness—Great Faith, and Power in Prayer—A Passage in Dean Milman's "Samor"—His Sermons a Kind of Silex Scintillans—Massive Preaching, but lightened by Beautiful Flowers—As an Orator—A Preacher in the Age of Faith—Seeing Great Truths—His Remarks on what was called "Welsh Jumping" in Religious Services.

THE character of Christmas Evans, it will be seen, from all that has gone before, appears to us to be eminently interesting as the most distinct, to us the most central, and realizable figure, in the religious life of his country, and his times: he is the central figure in a group of remarkable men. We shall not discuss the question as to whether he was the greatest,—greatness is so relative a term; he appears, to us, certainly, from our point of view, the most representative Welsh preacher of his time, perhaps of any time: in him seemed embodied not merely the imaginative, but the fanciful, the parable-loving spirit of his department of the great Celtic family; with this, that ardent devotion, that supersensuous absorption, which to our colder temperament looks like superstition.

One writer finely remarks of him, and with considerable truth, so far as his own country is concerned, "He is a connecting link between the beginning and the ending of the eighteenth century; he has the light, the talent, and the taste of the beginning, and has received every new light that has appeared since. He was enabled to accompany the career of religious knowledge in the morning, and also to follow its rapid strides in the evening. In this he is unlike every other preacher of the day: the morning and evening light of this wonderful century meet in him; he had strength to climb up to the top of Carmel in the morning, and remain there during the heat of the day, and see the consuming sacrifice, and the licking up of the water; his strength continued, by the hand of the Lord, so that he could descend from the mount in the evening, and run without fainting before the king's chariot to Jezreel."

On the whole, there is considerable truth in these words, although author and reader may alike take exception to some of them. The circumstances and situation of the life of this singular man have been set so clearly before the reader in these pages, that there can be no difficulty in apprehending the unpropitious and unfavourable atmosphere through which he was compelled to move. Few men can ever have more richly deserved the epithet of self-made: no systematic tuition could he ever have received; near to manhood before he even attempted to obtain, before he had even presented to him any inducements to attempt, the most rudimental elements of knowledge; we cannot gather that he had any teachers, who assisted him with more than hints, or the loan of a grammar, a lexicon, or some volume he desired to read; there are no indications of any particular kindness, no friendly hands, no wicket, or gate of school, or college opened to him. And as with the commencement of his career, so with its course; his intercourse was, probably, mostly with men, and minds inferior to his own; books, we have seen, he had few, although he read, with avidity, wherever he could borrow; and as with his mental training, so with his spiritual experience,—it appears all to have gone on within himself, very much unrelieved, and unaided; he had to fight his own doubts, and to gather strength in the wrestling, and the conflict. And as he thus formed himself, without assistance, so, apparently without any human assistance, he continued to labour on, amidst the popular acclamations of fame. The absence of all, and every exhibition of gratitude, is peculiarly affecting. Altogether, this strikes us as a grand, self-sustained, and much-enduring life, always hard, and necessitous; but its lines are very indelible, written as with a pen of iron, and as with the point of a diamond. It is natural that, in his old age, he should speak thus to a young man of the—

"VALUE OF INDUSTRY.

"I am an old man, my dear boy, and you are just entering the ministry. Let me now, and here tell you one thing, and I commend it to your attention, and memory. All the ministers that I have ever known, who have fallen into disgrace, or into uselessness, *have been idle men*. I never am much afraid of a young minister, when I ascertain that he can, and does, *fairly sit down to his book*. There is Mr. —, of whom we were talking just now, a man of such unhappy temper, and who has loved, for many years, to meddle in all sorts of religious disputes and divisions. He would have, long ago, been utterly wrecked, had not his habits of industry saved him. He has stuck to his book, and that has kept him from many dishonours, which, had he been an idle man, must have, by this time, overwhelmed him. An idle man is in the way of every temptation; temptation has no need to seek him; *he is at the corner of the street, ready, and waiting for it*. In the case of a minister of the Gospel, this peril is multiplied by his position, his neglected duties, the temptations peculiar to his condition, and his own superior susceptibility. *Remember this—stick to your book.*"

The foundations of the good man's character were laid in honest simplicity, real, and perfect sincerity; he was innocent, and unsuspecting as a child, and here, no doubt, lay the cause of many of his trials; his frank, and confiding disposition became the means by which his own peace was poisoned, when jealous men, malicious men,—and these sometimes Christian men,—took advantage of his simplicity. He once employed a person to sell a horse for him at a fair; after some time, Evans being there, he went out to see if the man was likely to succeed. He found that a bargain was going on for the horse, and nearly completed.

"Is this your horse, Mr. Evans?" said the purchaser.

"Certainly it is," he replied.

"What is his age, sir?"

"Twenty-three years."

"But this man tells me he is only fifteen."

"He is certainly twenty-three, for he has been with me these twenty years, and he was three years old when I bought him."

"Is he safe-footed?"

"Well, he is very far from that, and, indeed, that is the reason why I want to part with him; and he has never been put into harness since I bought him either."

"Please go into the house, Mr. Evans, and stop there," said the man whom he had employed to make the sale: "I never shall dispose of the horse while you are present."

But the dealer was, in this instance, mistaken, for the frank manner in which Mr. Evans had answered the questions, and told the truth, induced the buyer to make the purchase, even at a very handsome price. But the anecdote got abroad, and it added to Mr. Evans's reputation, and good name; and even the mention of the story in these pages, after these long years have passed away, is more to his memory than the gold would have been to his pocket.

Like all such natures, however, he was not wanting in shrewdness, and we have seen that, when irritated, he could express himself in sharp sarcasm. He had this power, but, upon principle, he kept it under control. It was a saying of his, "It is better to keep sarcasms pocketed, if we cannot use them without wounding friends." Once, two ministers of different sects were disputing upon some altogether trifling, and most immaterial point of ecclesiastical discipline. One of them said, "What is your opinion, Mr. Evans?" and he said, "To-day I saw two boys quarrelling over two snails: one of them insisted that his snail was the best, because it had horns; while the other as strenuously insisted that his was the best, because it had none. The boys were very angry, and vociferous, but the two snails were very good friends."

He comes before us with all that strength of character which he unquestionably possessed, as a spirit most affectionate, and especially forgiving. An anecdote goes about of a controversy he had with a minister of another sect, who so far forgot himself as to indulge in language utterly inconsistent with all Christian courtesy. But a short time elapsed, when the minister was charged with a crime: had he been convicted, degradation from the ministry must have been the smallest part of his punishment, but his innocence was made manifest, and perfectly clear. Mr. Evans always believed the charge to be false, and the attempt to prosecute to be unjust, and merely malicious. On the day when the trial came on he went, as was his wont, in all matters where he was deeply interested, into his own room, and fervently prayed that his old foe might be sustained, and cleared. He was in company with several friends and brother ministers, when a minister entered the room, and said, "Mr. B— is fully acquitted." Evans instantly fell on his knees, and with tears exclaimed, "Thanks be unto Thee, O Lord Jesus, for delivering one of Thy servants from the mouth of the lions." And he very soon joined his hearty congratulations with those of the other friends of the persecuted man.

It is certain the story of the Church recites very few instances of such an active life, so eminently devotional, and prayerful: we have seen this already illustrated in those remarkable covenants we have quoted. He had an old-fashioned faith in prayer. He was very likely never troubled much about the philosophy of it: his life passed in the practice of it. No Catholic monk or nun kept more regularly the hours, the matins, or the vigils than he. It appears, that for many years he was accustomed to retire for a short season, for prayer, three times during the day, and to rise at midnight, regularly, for the same purpose. He suffered much frequently from slander; he had disorders, and troubles in his churches; he had many afflictions, as we have seen, in life, and the frequent sense of poverty; but these all appeared to drive this great, good man to prayer, and his friends knew it, and felt it, and felt the serenity, and elevation of his character when in the social circle, even when it was also known that heavy trials were upon him. And one who appears to have known him applies to him, in such moments, the language of the Psalmist, "All thy garments smell of myrrh, aloes, and cassia, out of the ivory palaces."

And, perhaps, in this connection, we may say, without being misunderstood, that the especial necessities of his life gave to it something of a cloistered, and monastic character. He was not immured in the cell, or the monastery, but how little can we realize the profound solitude of those long journeys, so constantly renewed, through the silence of the lonely hills, across the desolation of the uninhabited moor! An intensely nervous, and meditative nature, no possibility of the book then, no retreat, we can believe no desire to retreat from the infinite stretched above him, and even the infinite seeming to spread all around him. In so devout a nature, how calculated all this to foster devotion, until it became at once the support, as well as the passion, of the soul!

And these perpetual wanderings among the mountains must have been a fine spiritual education, an education deepening emotion in the soul, and at the same time kindling the mind in thoughtful imagery. He reminds us of Dean Milman's hero, also a pilgrim through Wales:—

> "His path is 'mid the Cambrian mountains wild;
> The many fountains that well wandering down
> Plinlimmon's huge round side their murmurs smooth
> Float round him; Idris, that like warrior old
> His batter'd and fantastic helmet rears,
> Scattering the elements' wrath, frowns o'er his way,
> A broad irregular duskiness. Aloof
> Snowdon, the triple-headed giant, soars,
> Clouds rolling half-way down his rugged sides.
> Slow as he trod amid their dizzy heights,
> Their silences and dimly mingling sounds,
> Rushing of torrents, war of prison'd winds;
> O'er all his wounded soul flow'd strength, and pride,
> And hardihood; again his front soar'd up
> To commerce with the skies, and frank and bold,
> His majesty of step his rugged path
> Imprinted . . .
> . . . Whence, ye mountains, whence
> The spirit that within your secret caves
> Holds kindred with man's soul?"

Henry Vaughan delighted to call himself the Silurist, always proud of the country from whence he came: his was a different region of Wales from that which produced Christmas Evans. Henry Vaughan was the swan of the Usk; but the sermons of Evans, like the sacred poems of Vaughan, were a kind of *Silex Scintillans*, or sparks from the flint, sparks shot forth from the great mountains, and the overhanging stars, with both of which he held long communion: he had no opportunity for any other often in the course of his travel; they were as the streets of God, lighted with suns stretching across his way, in the green amphitheatre of day, and the blue amphitheatre of night.

And this was, no doubt, very greatly the secret of his preaching. It is not too strong a term to use, to say that, with all its brilliancy, its bardic, and poetic splendours, it was massive preaching. He usually laid the foundations of the edifice of a sermon, strong and secure in reason, and in Scripture, securing the understanding, and the convictions of his hearers, before he sketched those splendid allegories, or gave those descriptive touches; before even he appealed to those feelings, when he led the whole congregation captive by the chains of his eloquence.

We have said before, that like most of the preachers of his country, he delighted also in the use of sharp, rememberable sayings. That is a striking expression when he says, speaking of death, to the believer in Christ, "The crocodile of death shall be harnessed to the chariot of the daughter of Zion, to bring her home to her father's house." Again, "Our immortal souls, although in perishable bodies, are evidently originally birds of Paradise, and our faculties are the beautiful wings by which we understand, remember, fear, believe, love, hope, and delight in immortal, and eternal things." That is very pretty when he says, "Faith is the wedding-ring by which the poor daughter of the old Ammonite is married to the Prince of Peace: she is raised from poverty to opulence, from degradation to honour, not because of the intrinsic value of the ring, though it is a golden one, but on account of the union which it signifies, between her, and the beloved Prince." Again, "A cradle, a cross, and a grave, all of His Father's appointing, must Jesus have, in order to open a fountain of living water to the world." Such sentences as these the reader will find strewn along all his sermons, and many such in those which we have quoted more at length.

But it must always be remembered that Christmas Evans was, in a pre-eminent degree, the orator. He had a presence; he was nearly six feet high, and finely-proportioned; his whole bearing was dignified, and majestic; he had but one eye, it is true, but we can believe the testimony which describes it as singularly penetrating, and even burning with a wonderful effect, when the strong inspiration of his eloquence was upon him. Then his voice was one of marvellous compass, and melody; like his sermons themselves, which were able to touch the hearts of mighty multitudes, so his voice was able to reach their ears.

When he heard Robert Hall, the marvellous enchantment of that still, small voice, a kind of soprano in its sweet, and cleaving clearness, so overwhelmed him, that he longed to preach in that tone, and key; but the voices of the men were fitted to their words,—Hall's to his own exquisitely-finished culture, and to the sustained, and elevated culture either of spirit, or intelligence of those whom he addressed; Evans's words we suppose rolled like the thunder of a mighty sea, with all its amplitude of many-voiced waves. Singers differ, and, no doubt, while we are able to admire the evangelical force, and fervour, and even the fine pictorial imagery of the sermons of Christmas Evans, it is something like looking at the painting on the glass, which may be very pretty, and exquisite, but in order really to see it, it should be in the camera, with the magnifying lens, and the burning lamp behind it. Alas! it is so with all reported and written eloquence: the figures, and the words are almost as cold as the paper upon which they are printed, as they pass before the eye; they need the inspiration of the burning genius, and that inspired by a Divine affection, or afflatus, in their utterance, to give them a real effect.

And in the case of Christmas Evans's sermons, this is not all: to us they are only translations,—translations from the difficult Welsh language,—translations without the wonderful atmospheric accent of the Welsh vowel; so that the very best translation of one of Christmas Evans's performances can only be the skeleton of a sermon. We may admire the structure, the architecture of the edifice, but we can form little idea of the words which were said to have set Wales on fire.

We recur to the expression we used a few sentences since. We are able to appreciate the massive character of these sermons: it is very true they are cyclopean,—they have about them a primæval rudeness; but then the cyclopean architecture, although primitive, is massive. Here are huge thoughts, hewn out of the primæval, but ever-abiding instincts of our nature, or, which is much the same thing, from the ancient, and granite flooring of the Divine Word. We must make this allowance for our preacher: he took up his testimony from the grand initial letters of Faith; he knew something of the other side of thought; the belief of his country, in his time, in the earlier days of his ministry, had been very much vexed by Sabellianism.

The age of systematic, and scientific doubt had not set in on the Principality; but he met the conscience of man as a conscience, as that which was a trouble, and a sorrow to the thoughtful mind, and where it was still untroubled, he sought to alarm it, and awaken it to terror, and to fear; and he preached the life, and work of Christ as a legitimate satisfaction, and rest to the troubled conscience. This was, no doubt, the great burden of his ministry; these are the subjects of all his sermons. He used the old words, the old nomenclature.

Since the day of Christmas Evans, theological language is so altered, that the theological lexicon of the eighteenth century would seem very poorly to represent theological ideas in this close of the nineteenth. But we have often thought, that, perhaps, could the men of that time be brought face to face with the men of this, it might be found that terms had rather enlarged their signification, than essentially altered their meaning,—this in many instances, of course, not in all. But it would often happen, could we but patiently analyze the meaning of theological terms, we should often find a brother where we had suspected an alien, and a friend where we had imagined a foe.

Thus Christmas Evans dealt with great truths. He was a wise master-builder, and all the several parts of his sermons were related together in mutual dependence. The reader will notice that there was always symmetry in their construction: he obeys an order of thought; we feel that he speaks of that which, to the measure of the revelation given, and his entrance into the mind of the Spirit, he distinctly understands. A mind, which itself lives in the light, will, by its own sincerity, make the subject which it attempts to expound clear; and he had this faculty, eminently, of making abstruse truths shine out with luminous, and distinct beauty. This is always most noble when the mind of a preacher rises to the highest truths in the Christian scheme. A great deal of our preaching, in the present day, well deserves the name of pretty: how many men, whose volumes of sermons are upon our shelves, both in England, and America, seem as if their preachers had been students in the natural history of religion, gathering shells, pretty rose-tinted shells, or leaves, and insects for a theological museum! And a very pretty occupation, too, to call attention to the lily-work of the temple. But there are others, whose aim has been—

> "Rather to see great truths
> Than touch and handle little ones."

And, certainly, Christmas Evans was of that order who occupied the mind, and single eye, rather on the pathway of the planet beyond him, than in the study of the most exquisite shell on the sea-shore. Among religious students, and even among eminent preachers, there are some, who may be spoken of as Divine, and spiritual astronomers,—they study the laws of the celestial lights; and there are others, who may be called religious entomologists,—they find themselves at home amidst insectile prettinesses. Some minds are equal to the infinitely large, and the infinitely small, the remote not more than the near; but such instances are very rare.

The power of great truths overwhelms the man who feels them; this gives rise to that impassioned earnestness which enables a great speaker to storm, and take possession of the hearts of his hearers: the man, it has been truly said, was lost in his theme, and art, was swallowed up in excited feeling, like a whirlpool, bearing along the speaker, and his hearers with him, on the current of the strong discourse. The histories of the greatest orators,—for instance, Massillon, Bossuet, and Robert Hall,—show how frequently it was the case, that the excited feelings of an audience manifested themselves by the audience starting from their seats, and, sometimes, by loud expressions of acclamation, or approbation. Some such scenes appear to have manifested themselves, even beneath Christmas Evans's ministry. Some such scenes as these led to the report of those excitements in Wales, which many of our readers have heard of as "Welsh jumping." Evans appears to have been disposed to vindicate from absurdity this phenomenon,—the term used to describe it was, no doubt, employed as a term of contempt. He says,—

"Common preaching will not do to arouse sluggish districts from the heavy slumbers into which they have sunk; indeed, formal prayers, and lifeless sermons are like bulwarks raised against these things: five, or six stanzas will be sung as dry as Gilboa, instead of one, or two verses, like a new song full of God, of Christ, and the Spirit of grace, until the heart is attuned for worship. The burying grounds are kept in fine order in Glamorganshire, and green shrubs, and herbs grow on the graves; but all this is of little value, for the inhabitants of them are all dead. So, in every form of godliness, where its power is not felt, order without life is exceedingly worthless: you exhibit all the character of human nature, leaving every bud of the flower to open in the beams of the sun, except in Divine worship. On other occasions, you English appear to have as much fire in your affections as the Welsh have, if you are noticed. In a court of law, the most efficient advocate, such as Erskine, will give to you the greatest satisfaction; but you are contented with a preacher speaking so lifelessly, and so low, that you can hardly understand a third part of what he says, and you will call this decency in the sanctuary. To-morrow I shall see you answering fully to the human character in your own actions. When the speakers on the platform will be urging the claims of missions, you will then beat the boards, and manifest so much life, and cheerfulness that not one of you will be seen to take up a note-book, nor any other book, while the speaker shall be addressing you. A Welshman might suppose, by hearing your noise, that he had been silently conveyed to one of the meetings of the Welsh jumpers, with this difference, that you would perceive many more tears shed, and hear many more 'calves of the lips' offered up, in the rejoicing meetings of Wales; but you use your heels well on such occasions, and a little of your tongues; but if even in Wales, in certain places,—that is, places where the fervent gales are not enjoyed which fill persons with fear, and terror, and joy, in approaching the altar of God,—you may see, while hearing a sermon, one looking into his hymn-book, another into his note-book, and a third turning over the leaves of his Bible, as if he were going to study a sermon in the sanctuary, instead of attending to what is spoken by the preacher as the mouth of God."

He proceeds, at considerable length, in this strain, in a tone of apology which, while it is frank, and ingenuous, certainly seems to divest the excitement of the Welsh services of those objectionable features which, through a haze of ignorant prejudice, had very much misrepresented the character of such gatherings in England. It was, as Mr. Evans shows, the stir, and excitement, the more stereotyped acclamation, of an English meeting manifesting itself in the devotional services of these wild mountain solitudes. He continues,—

> "It is an exceedingly easy matter for a minister to manage a congregation while Christian enjoyment keeps them near to God; they are diligent, and zealous, and ready for every good work; but it is very easy to offend this joyous spirit—or give it what name you please, enthusiasm, religious madness, or Welsh jumping,—its English name,—and make it hide itself; a quarrel, and disagreement in the Church, will occasion it to withdraw immediately; indulging in sin, in word or deed, will soon put it to flight: it is like unto the angel formerly, who could not behold the sin of Israel without hiding himself,—so is the angel of the religious life of Wales, which proves him to be a holy angel, though he has the name of a Welsh jumper. My prayer is, that this angel be a guard upon every congregation, and that none should do anything to offend him. It is an exceedingly powerful assistant to accompany us through the wilderness, but the individual that has not felt its happy influences has nothing to lose; hence he does not dread a dry meeting, and a hard prayer, for they are all the same to him; but the people of this enjoyment pray before prayer, and before hearing, that they may meet with God in them.
>
> "The seasons when these blessings are vouchsafed to the churches of Wales are to be noticed: it is generally at a time when the cause of religion is at a low ebb, all gone to slumber; this happy spirit of enjoyment in religion, like the angel of the pillar of fire, appears when there is distress, and everything at the worst; its approach to the congregation is like the glory of God returning to the temple of old; it creates a stir among the brethren; they have a new prayer, and a new spirit given them to worship God; this will lay hold of another; some new strength, and light will appear in the pulpit, until it will be imagined that the preacher's voice is altered, and that his spirit has become more evangelical,

and that he preaches with a more excellent savour than usual; tenderness will descend upon the members, and it will be seen that Mr. Wet-eyes, and Mr. Amen, have taken their place among them; the heavenly gale will reach some of the old backsliders, and they are brought, with weeping, to seek their forfeited privilege; by this time the sound of Almighty God will be heard in the outer court, beginning to move the hearers like a mighty wind shaking the forest; and as the gale blows upon the outer court, upon the hearers, and the young people, and afterwards making its way through the outer court, to rouse the inner court, until a great concern is awakened for the state of the soul. And, see, how these powerful revivals evince their nature: they are certain, where they are strong, to bend the oaks of Bashan, men of strong, and sturdy minds, and haughty hearts; they bring all the ships of Tarshish, and the merchants of this world, in the harbour hearing; the power of the day of the Lord will raze all the walls of bigotry to the foundation; thoughts of eternal realities, and the spirit of worship, are by these blessings diffused abroad, and family worship is established in scores of families; the door of such a district, opened by the powers of the world to come, creates the channel where the living waters flow, and dead fish are made alive by its virtues."

So Christmas Evans vindicated the excitements of religious services in Wales from English aspersions.

CHAPTER XII.
SUMMARY OF GENERAL CHARACTERISTICS OF CHRISTMAS EVANS AS A PREACHER.

Remarks renewed in Vindication of his Use of Parable in the Pulpit—His Sermons appear to be born of Solitude—His Imitators—His Probable Acquaintance with "the Sleeping Bard" of Elis Wyn—A Dream—Illustrations—The Gospel Mould—Saul of Tarsus and his Seven Ships—The Misplaced Bone—The Man in the House of Steel—The Parable of the Church as an Ark among the Bulrushes of the Nile—The Handwriting—Death as an Inoculator—Time—The Timepiece—Parable of the Birds—Parable of the Vine-tree, the Thorn, the Bramble, and the Cedar—Illustrations of his more Sustained Style—The Resurrection of Christ—They drank of that Rock which followed them—The Impossibility of Adequate Translation—Closing Remarks on his Place and Claim to Affectionate Regard.

FROM the extracts we have already given, it will be seen that Christmas Evans excelled in the use of parable in the pulpit. Sometimes he wrought his mine like a very Bunyan, and we believe no published accounts of these sermons in Welsh, and certainly none that we have found translated into English, give any idea of his power. With what amazing effect some of his sermons would tell on the vast audiences which in these days gather together in London, and in our great towns! This method of instruction is now usually regarded as in bad taste; it does not seem to be sanctioned by the great rulers, and masters of oratorical art. If a man could create a "Pilgrim's Progress," and recite it, it would be found to be a very doubtful article by the rhetorical sanhedrim. Yet our Lord used this very method, and without using some such method—anecdote, or illustration—it is doubtful whether any strong hold can be obtained over the lower orders of mind. Our preacher entered into the spirit of Scripture parable, and narrative. One of the most famous of his discourses is that on the Demoniac of Gadara, which we have already given in preceding pages. Some of our readers will be shocked to know that, in the course of some of his descriptions in it, he convulsed his audience with laughter in the commencement. Well, he need not be imitated there; but he held it sufficiently subdued before the close, and an alternation of tears, and raptures, not only testified to his powers, but to his skill in giving an allegorical reading of the narrative.

For the purpose of producing effect,—and we mean, by effect, visible results in crushed, and humbled hearts, and transformed lives,—it would be a curious thing to try, in England, the preaching of some of the great Welshman's sermons. What would be the effect upon any audience of that great picture of the Churchyard World, and the mighty controversy of Justice, and Mercy? Let it be admitted that there are some things in it, perhaps many, that it would not demand a severe taste to expel from the picture, but take it as the broad, bold painting of a man not highly educated,—indeed, highly educated men, as we have said, could not perform such things: a highly-educated man could never have written the "Pilgrim's Progress"—let it be remembered that it was delivered to men, perhaps, we should say, rather educated than instructed, men illiterate in all things *except* the Bible. We ourselves have, in some very large congregations, tried the preaching of one of the most famous of Evans's sermons, "The Spirit walking in dry places, seeking rest, and finding none."

Christmas Evans's preaching was by no means defective in the bone, and muscle of thought, and pulpit arrangement; but, no doubt, herein lay his great *forte*, and power,—he could paint soul-subduing pictures. They were not pieces of mere word-painting, they were bathed in emotion, they were penetrated by deep knowledge of the human heart. He went into the pulpit, mighty from lonely wrestlings with God in mountain travellings; he went among his fellow-men, his audiences, strong in his faith in the reality of those covenants with God, whose history, and character we have already presented to our readers.

There was much in his preaching of that order which is so mighty in speech, but which loses so much, or which seems to acquire such additional coarseness, when it is presented to the eye. Preachers now live too much in the presence of published sermons, to be in the highest degree effective. He who thinks of the printing-press cannot abandon himself. He who uses his notes slavishly cannot abandon himself; and, without abandonment, that is, forgetfulness, what is oratory? what is action? what is passion? If we were asked what are the two greatest human aids to pulpit power, we should say, Self-possession and Self-abandonment; the two are perfectly compatible, and in the pulpit the one is never powerful without the other. Knowledge, Belief, Preparation, these give self-possession; and Earnestness, and Unconsciousness, these give self-abandonment. The first, without the last, may make a preacher like a stony pillar, covered with runes and hieroglyphics; and the last, without the first, may make a mere fanatic, with a torrent of speech, plunging lawlessly, and disgracefully abroad. The two, in combination in a noble man, and teacher, become sublime. Perhaps they reached their highest realization, among us, in Robertson of Brighton. In another, and in a different department, and scarcely inferior order of mind, they were nobly realized in Christmas Evans.

Perhaps there never was a time when ministers were more afraid of their audiences than in this day; afraid of the big man, with his wealth, afraid of the highly-cultured young man with the speculative eyeglasses, who has finished his education in Germany; afraid lest there should be the slightest departure from the most perfect, and elegant taste. The fear of man has brought a snare into the pulpit, and it has paralysed the preacher. And in this highly-furnished, and cultivated time we have few instances of preachers who, in the pulpit, can either possess their souls, or abandon them to the truth, in the text they have to announce.

It must have been, one thinks, a grand thing to have heard Christmas Evans; the extracts from his journal, the story they tell of his devout, and rapt communions of soul with God, among the mountains, the bare, and solitary hills, reveal sufficiently how, in himself, the preacher was made. When he came into the pulpit, his soul was kindled, and inflamed by the live coals from the altar. Some men of his own country imitated him, of course. Imitations are always ludicrous,—some of these were especially so. There was, says one of his biographers, the shrug, the shake of the head, the hurried, undertoned exclamation, "Bendigedig," etc., etc., always reminding us, by verifying it, of Dr. Parr's description of the imitators of Johnson: "They had the nodosities of the oak without its vigour, and the contortions of the sibyl without her inspiration."

It was not so with him: he had rare, highly spiritual, and gifted sympathies; but even in his very colloquies in the pulpit, there was a wing, and sweep of majesty. He preached often amidst scenes of wildness, and beauty, in romantic dells, or on mountain sides, and slopes, amidst the summer hush of crags, and brooks, all ministering, it may be thought, to the impression of the whole scene; or it was in rude, and unadorned mountain chapels, altogether alien from the æsthetics so charming to modern religious sensibilities; but he never lowered his tone, his language was always intelligible; but both it, and the imagery he employed, even when some circumstances gave to it a homely light, and play, always ascended; he knew the workings of the heart, and knew how to lay his finger impressively upon all its movements, and every kind of sympathy attested his power.

It is a great thing to bear men's spirits along through the sublime reaches, and avenues of thought, and emotion; and majesty, and sublimity seem to have been the common moods of his mind; never was his speech, or his pulpit, like a Gilboa, on which there was no dew. He gave it as his advice to a young preacher, "Never raise the voice while the heart is dry; let the heart, and affections shout first,—let it commence within." A man who could say, "Hundreds of prayers bubble from the fountain of my mind,"—what sort of preacher was he likely to make? He "mused, and the fire burned;" like the smith who blows upon the furnace, until the iron is red hot, and then strikes on the anvil till the sparks fly all round him, so he preached. His words, and thoughts became radiant with fire, and metaphor; they flew forth rich, bright, glowing, like some rich metal in ethereal flame. As we have said, it was the nature, and the habit of his mind, to embody, and impersonate; attributes, and qualities took the shape, and form of persons; he seemed to enter mystic abodes, and not to talk of things as a metaphysician, or a theologian, but as a spectator, or actor. The magnificences of nature crowded round him, bowing in homage, as he selected from them to adorn, or illustrate his theme; all things beautiful, and splendid, all things fresh, and young, all things old, and venerable. Reading his discourses, for instance, the *Hind of the Morning*, we are astonished at the prodigality, and the unity of the imagination, the coherency with which the fancies range themselves, as gems, round some central truth, drinking, and reflecting its corruscations.

Astounded were the people who heard; it was minstrelsy even more than oratory; the truths were old and common, there was no fine discrimination, and subtle touch of expression, as in Williams, and there was no personal majesty, and dignity of sonorous swell of the pomp of words, as in John Elias; but it was more,—it was the wing of prophecy, and poetry, it was the rapture of the seer, or the bard; he called up image after image, grouped them, made them speak, and testify; laden by grand, and overwhelming feelings, he bore the people with him, through the valley of the shadow of death, or across the Delectable Mountains. There is a spell in thought, there is a spell in felicitous language; but when to these are added the vision which calls up sleeping terror, the imagination which makes living nature yet more alive, and brings the solemn, or the dreadful people of the Book of God to our home, and life of to-day, how terribly majestic the preacher becomes!

The sermons of Christmas Evans can only be known through the medium of translation. They, perhaps, do not suffer as most translations suffer; but the rendering, in English, is feeble in comparison with the at once nervous, bony, and muscular Welsh language. The sermons, however, clearly reveal the man; they reveal the fulness, and strength of his mind; they abound in instructive thoughts; their building, and structure is always good; and many of the passages, and even several of the sermons, might be taken as models for strong, and effective pulpit oratory. Like all the preachers of his day, and order of mind, and peculiarity of theological sentiment, and training, his usage of the imagery of Scripture was remarkably free; his use also of texts often was as significant, and suggestive as it was, certainly, original.

No doubt, for the appreciation of his purpose, and his power in its larger degree, he needed an audience well acquainted with Scripture, and sympathetic, in an eminent manner, with the mind of the preacher. There seem to have been periods, and moments when his mind soared aloft, into some of the highest fields of truth, and emotion. Yet his wing never seemed little, or petty in its flight. There was the firmness, and strength of the beat of a noble eagle. Some eloquence sings, some sounds; in one we hear the voice of a bird hovering in the air, in the other we listen to the thunder of the plume: the eloquence of Christmas Evans was of the latter order.

We have remarked it before,—there is a singular parable-loving instinct in Wales. Its most popular traditional, and prose literature, is imbued with it; the "Mabinogion," the juvenile treasures of Welsh legend, corresponding to the Grimm of Germany, and the other great Teutonic and Norse legends, but wholly unlike them, prove this. But we are told that the most grand prose work in Wales, of modern date, and, at the same time, the most pre-eminently popular, is the "Sleeping Bard," by Elis Wyn. He was a High Church clergyman, and wrote this extraordinary allegory at the commencement of the last century. Christmas Evans must have known it, have known it well. It portrays a series of visions, and if Mr. Borrow's testimony may be relied upon, they are thoroughly Dantesque. He says, "It is a singular mixture of the sublime, and the coarse, the terrible, and the ludicrous, of religion, and levity, and combines Milton, Bunyan, and Quevedo."

This is immense praise. The Vision of the World, the first portion, leads the traveller down the streets of Pride, Pleasure, and Lucre; but in the distance is a cross street, little and mean, in comparison with the others, but clean, and neat, and on a higher foundation than the other streets; it runs upwards, towards the east; they sink downwards, towards the north—this is the street True Religion. This is very much in the style of Christmas Evans, and so also is the vision of Death, the vision of Perdition, and the vision of Hell. This singular poem appears to have been exceedingly popular in Wales when Christmas Evans was young.

But our preacher has often been called the Bunyan of Wales—the Bunyan of the pulpit. In some measure, the epithet does designate him; he was a great master of parabolic similitude, and comparison. This is a kind of preaching ever eminently popular with the multitude; it requires rather a redundancy of fancy, than imagination—perhaps a mind considerably disciplined, and educated would be unable to indulge in such exercises—a self-possession, balanced by ignorance of many of the canons of taste, or utterly oblivious, and careless of them; for this is a kind of teaching of which we hear very little. Now we have not one preacher in England who would, perhaps, dare to use, or who could use well, the parabolic style. This was the especial power of Christmas Evans. He excelled in personification; he would seem frequently to have been mastered by this faculty. The abstraction of thought, the disembodied phantoms of another world, came clothed in form, and feature, and colour; at his bidding they came—

> "Ghostly shapes
> Met him at noontide; Fear, and trembling Hope,

>Silence, and Foresight; Death, the skeleton,
>And Time, the shadow."

Thus, he frequently astounded his congregations, not merely by pouring round his subject the varied hues of light, or space, but by giving to the eye defined shapes, and realizations. We do not wonder to hear him say, "If I only entered the pulpit, I felt raised, as it were, to Paradise, above my afflictions, until I forgot my adversity; yea, I felt my mountain strong. I said to a brother once, 'Brother, the doctrine, the confidence, and strength I feel, will make persons dance with joy in some parts of Wales.' 'Yea, brother,' said he, with tears flowing from his eyes." He was visited by remarkable dreams. Once, previous to a time of great refreshing, he dreamt:—

"He thought he was in the church at Caerphilly, and found many harps hanging round the pulpit, wrapped in coverings of green. 'Then,' said he, 'I will take down the harps of heaven in this place.' In removing the covering, he found the ark of the covenant, inscribed with the name of Jehovah. Then he cried, 'Brethren, the Lord has come to us, according to His promise, and in answer to our prayers.'" In that very place, he shortly afterwards had the satisfaction of receiving one hundred and forty converts into the Church, as the fruit of his ministry.

As we have said, nothing can well illustrate, on paper, the power of the orator's speech, but the following may serve, as, in some measure, illustrating his method:—

"THE GOSPEL MOULD.

> "I compare such preachers to a miner, who should go to the quarry where he raised the ore, and, taking his sledge in his hand, should endeavour to form bars of iron of the ore in its rough state, without a furnace to melt it, or a rolling mill to roll it out, or moulds to cast the metal, and conform the casts to their patterns. The Gospel is like a form, or mould, and sinners are to be melted, as it were, and cast into it. 'But ye have obeyed from the heart that form of doctrine which was delivered you,' or into which you were delivered, as is the marginal reading, so that your hearts ran into the mould. Evangelical preachers have, in the name of Christ, a mould, or form to cast the minds of men into; as Solomon the vessels of the temple. The Sadducees and Pharisees had their forms, and legal preachers have their forms; but evangelical preachers should bring with them the 'form of sound words,' so that, if the hearers believe, or are melted into it, Christ may be formed in their hearts,—then they will be as born of the truth, and the image of the truth will

appear in their sentiments, and experience, and in their conduct in the Church, in the family, and in the neighbourhood. Preachers without the mould are all those who do not preach all the points of the Gospel of the Grace of God."

We will now present several extracts, derived from a variety of sources, happily illustrating the general character of his sermons.

"SAUL OF TARSUS AND HIS SEVEN SHIPS.

"Saul of Tarsus was once a thriving merchant and an extensive ship-owner; he had seven vessels of his own, the names of which were—1. Circumcised the Eighth Day; 2. Of the Stock of Israel; 3. Of the Tribe of Benjamin; 4. A Hebrew of the Hebrews; 5. As touching the Law, a Pharisee; 6. Concerning Zeal, persecuting the Church. The seventh was a man-of-war, with which he one day set out from the port of Jerusalem, well supplied with ammunition from the arsenal of the Chief Priest, with a view to destroy a small port at Damascus. He was wonderfully confident, and breathed out threatenings and slaughter. But he had not got far from port before the Gospel Ship, with Jesus Christ Himself as Commander on board, hove in sight, and threw such a shell among the merchant's fleet that all his ships were instantly on fire. The commotion was tremendous, and there was such a volume of smoke that Paul could not see the sun at noon. While the ships were fast sinking, the Gospel Commander mercifully gave orders that the perishing merchant should be taken on board. 'Saul, Saul, what has become of all thy ships?' 'They are all on fire.' 'What wilt thou do now?' 'Oh that I may be found in Him, not having my own righteousness, which is of the law, but that which is through the faith of Christ, the righteousness which is of God. by faith.'"

"THE MISPLACED BONE.

"Let every one keep his own place, that there be no schism in the body. There arose a fierce contention in the human body; every member sought another place than the one it found itself in, and was fitted for. After much controversy, it was agreed to refer the whole matter to one whose name was Solomon Wise-in-his-own-conceit. He was to arrange, and adjust the whole business, and to place every bone in its proper position. He received the appointment gladly, and was filled with joy, and confidence. He commenced with finding a place for himself. His proper post was the heel; but where do you think he found it? He must needs be the golden bowl in which the brains were deposited. The natural consequences followed. The coarse heel bone was not of the right quality, nor of the suitable dimensions to contain the brains, nor could the vessel intended for that purpose form a useful, or comely part of the foot. Disorder ensued in foot, head, face, legs, and arms. By the time Solomon Wise-in-his-own-conceit had reconstructed the body, it could neither walk, nor speak, nor smell, nor hear, nor see. The body was, moreover, filled with intolerable agony, and could find no rest, every bone crying for restoration to its own place, that is to say, every one but the heel-bone; that was mightily pleased to be in the head, and to have the custody of the brains. Sin has introduced similar disorder amongst men, and even amongst professors of religion, and into congregations. 'Let every one keep his own place, that there be no schism in the body.' The body can do much, can bear heavy burdens, all its parts being in their own positions. Even so in the Church; much good can be done by every member keeping and filling his own place without high-mindedness."

"THE MAN IN THE HOUSE OF STEEL.

"A man in a trance saw himself locked up in a house of steel, through the walls of which, as through walls of glass, he could see his enemies assailing him with swords, spears, and bayonets; but his life was safe, for his fortress was locked within. So is the Christian secure amid the assaults of the world. His 'life is hid with Christ in God.'

"The Psalmist prayed, 'When my heart is overwhelmed within me, lead me to the Rock that is higher than I.' Imagine a man seated on a lofty rock in the midst of the sea, where he has everything necessary for his support, shelter, safety, and comfort. The billows heave and break beneath him, and the hungry monsters of the deep wait to devour him; but he is on high, above the rage of the former, and the reach of the latter. Such is the security of faith.

"But why need I mention the rock, and the steel house? for the peace that is in Christ is a tower ten thousand times stronger, and a refuge ten thousand times safer. Behold the disciples of Jesus exposed to famine, nakedness, peril, and sword—incarcerated in dungeons; thrown to wild beasts; consumed in the fire; sawn asunder; cruelly mocked, and scourged; driven from friends, and home, to wander among the mountains, and lodge in dens, and caves of the earth; being destitute, afflicted, tormented; sorrowful, but always rejoicing; cast down, but not destroyed; an ocean of peace within, which swallows up all their sufferings.

"'Neither death,' with all its terrors; 'nor life,' with all its allurements; 'nor things present,' with all their pleasure, 'nor things to come,' with all their promise; 'nor height' of prosperity; 'nor depth' of adversity; 'nor angels' of evil; 'nor principalities' of darkness; 'shall be able to separate us from the love of God which is in Christ Jesus.' 'God is our refuge, and strength; a very present help in trouble. Therefore will we not fear, though the earth be removed, and though the mountains be carried into the midst of the sea—though the waters thereof roar and be troubled, though the mountains shake with the swelling thereof.' This is the language of strong faith in the peace of Christ. How is it with you amid such turmoil, and commotion? Is all peaceful within? Do you feel secure in the name of the Lord, as in a strong fortress, as in a city well supplied, and defended?

"'There is a river, the streams whereof shall make glad the city of God, the holy place of the tabernacles of the most high. God is in the midst of her; she shall not be moved. God shall help her, and that right early.' 'Unto the upright, there ariseth light in the darkness.' The bright and morning star, shining upon their pathway, cheers them in their journey home to their Father's house. And when they come to pass over Jordan, the Sun of Righteousness shall have risen upon them, with healing in His wings. Already they see the tops of the mountains of immortality, gilded with his beams, beyond the valley of the shadow of death. Behold, yonder, old Simeon hoisting his sails, and saying, 'Lord, now lettest thou Thy servant depart in peace, according to Thy word; for mine eyes have seen Thy salvation.' Such is the peace of Jesus, sealed to all them that believe by the blood of His cross.

"When we walk through the field of battle, slippery with blood, and strewn with the bodies of the slain—when we hear the shrieks, and the groans of the wounded, and the dying—when we see the country wasted, cities burned, houses pillaged, widows, and orphans wailing in the track of the victorious army, we cannot help exclaiming, 'Oh, what a blessing is peace!' When we are obliged to witness family turmoils, and strifes—when we see parents, and children, brothers, and sisters, masters, and servants, husbands, and wives, contending with each other like tigers—we retire as from a smoky house, and exclaim as we go, 'Oh, what a blessing is peace!' When duty calls us into that church, where envy, and malice prevail, and the spirit of harmony is supplanted by discord, and contention—when we see brethren, who ought to be bound together in love, full of pride, hatred, confusion, and every evil work—we quit the unhallowed scene with painful feelings of repulsion, repeating the exclamation, 'Oh, what a blessing is peace!'

"But how much more precious in the case of the awakened sinner! See him standing, terror-stricken, before Sinai. Thunders roll above him—lightnings flash around him—the earth trembles beneath him, as if ready to open her mouth, and swallow him up. The sound of the trumpet rings through his soul, 'Guilty! guilty! guilty!' Pale and trembling, he looks eagerly around him, and sees nothing but revelations of wrath. Overwhelmed with fear, and dismay, he cries out—'O wretched man that I am! who shall deliver me! What shall I do?' A voice reaches his ear, penetrates his heart—'Behold the Lamb of God, that taketh away the sin of the world!' He turns his eyes to Calvary. Wondrous vision! Emmanuel expiring upon the cross! the sinner's Substitute satisfying the demand of the law against the sinner! Now all his fears are hushed, and rivers of peace flow into his soul. This is the peace of Christ.

"How precious is this peace, amid all the dark vicissitudes of life! How invaluable this jewel, through all the dangers of the wilderness! How cheering to know that Jesus, who hath loved us even unto death, is the pilot of our perilous voyage; that He rules the winds, and the waves, and can hush them to silence at His will, and bring the frailest bark of faith to the desired haven! Trusting where he cannot trace his Master's footsteps, the disciple is joyful amid the darkest dispensations of Divine Providence; turning all his sorrows into songs, and all his tribulations into triumphs. 'Thou wilt keep him in perfect peace, whose mind is stayed on Thee, because he trusteth in Thee.'"

"THE PARABLE OF THE CHURCH AS AN ARK AMONG THE BULRUSHES OF THE NILE.

"I see an ark of bulrushes, daubed with slime, and pitch, placed on the banks of the Nile, which swarmed with fierce crocodiles. Pharaoh's daughter espies it, and sends her maidens to find out what there can be in it. Little Moses was there, with a face of miraculous beauty, to charm the princess of Egypt. She determined to adopt him as her son. Behold, a great wonder. On the brink of the river, where the three great crocodiles—the Devil, Sin, and Death—have devoured their millions, there lay those who it was seen, before the foundation of the world, would be adopted into the court of heaven. The Gospel comes forth like a royal princess, with pardon in her hand, and mercy in her eye; and hastening with her handmaidens, she glances at the thousands asleep in the perils of sin. They had favour in her sight, and she sent for her maidens, called Justification, and Sanctification, to train them for the inheritance of the saints."

"THE HANDWRITING.

"When Adam sinned, there was issued against him the writ of death, written by the finger of God in the book of the moral law. Adam had heard it read before his fall, but in seeking to become a god, by eating of the fruit of the tree, had forgotten it. Now God read it in his conscience, and he was overwhelmed with fear. But the promise of a Redeemer having been given, Mercy arranged that sacrifices should be offered as a typical payment of the debt. When God appeared on Sinai, to enter into covenant with His people, He brought this writ in His hand, and the whole camp understood, from the requirements of the law, that they must perish; their lives had been forfeited. Mercy devised that a bullock's blood should be shed, instead of the blood of man. The worshippers in the temple were bound to offer living sacrifices to God, that they might die in their stead, and be consumed. Manoah feared the flames of the sacrifice that was offered upon the rock; but his wife understood that, since the angel had ascended in the flame, in their stead, it was a favourable omen. Every worshipper, by offering other lives instead of their own on the altars of God, acknowledged that the 'handwriting' was in force against them, and their high priest had minutely to confess all their sins 'over' the victim. Yet, by all the blood that ever crimsoned Levi's robe, and the altars of God, no real atonement was made for sin, nor forgiveness procured for the smallest crime. All the sacrifices made a remembrance of sin, but were no means of pardon. More than two thousand years the question had been entertained, how to reconcile man with God. The 'handwriting' was real on Mount Ebal every year; meanwhile the debt was fast accumulating, and new bills were being constantly filed. The books were opened from time to time; but to meet the claims there was nothing brought to the altar but the blood of sacrifices, as a sort of draft in the name of Christ upon the Bank of Gold. When Heaven, and earth had grown weary of this fictitious or seeming, pardon of sin, I hear a voice exclaim: 'Away with sacrifices, and burnt-offerings: Heaven has no pleasure in them; a body has been prepared for me. Lo, I come to reconcile man with God by one sacrifice.' He came, 'leaping upon the mountains, and skipping upon the hills.' Calling at the office where the 'handwriting' lay, when only eight days old, He signed with His own blood an acknowledgment of the debt, saying: 'This is an earnest, and a pledge that my heart's blood shall be freely given.' The three-and-thirty years have expired; I see Him in Gethsemane, with the priceless purse of gold which He had borne with Him through the courts of Caiaphas and Pilate; but to them the image, and the superscription on the coin was a mystery. The Father, however, recognised them in the court of Sinai, where the 'handwriting' was that demanded the life of the whole world. The day following, 'the Virgin's Son' presented Himself to pay the debt in liquid gold; and the treasure which He bore would have set free a myriad worlds. He passes along the streets of Jerusalem towards Sinai's office; the mercy-seat is removed to 'the place of skulls;' as He proceeds, He exclaims: 'I am come not to destroy, but to fulfil the law.' Send in, before the hour of three, each curse, and threat ever pronounced against my people. Bring in the first old bill against Adam as their head. I will redeem a countless host of infants to-day; their names shall be taken out of old Eden's accounts. Bring in the many transgressions which have been filed through the ages, from Adam until now; include Peter's denial of me last night; but as to Judas, he is a son of perdition, he has no part in me, having sold me for thirty pieces of silver. We have here an exhaustless crimson treasure,—enough to meet the demand; enough to fill every promise, and every prophecy with mercy; enough to make my beloved, and myself happy, and blest for ever! By three in the afternoon of that day, there was not a bill in all Eden, or Sinai, that had not been brought to the cross. And when all was settled, Christ bowed down His head, but cried with a loud voice: 'It is finished!' The gates of death, and hell trembled, and shook. 'The posts of the doors moved at the voice.' The great gulf between God, and His people was closed up. Sinai appeared with the offering, and grew still; the lightnings no longer flashed, and the thunder ceased to roar."

"DEATH AS AN INOCULATOR.

"Death may be conceived of as a gigantic inoculator. He carries about with him a monstrous box, filled with deadly matter, with which he has infected every child of Adam. The whole race of man is doomed by this law of death. But see! This old inoculator gets paid back in his own coin. The Son of Man, humbling Himself to death, descends into the tomb, but rises immortal. He seized death in Joseph's grave. But, amazing spectacle! with the matter of His own immortality He inoculated mortality with death, whose lifeless corpse will be seen, on the resurrection morning, among the ruins of His people's graves; while they, with one voice, will rend the air as if eternity opened its mouth, exclaiming: 'O death, where is thy sting? O grave, where is thy victory?'"

"TIME.

"Time, considered as a whole, is the age of the visible creation. It began with the fiat, 'Let there be light;' and it will end with the words: 'Come, ye blessed of my Father,' and 'Go, ye cursed.' Each river, and mountain, town, and city, hovel, and palace, every son, and daughter of Adam, must undergo the change, pass away, for whatever is seen is only for a time. The time of restoration, by the presence of the glory of Christ, will be the morning of judgment, and resurrection. That morning will be the last of time: then eternity begins. From that time, each man will dwell in his everlasting home: the ungodly in a lake of fire, that will burn for ever; while the joy, and happiness of the blest will know no end.

"Oh the fearfulness of the word *everlasting*, written over the door of the lake of fire! Oh the happiness it will create when read above the eternal kingdom!

"Time is the age of the visible world; but eternity is the age of God. This limitless circle centres in Him. The age of the visible world is divided into years, and days, according to the revolutions of the earth, and sun,—into weeks, in memory of the world's creation, and the resurrection of Christ,—into hours, minutes, seconds, and moments. These last can scarcely be distinguished, yet they are parts of the great body of time; but seven thousand years constitute no part of eternity. One day, and a thousand years, yea, millions of years, are alike, compared with the age of God, forming no part of the vast changeless circle that knows neither loss, nor gain. The age of time is winding up by minutes, days, and years: the age of God is one endless to-day; and such will be your age, and mine, when we have once passed the limits of time, beyond which Lazarus is blessed, and the rich man tormented. My brethren in the ministry, who in years gone by travelled with me from one Association to another, are to-day living in that great endless hour!

"Time is an age of changes, revolutions, and reforms; but eternity is calm, stationary, and changeless. He who enters upon it an enemy to God, faithless, prayerless, unpardoned, and unregenerate, remains so for ever. Great changes take place in time, for which the new song in eternity will never cease. Natures have been changed, and enmity has been abolished. In time, the life covenant was broken, and man formed, and sealed his compact with hell. One, equal with God, died upon the cross, in the form of a servant, to destroy the works of the devil, and to unite man, and God in the bond of peace through His own blood. Time, and language would fail to recount what in time has been accomplished, involving changes from life, to death, and from death, to life. Here the pure have become denied, and the guiltless condemned; and here, also, the sinner has been justified, the polluted cleansed, the poor enriched, the enemy reconciled, and the dead have been made alive, where one paradise has been lost, and a better regained. The new song from the midst of eternity sounds in our ears. Hear it! It has for its subjects one event that took place in eternity, and three that have transpired in time: 'Unto Him that loved us, and washed us from our sins in His own blood, and hath made us kings, and priests unto God, and His Father: to Him be glory, and dominion for ever, and ever. Amen.'"

"THE TIMEPIECE.

"You may move the hands on the dial-plate this way, and the other, and finger as you please the machinery within, but if there be no mainspring there your labour will be in vain. So the 'hands' of men's lives will not move, in holy obedience, at the touch of the law, unless the mainspring be supplied by God through the Gospel; then only will the whole life revolve on the pivot of the love of Christ, as upon an imperishable diamond. It is not difficult to get the timepiece to act well, if the internal machinery be in proper order; so, with a right spirit within, Lydia attends to the word, Matthew leaves 'the receipt of custom,' Saul of Tarsus prays; and the three thousand repent, believe, and turn unto the Lord.

"A gentleman's timepieces were once out of order, and they were examined, when it was found that in one of them the mainspring was injured; the glass which protected the dial-plate of the other was broken; while the machinery of the third had got damp, and rusty, although the parts were all there. So the lack of holiness, in some cases, arises from the want of heart to love God; another man has not the glass of watchfulness in his conduct; another has got rusty with backsliding from God, and the sense of guilt so clogs the wheels of his machinery, that they must be well brushed with rebuke, and correction, and oiled afresh with the Divine influence, before they will ever go well again.

"The whole of a Christian's life is a reaching forward; but he has to begin afresh, like the people of Israel in the wilderness; or, like a clock, he has constantly to recommence at the figure one, and go on to that of twelve, through all the years of his experience on earth. But after the resurrection, he will advance, body, and soul, to the figure of million of millions, never to begin again throughout eternity. The sun in that world will never rise, nor set; it will have neither east, nor west! How often has an invisible hand wound up thy religious spirit below, but there the weights will never come down again!"

"PARABLE OF THE BIRDS.

"A gentleman kept in his palace a dove, a raven, and an eagle. There was but little congeniality, or friendship amongst them. The dove ate its own proper food, and lodged in the aviary. The raven fed on carrion, and sometimes would pick out the eyes of an innocent lamb, and had her nest in the branches of a tree. The eagle was a royal bird; it flew very high, and was of a savage nature; it would care nothing to eat half-a-dozen doves for its breakfast. It was considered the chief of all birds, because it could fly higher than all. All the doves feared its beak, its angry eyes, and sharp talons. When the gentleman threw corn in the yard for the dove, the raven would be engaged in eating a piece of flesh, a part of a lamb haply; and the eagle in carrying a child from the cradle to its eyrie. The dove is the evangelical, industrious, godly professor; the raven is the licentious, and unmanageable professor; and the eagle the high-minded, and self-complacent one. These characters are too often amongst us; there is no denomination in church, or meeting-house, without these three birds, if there be birds there at all. These birds, so unlike, so opposed, never can live together in peace. Let us pray, brethren, for union of spirit in the bond of peace."

"PARABLE OF THE VINE-TREE, THE THORN, THE BRAMBLE, AND THE CEDAR.

"The trees of Lebanon held a council to elect a king, on the death of their old sovereign, the Yew-tree. It was agreed to offer the sovereignty to the Cedar; at the same time, in the event of the Cedar's declining it, to the Vine-tree, and then to the Olive-tree. They all refused it. The Cedar said, 'I am high enough already.' The Vine said, 'I prefer giving forth my rich juice to gladden man's heart.' In like manner, the Olive was content with giving its fruit, and would receive no other honour. Recourse was then had to the Thorn. The Thorn gladly received the office; saying to itself, 'I have nothing to lose but this white dress, and a berry for pigs, while I have prickles enough to annoy the whole wood.' The Bramble rebelled against the Thorn, and a fire of pride, and envy was kindled, which, at length, wrapped the whole forest in one blaze. Two or three vain, and high-minded men have frequently broken up the peace of congregations; and, by striving for the mastery, have inflicted on the cause of religion incalculable injuries; when they have had no more fitness for rule than the white-thorn, or the prickly bramble."

The following extract is of another order; it is more lengthy, and it is upon a theme which always drew forth the preacher's most exulting notes:—

"THE RESURRECTION OF OUR LORD.

"Let us now consider the fact of our Lord's resurrection, and its bearing upon the great truths of our holy religion.

"This most transcendent of miracles is sometimes attributed to the agency of the Father; who, as the Lawgiver, had arrested, and imprisoned in the grave the sinner's Surety, manifesting at once His benevolence, and His holiness; but by liberating the prisoner, proclaimed that the debt was cancelled, and the claims of the law satisfied. It is sometimes attributed to the Son Himself; who had power both to lay down His life, and to take it again; and the merit of whose sacrifice entitled Him to the honour of thus asserting His dominion over death, on behalf of His people. And sometimes it is attributed to the Holy Spirit, as in the following words of the Apostle:—'He was declared to be the Son of God with power, according to the Spirit of Holiness, by the resurrection from the dead.'

"*The resurrection of Christ is a clear and incontestable proof of His Divinity.*

"He had declared Himself equal with God the Father, and one with Him in nature, and in glory. He had told the people that He would prove the truth of this declaration, by rising from the grave three days after His death. And when the morning of the third day began to dawn upon the sepulchre, lo! there was an earthquake, and the dead body arose, triumphant over the power of corruption.

"This was the most stupendous miracle ever exhibited on earth, and its language is:—'Behold, ye persecuting Jews and murdering Romans, the proof of my Godhead! Behold, Caiaphas, Herod, Pilate, the power, and glory of your Victim!' 'I am He that liveth, and was dead; and lo! I am alive for evermore!' 'I am the root, and the offspring of David, and the Bright, and Morning Star!' 'Look unto Me, and be ye saved, all ye ends of the earth; for I am God, and besides Me there is none else!'

"Our Lord's resurrection affords incontrovertible evidence of the truth of Christianity.

"Pilate wrote the title of Christ in three languages on the cross; and many have written excellent, and unanswerable things, on the truth of the Christian Scriptures, and the reality of the Christian religion; but the best argument that has ever been written on the subject was written by the invisible hand of the Eternal Power, in the rocks of our Saviour's sepulchre. This confounds the sceptic, settles the controversy, and affords an ample, and sure foundation for all them that believe.

"If any one asks whether Christianity is from heaven, or of men, we point him to the 'tomb hewn out of the rock,' and say—'There is your answer! Jesus was crucified, and laid in that cave; but on the morning of the third day it was found empty; our Master had risen, and gone forth from the grave victorious.'

"This is the pillar that supports the whole fabric of our religion; and he who attempts to pull it down, like Samson, pulls ruin upon himself. 'If Christ is not risen, then is our preaching vain, and your faith is also vain, ye are yet in your sins;' but if the fact is clearly proved, then Christianity is unquestionably true, and its disciples are safe.

"This is the ground on which the Apostle stood, and asserted the divinity of his faith:—'Moreover, I testify unto you the gospel, which I preached unto you; which also ye have received, and wherein ye stand; by which also ye are saved, if ye keep in memory what I preached unto you, unless ye have believed in vain; for I delivered unto you first of all that which I also received, how that Christ died for our sins according to the Scriptures, and that He was buried, and that He rose again the third day, according to the Scriptures.'

"The resurrection of Jesus is the most stupendous manifestation of the power of God, and the pledge of eternal life to His people.

"The apostle calls it 'the exceeding greatness of His power to usward, who believe, according to the working of His mighty power, which He wrought in Christ when He raised Him from the dead.' This is a river overflowing its banks—an idea too large for language. Let us look at it a moment.

"Where do we find 'the exceeding greatness of His power'? In the creation of the world? in the seven Stars and Orion? in the strength of Behemoth and Leviathan? No! In the Deluge? in the fiery destruction of Sodom? in the overthrow of Pharaoh, and his host? in hurling Nebuchadnezzar, like Lucifer, from the political firmament? No! It is the power which He wrought in Christ. When? When He healed the sick? when He raised the dead? when He cast out devils? when He blasted the fruitless fig-tree? when He walked upon the waters of Galilee? No! It was 'when He raised Him from the dead.' Then the Father placed the sceptre in the hands of the Son, 'and set Him above all principality, and power, and might, and dominion, and every name that is named, not only in this world, but also in that which is to come; and put all things under His feet, and gave Him to be Head over all things to the Church.'

"This is the source of our spiritual life. The same power that raised the dead body of our Lord from the grave, quickens the soul of the believer from the death in trespasses, and sins. His riven tomb is a fountain of living waters; whereof, if a man drink, he shall never die. His raised, and glorified body is the sun, whence streams eternal light upon our spirits; the light of life, that never can be quenched.

"Nor here does the influence of His resurrection end. 'He who raised up Jesus from the dead shall, also, quicken our mortal bodies.' His resurrection is the pledge, and the pattern of ours. 'Because He lives, we shall live also.' 'He shall change our vile body, that it may be fashioned like unto His glorious body.' We hear Him speaking in the Prophet:—'Thy dead shall live; together with my dead body shall they arise. Awake, and sing, ye that dwell in the dust; for thy dew is as the dew of herbs, and the earth shall cast out her dead.'

"How divinely does the Apostle speak of the resurrection-body of the saints! 'It is sown in corruption, it is raised in incorruption; it is sown in dishonour, it is raised in glory; it is sown in weakness, it is raised in power; it is sown a natural body, it is raised a spiritual body. For this corruptible must put on incorruption, and this mortal must put on immortality. Then shall be brought to pass the saying that is written: 'Death is swallowed up in victory! O death, where is thy victory? O grave, where is thy sting? Thanks be unto God that giveth us the victory, through our Lord Jesus Christ.'

"Ever since the fall in Eden, man is born to die. He lives to die. He eats, and drinks, sleeps, and wakes, to die. Death, like a dark steel-clad warrior, stands ever before us; and his gigantic shadow comes continually between us, and happiness. But Christ hath 'abolished death, and brought life, and immortality to light through the gospel.' He was born in Bethlehem, that He might die on Calvary. He was made under the law, that He might bear the direst penalty of the law. He lived thirty-three years, sinless, among sinners, that He might offer Himself a sin-offering for sinners upon the cross. Thus 'He became obedient unto death,' that He might destroy the power of death; and on the third morning, a mighty angel, rolling away the stone from the mouth of the sepulchre, makes the very door of death's castle the throne whence He proclaims 'the resurrection, and the life.'

"The Hero of our salvation travelled into Death's dominion, took possession of the whole territory on our behalf, and returning, laden with spoils, ascended to the Heaven of heavens. He went to the palace, seized the tyrant, and wrested away his sceptre. He descended into the prison-house, knocked off the fetters of the captives; and when He came up again, left the door of every cell open, that they might follow Him. He has gone over into our promised inheritance, and His glory illuminates the mountains of immortality; and through the telescope which He has bequeathed us we 'see the land which is very far off.'

"I recollect reading, in the writings of Flavel, this sentiment—that the souls in Paradise wait, with intense desire, for the reanimation of their dead bodies, that they may be united to them in bliss for ever. Oh what rapture there shall be among the saints, when those frail vessels, from which they escaped with such a struggle, as they foundered in the gulf of death, shall come floating in, with the spring-tide of the resurrection, to the harbour of immortality! How glorious the reunion, when the seeds of affliction, and death are left behind in the tomb! Jacob no longer lame, nor Moses slow of speech, nor Lazarus covered with sores, nor Paul troubled with a thorn in the flesh!

"'It doth not yet appear what we shall be; but we know that, when He shall appear, we shall be like Him; for we shall see Him as He is.' The glory of the body of Christ is far above our present conception. When He was transfigured on Tabor, His face shone like the sun, and His raiment was white as the light. This is the pattern shown to His people on the mount. This is the model after which the bodies of believers shall be fashioned in the resurrection. 'They that be wise shall shine as the brightness of the firmament; and they that turn many to righteousness, as the stars for ever, and ever.'

"In conclusion:—The angel said to the woman, 'Go quickly, and tell His disciples that He is risen from the dead; and behold, He goeth before you into Galilee; there shall ye see Him; lo! I have told you. And they departed quickly from the sepulchre, with fear, and great joy; and did run to bring His disciples word.'

"Brethren! followers of Jesus! be ye also preachers of a risen Saviour! Go quickly—there is no time for delay—and publish the glad tidings to sinners! Tell them that Christ died for their sins, and rose again for their justification, and ascended to the right hand of the Father to make intercession for them, and is now able to save unto the uttermost all that come unto God by Him!

"And you, impenitent, and unbelieving men! hear this blessed message of salvation! Do you intend ever to embrace the proffered mercy of the Gospel? Make haste! Procrastination is ruin! Now is the accepted

> time! Oh, fly to the throne of grace! Time is hastening; you will soon be swallowed up in eternity! May the Lord have mercy upon you, and rouse you from your indifference, and sloth! It is my delight to invite you to Christ; but I feel more pleasure, and more confidence in praying for you to God. I have besought, and entreated you, by every argument, and every motive in my power; but you are yet in your sins, and rushing on toward hell. Yet I will not give you up in despair. If I cannot persuade you to flee from the wrath to come, I will intercede with God to have mercy upon you, for the sake of His beloved Son. If I cannot prevail in the pulpit, I will try to prevail at the throne."

This must be regarded as a very noble piece; the words make themselves felt; evidently, the resurrection of our Lord, to this preacher, was a great reality; it is now, by many, regarded only as a charming myth; a very curious eschatology in our day has found its way even into our pulpits, and we have eminent ministers of the Church of England, well-known Congregational, and other ministers, who affect to believe, and to preach the Resurrection of Christ; but a careful listener in the pew, or a converser by the fireside, will find, to his amazement, that the resurrection, as believed by them, is no honest resurrection at all: it is a spiritual resurrection which leaves the body of Jesus unrisen, and in the possession of death, and the grave. In that view, which has just passed before us, a very different, and most absolutely real resurrection is preached; indeed, it is the only view which leaves a heart of immortal hope in the Christian faith, the only view which seems at all tenable, if we are to believe in the power of Christ's resurrection.

We will close these extracts by one of yet another order,—a vivid descriptive picture of the smiting of the rock, the streams flowing through the desert, and the joy of the mighty caravan of pilgrims on their way to the promised land.

"'THEY DRANK OF THAT ROCK WHICH FOLLOWED THEM.'

> "Having spoken of *the smiting*, let us, *now*, look at *the result*, the flowing of the waters; a timely mercy to 'the many thousands of Israel,' on the point of perishing in the desert; shadowing forth a far greater mercy, the flowing of living waters from the 'spiritual rock,' which is Christ.

> "In the death of our Redeemer, we see three infinite depths moved for the relief of human misery: the love of the Father, the merit of the Son, and the energy of the Holy Spirit. These are the depths of wonder whence arise the rivers of salvation.

"*The waters flowed in the presence of the whole assembly.* The agent was invisible, but His work was manifest.

"The water flowed *in great abundance,* filling the whole camp, and supplying all the people. Notwithstanding the immense number, and the greatness of their thirst, there was enough for each, and for all. The streams ran in every direction to meet the sufferers, and their rippling murmur seemed to say—'Open thy mouth, and I will fill it.' Look to the cross! See there the gracious fountain opened, and streams of pardoning, and purifying mercy flowing down the rock of Calvary, sweeping over the mount of Olives, and cleaving it asunder, to make a channel for the living waters to go out over the whole world, that God may be glorified among the Gentiles, and all the ends of the earth may see His salvation.

"The water flowed *from the rock,* not pumped by human labour, but drawn by the hand of God. It was the same power that opened the springs of mercy upon the cross. It was the wisdom of God that devised the plan, and the mercy of God that furnished the Victim. His was the truth, and love that gave the promise by the prophet—'In that day there shall be a fountain opened to the house of David, and to the inhabitants of Jerusalem, for sin, and uncleanness.' His was the unchanging faithfulness that fulfilled it in His Son—'Not by works of righteousness which we have done, but according to His mercy He saved us, by the washing of regeneration, and renewing of the Holy Ghost, which He shed on us abundantly, through Jesus Christ our Lord.' Our salvation is wholly of God; and we have no other agency in the matter than the mere acceptance of His proffered grace.

"The water flowed *in twelve different channels*; and, according to Dr. Pococke, of Scotland, who visited the place, the deep traces in the rock are visible to this day. But the twelve streams, one for each tribe, all issued from the same fountain, in the same rock. So the great salvation flowed out through the ministry of the twelve apostles of the Lamb, and went abroad over all the earth. But the fountain is one. All the apostles preached the same Saviour, and pointed to the same cross. 'Neither is there salvation in any other, for there is no other name under heaven, given among men, whereby we must be saved.' We must come to this spring, or perish.

"The flowing of the waters *was irresistible by human power.* Who can close the fountain which God hath opened? can Edom, or Moab, or Sihon, or Og dam up the current which Jehovah hath drawn from the rock? Can Caiaphas, and all the Jews, aided by the prince of this world—can all the powers of earth and hell combined—arrest the work of redemption, and dry up the fountain of mercy which Christ is opening on Calvary? As soon might they dry up the Atlantic, and stop the revolutions of the globe. It is written, and must be fulfilled. Christ must suffer, and enter into His glory—must be lifted up, and draw all men unto Him—and repentance, and remission of sins must be preached in His name among all nations, beginning at Jerusalem.

"*The water flowing from the rock was like a river of life to the children of Israel.* Who can describe the distress throughout the camp, and the appearance of the people, when they were invited to approach a flinty rock, instead of a fountain, or a stream, to quench their thirst? What angry countenances were there, what bitter censures, and ungrateful murmurings, as Moses went up to the rock, with nothing in his hand but a rod! 'Where is he going,' said they, 'with that dry stick? What is he going to do on that rock? Does he mean to make fools of us all? Is it not enough that he has brought us into this wilderness to die of thirst? Will he mock us now by pretending to seek water in these sands, or open fountains in the solid granite?' But see! he lifts the rod, he smites the rock; and lo, it bursts into a fountain; and twelve crystal streams roll down before the people! Who can conceive the sudden transport? Hear the shout of joy ringing through the camp, and rolling back in tumultuous echoes from the crags, and cliffs of Horeb,—'Water! water! A miracle! a miracle! Glory to the God of Israel! glory to His servant Moses!' It was a resurrection-day to Israel, the morning light bursting upon the shadow of death. New life, and joy are seen throughout the camp. The maidens are running with cups, and pitchers, to the rock. They fill, and drink; then fill again, and haste away to their respective tents, with water for the sick, the aged, and the little ones, joyfully exclaiming—'Drink, father! Drink, mother! Drink, children! Drink, all of you! Drink abundantly! Plenty of water now! Rivers flowing from the rock!' Now the oxen are coming, the asses, the camels, the sheep, and the goats—coming in crowds to quench their thirst, and plunging into the streams before them. And the feathered tribes are coming, the turtle-dove, the pigeon, the swallow, the sparrow, the robin, and the wren; while the croaking raven, and the fierce-eyed eagle, scenting the water from afar, mingle with them round the rock.

"Brethren, this is but a faint emblem of the joy of the Church, in drinking the waters that descend from Calvary, the streams that gladden the city of our God. Go back to the day of Pentecost for an instance. Oh what a revolution of thought, and feeling, and character! What a change of countenance, and conscience, and heart! Three thousand men, that morning full of ignorance, and corruption, and guilt—idolaters, sensualists, blasphemers, persecutors— before night were perfectly transformed—the lions converted into lambs—the hard heart melted, the dead conscience quickened, and the whole man become a new creature in Christ Jesus! They thirsted, they found the 'Spiritual rock,' tasted its living waters, and suddenly leaped into new life, like Lazarus from the inanition of the grave!

"This is the blessing which follows the Church through all her wanderings in the wilderness, accompanies her through the scorching desert of affliction, and the valley of the shadow of death; and when, at last, she shall come up out of great tribulation, her garments shall be found washed and made white in the blood of the Lamb; and the Lamb, who is in the midst of the throne, shall lead her to everlasting fountains, and she shall thirst no more!"

Among the great Welsh preachers, then, in closing, it will now be enough to say, that, without claiming for Christmas Evans pre-eminence above all his contemporaries, or countrymen, it may, with truth, be said, we have yet better means of forming an opinion of him than of any other. We have attempted to avail ourselves of such traditions, and stories of their pulpit ministration, and such fragments of their spoken words, as may convey some, if faint, still fair, idea of their powers. Even of Christmas Evans our knowledge is, by no means, ample, nor are there many of his sermons left to us; but such as we possess seem sufficient for the formation of as high an estimate, through the medium of criticism, and the press, as that which was formed by the flocking crowds, and thousands who deemed it one of their greatest privileges, and pleasures to listen to his living voice. And it must be admitted, we think, that these sermons are of that order which retains much of its power, when the voice through which it spoke is still. Welsh sermons, beyond almost any others, lose their vitality by the transference to the press, and no doubt this preacher suffers in this way, too; some, however, will not bear the printing machine at all, and when the voice ceases to speak, all which made them effective is gone. With these sermons it is, undoubtedly, otherwise, and from some of them it may, perhaps, even be possible to find models of the mould of thought, and the mode at once of arrangement, as well as the qualities of emotion, and expression, which make preaching successful, whether for converting, or comforting the souls of men. Nor is it less significant that this man, who exercised a ministry of immense usefulness for more than half a century, and retained his power over men, with the same average freshness, and splendour until within four days of his death, did so in virtue of the living freshness of his heart, and mind. Like such men as John Bunyan, and Richard Baxter, no University could claim him, for he was of none; he had graduated in no college, had sat before no academical prelections, and was decorated with no diplomas,—only the Divine Spirit was master of the college in which he was schooled. We write this with no desire to speak disparagingly of such training, but, rather, to bring out into conspicuous honour the strength of this self-formed, severely toiling, and nobly suffering man. He was a spiritual athlete in labours more abundant; perhaps it might seem that the "one-eyed man of Anglesea," as he was so familiarly called, until this designation yielded to the more affectionate term of "Old Christmas," throughout the Principality—must have been in bodily presence contemptible; but if his appearance was rugged, we suppose it could scarcely have been less than royal,—a man the spell of whose name, when he came into a neighbourhood, could wake up all the sleepy villages, and bid their inhabitants pour along, up by the hills, and down by the valleys, expectant crowds watching his appearance with tears, and sometimes hailing him with shouts—must have been something like a king among men. We have seen how poor he was, and how indifferent to all that the world regarded as wealth, but he was one of those of whom the apostle speaks "as poor, yet making many rich, as having nothing, and yet possessing all things." And thus, from every consideration, whether we regard his singular genius, so truly national, and representative of the mind, and character of his country, his indomitable struggles, and earnest self-training, his extraordinary power over his congregations, his long, earnest life of self-denying usefulness, especially his intense reality, the holy purity, and consecration of his soul, Christmas Evans deserves our reverent memory while we glorify God in him.

APPENDATORY.
SELECTION OF ILLUSTRATIVE SERMONS.

AND now, although the various, and several selections we have given in the different preceding sections of this volume, may assist the reader in forming some idea of the manner, and method of Christmas Evans, before closing the volume we will present some selections from entire sermons, translated from the Welsh; and while, of course, labouring beneath the disadvantages of translation, we trust they will not unfavourably represent those various attributes of pulpit power, for which we have given the great preacher credit.

SERMON I.—THE TIME OF REFORMATION.

SERMON II.—THE PURIFICATION OF THE CONSCIENCE.

SERMON III.—FINISHED REDEMPTION.

SERMON IV.—THE FATHER AND SON GLORIFIED.

SERMON V.—THE CEDAR OF GOD.

SERMON I.
THE TIME OF REFORMATION.

"Until the time of reformation."—HEB. ix. 10.

The ceremonies pertaining to the service of God, under Sinaitic dispensation, were entirely typical in their character; mere figures of Christ, the "Highpriest of good things to come, by a greater, and more perfect tabernacle, not made with hands;" who, "not by the blood of goats, and calves, but by His own blood, has entered once into the holy place, having obtained eternal redemption for us." Sustaining such a relation to other ages, and events, they were necessarily imperfect, consisting "only in meats, and drinks, and divers washings, and carnal ordinances," not intended for perpetual observance, but imposed upon the Jewish people merely "until the time of reformation," when the shadow should give place to the substance, and a Greater than Moses should "make all things new." Let us notice the time of reformation, and the reformation itself.

I. Time may be divided into three parts; the Golden Age before the fall, the Iron Age after the fall, and the Messiah's Age of Jubilee.

In the Golden Age, the heavens, and the earth were created; the Garden of Eden was planted; man was made in the image of God, and placed in the garden, to dress, and keep it; matrimony was instituted; and God, resting from His labour, sanctified the seventh day, as a day of holy rest to man.

The Iron Age was introduced by the temptation of a foreigner, who obtruded himself into Paradise, and persuaded its happy denizens to cast off the golden yoke of obedience, and love to God. Man, desiring independence, became a rebel against heaven, a miserable captive of sin, and Satan, obnoxious to the Divine displeasure, and exposed to eternal death. The law was violated; the image of God was lost, and the enemy came in like a flood. All communication between the island of Time, and the continent of Immortality was cut off, and the unhappy exiles saw no hope of crossing the ocean that intervened.

The Messiah's Age may be divided into three parts; the time of Preparation, the time of Actual War, and the time of Victory and Triumph.

The Preparation began with the dawning of the day in Eden, when the Messiah came in the ship of the Promise, and landed on the island of Time, and notified its inhabitants of His gracious intention to visit them again, and assume their nature, and live and die among them; to break their covenant allegiance to the prince of the iron yoke; and deliver to them the charter, signed, and sealed with His own blood, for the redemption, and renovation of their island, and the restoration of its suspended intercourse with the land of Eternal Life. The motto inscribed upon the banners of this age was,— "He shall bruise thy heel, and Thou shalt bruise his head." Here Jehovah thundered forth His hatred of sin from the thick darkness, and wrote His curse in fire upon the face of heaven; while rivers of sacrificial blood proclaimed the miserable state of man, and his need of a costlier atonement than mere humanity could offer. Here, also, the spirit of Messiah fell upon the prophets, leading them to search diligently for the way of deliverance, and enabling them to "testify beforehand of the sufferings of Christ, and the glory that should follow."

Then came the season of Actual War. "Messiah the Prince" was born in Bethlehem, wrapped in swaddling bands, and laid in a manger,—the Great Deliverer, "made of a woman, made under the law, to redeem those that were under the law, that we might receive the adoption of sons." With His almighty hand, He laid hold on the works of the devil, unlocked the iron furnace, and broke the brazen bands asunder. He opened His mouth, and the deaf heard, the blind saw, the dumb spoke, the lame walked, and the lepers were cleansed. In the house of Jairus, in the street of Nain, and in the burial ground of Bethany, His word was mightier than death; and the damsel on her bed, the young man on his bier, and Lazarus in his tomb, rising to second life, were but the earnests of His future triumph. The diseases of sin He healed, the iron chains of guilt He shattered, and all the horrible caves of human corruption, and misery were opened by the Heavenly Warrior. He took our yoke, and bore it away upon His own shoulder, and cast it, broken, into the bottomless pit. He felt in His hands, and feet, the nails, and in His side the spear. The iron entered into His soul, but the corrosive power of His blood destroyed it, and shall ultimately eat away all the iron in the kingdom of death. Behold Him hanging on Calvary, nailing upon His cross three bills, the handwriting of the law which was against us, the oath of our allegiance to the prince of darkness, and the charter of the "everlasting covenant;" fulfilling the first, breaking the second, and sealing the third with His blood!

Now begins the scene of Victory and Triumph. On the morning of the third day, the Conqueror is seen "coming from Edom, with dyed garments from Bozrah." He has "trodden the winepress alone." By the might of His single arm He has routed the hosts of hell, and spoiled the dominions of death. The iron castle of the foe is demolished, and the Hero returns from the war, "glorious in His apparel, travelling in the greatness of His strength." He enters the gates of the everlasting city, amid the rejoicing of angels, and the shouts of His redeemed. And still He rides forth in the chariot of His grace, "conquering, and to conquer." A two-edged sword issues from His mouth, and, in His train, follow the victorious armies of heaven. Lo! before Him fall the altars of idols, and the temples of devils; and the slaves of sin are becoming the servants, and sons of the living God; and the proud sceptic beholds, wonders, believes, and adores; and the blasphemer begins to pray, and the persecutor is melted into penitence, and love, and the wolf comes, and lays him down gently by the side of the lamb. And Messiah shall never quit the field, till He has completed the conquest, and swallowed up death in victory. In His "vesture dipped in blood," He shall pursue the armies of Gog and Magog on the field of Amageddon, and break the iron teeth of the beast of power, and cast down Babylon as a mill-stone into the sea, and bind the old serpent in the lake of fire, and brimstone, and raise up to life immortal the tenants of the grave. Then shall the New Jerusalem, the metropolis of Messiah's golden empire, descend from heaven, adorned with all the jewellery of creation, guarded at every gate by angelic sentinels, and enlightened by the glory of God, and of the Lamb; and the faithful shall dwell within its walls, and sin, and sorrow, and death, shall be shut out for ever!

Then shall Time be swallowed up in Eternity. The righteous shall inherit life everlasting, and the ungodly shall find their portion in the second death. Time is the age of the visible world; eternity is the age of the invisible God. All things in time are changeful; all things in eternity are immutable. If you pass from time to eternity, without faith in Christ, without love in God, an enemy to prayer, an enemy to holiness, "impurged and unforgiven," so you must ever remain. Now is the season of that blessed change, for which myriads shall sing everlasting anthems of praise. "To-day, if ye will hear His voice, harden not your hearts." To-day the office is open: if you have any business with the Governor, make no delay. Now He has time to talk with the woman of Samaria by the well, and the penitent thief upon the cross. Now He is ready to forgive your sins, and renew your souls, and make you meet to become the partakers of the inheritance of the saints in light. Now He waits to wash the filthy, and feed the hungry, and clothe the naked, and raise the humble, and quicken the spiritually dead, and enrich the poor, and wretched, and reconcile enemies by His blood. He came to unloose your bands, and open to you the gates of Eden; condemned for your acquittal, and slain for the recovery of your forfeited immortality. The design of all the travelling from heaven to earth, and from earth to heaven, is the salvation of that which was lost, the restoration of intercourse, and amity between the Maker and the worm. This is the chief of the ways of God to man, ancient in its origin, wise in its contrivance, dear in its accomplishment, powerful in its application, gracious in its influence, and everlasting in its results. Christ is riding in His chariot of salvation, through the land of destruction, and death, clothed in the majesty of mercy, and offering eternal life to all who will believe. O captives of evil! now is the accepted time; now is the day of salvation; now is the year of Jubilee; now is the age of deliverance; now is "the time of reformation."

II. All the prophets speak of something within the veil, to be manifested in due time; the advent of a Divine agent in a future age, to accomplish a glorious "reformation." They represent him as a prince, a hero, a high priest, a branch growing out of dry ground, a child toying with the asp, and the lion, and leading the wolf, and the lamb together. The bill of the reformation had been repeatedly read by the prophets, and its passage required the descent of the Lord from heaven. None but Himself could effect the change of the dispensation. None but Himself had the authority and the power to remove the first, and establish the second. He whose voice once shook the earth, speaks again, and heaven is shaken. He whose footsteps once kindled Sinai into flame, descends again, and Calvary is red with blood. The God of the ancient covenant introduces anew, which is to abide for ever. The Lord of the temple alone could change the furniture, and the service from the original pattern shown to Moses on the mount; and six days before the rending of the veil, significant of abrogation of the old ceremonial, Moses came down upon a mountain in Palestine to deliver up the pattern to Him of whom he had received it on Sinai, that He might nail it to the cross on Calvary; for the "gifts and sacrifices" belonging to the legal dispensation, "could not make him that did the service perfect, as pertaining to the conscience; which stood only in meats, and drinks, and divers washings, and carnal ordinances, imposed on them until the time of reformation."

This reformation signifieth "the removal of those things that are shaken, as of things that are made, that those things which cannot be shaken may remain;" the abrogation of "carnal ordinances," which were local, and temporal in their nature, to make room for a spiritual worship, of universal, and perpetual adaptation. Henceforth the blood of bulls, and goats is superseded by the great reconciling sacrifice of the Lamb of God, and outward forms, and ceremonies give place to the inward operations of a renovating, and purifying Spirit.

To the Jewish Church, the covenant of Sinai was a sort of starry heaven. The Shekinah was its sun; the holy festivals, its moon; and prophets, priests, and kings, its stars. But Messiah, when He came, shook them all from their spheres, and filled the firmament Himself. He is our "Bright and Morning Star;" the "Sun of Righteousness," rising upon us "with healing in His wings."

The old covenant was an accuser, and a judge, but offered no pardon to the guilty. It revealed the corruption of the natural heart, but provided no renovating, and sanctifying grace. It was a natural institution, for special benefit of the seed of Abraham. It was a small vessel, trading only with the land of Canaan. It secured, to a few, the temporal blessings of the promised possession, but never delivered a single soul from eternal death, never bore a single soul over to the heavenly inheritance. But the new covenant is a covenant of grace, and mercy, proffering forgiveness, and a clean heart, not on the ground of any carnal relationship, but solely through faith in Jesus Christ. Christianity is a personal concern between each man, and his God, and none but the penitent believer has any right to its spiritual privileges. It is adapted to Gentiles, as well as Jews, "even as many as the Lord our God shall call." Already has it rescued myriads from the bondage of sin, and conveyed them over to the land of immortality; and its voyages of grace shall continue to the end of time, "bringing many sons to glory."

"Old things are passed away, and all things are become new." The circumcision of the flesh, made with hands, has given place to the circumcision of the heart by the Holy Ghost. The Shekinah has departed from Mount Zion, but its glory is illuminating the world. The Sword of Joshua is returned to its scabbard; and "the sword of the Spirit, which is the word of God," issues from the mouth of Messiah, and subdues the people under Him. The glorious High-priesthood of Christ has superseded sacerdotal office among men. Aaron was removed from the altar by death before his work was finished; but our High-priest still wears His sacrificial vestments, and death hath established Him before the mercy-seat, "a Priest for ever, after the order of Melchisedec." The earthquake which shook Mount Calvary, and rent the veil of the temple, demolished "the middle wall of partition" between Jews and Gentiles. The incense which Jesus offered fills the temple, and the land of Judea cannot confine its fragrance. The fountain which burst forth in Jerusalem, has sent out its living streams into every land; and the heat of summer cannot dry them up, nor the frosts of winter congeal them.

In short, all the vessels of the sanctuary are taken away by the Lord of the temple. The "twelve oxen," bearing the "molten sea," have given place to "the twelve Apostles of the Lamb," proclaiming "the washing of regeneration, and renewing of the Holy Ghost." The sprinkled mercy-seat, with its over-shadowing, and intensely-gazing cherubim, has given place to "the throne of grace," stained with the blood of a costlier sacrifice, into which the angels desire to look. The priest, the altar, the burnt-offering, the table of shew-bread, and the golden candlestick, have given place to the better things of the new dispensation introduced by the Son of God, of which they were only the figures, and the types. Behold, the glory has gone up from the temple, and rests upon Jesus on Mount Tabor; and Moses, and Elias are there, with Peter, and James, and John; and the representatives of the old covenant are communing with the Apostles of the new, and the transfigured Christ is the medium of the communication; and a voice of majestic music, issuing from "the excellent glory," proclaims—"This is my beloved Son, hear ye Him."

"God, who at sundry times, and in divers manners spake unto our fathers by the prophets, hath in these last days spoken unto us by His Son." Behold Him nailed to the Cross, and hear Him cry—"It is finished!" The voice which shook Sinai is shaking Calvary. Heaven and hell are in conflict, and earth trembles at the shock of battle. The Prince of Life expires, and the sun puts on his robes of mourning. Gabriel! descend from heaven, and explain to us the wondrous emblem! As set the sun at noon on Golgotha, making preternatural night throughout the land of Palestine, so shall the empire of sin, and death be darkened, and their light shall be quenched at meridian. As the Sun of Righteousness, rising from the night of the grave on the third morning, brings life, and immortality to light; so shall "the day-spring from on high" yet dawn upon our gloomy vale, and "the power of His resurrection" shall reanimate the dust of every cemetery!

He that sitteth upon the throne hath spoken—"Behold, I make all things new." The reformation includes not only the abrogation of the old, but also the introduction of the new. It gives us a new Mediator, a new covenant of grace, a new way of salvation, a new heart of flesh, a new heaven and a new earth. It has established a new union, by a new medium, between God, and man. "The Word was made flesh, and dwelt among us, and we beheld His glory, the glory as of the only-begotten of the Father, full of grace and truth." "Forasmuch as the children were partakers of flesh and blood, He also Himself likewise took part of the same." "God was manifest in the flesh, justified in the spirit, seen of angels, preached unto the Gentiles, believed on in the world, received up into glory." Here was a new thing under the sun;

the "Son of man" bearing the "express image" of the living God; bearing it untarnished through the world; through the temptations and sorrows of such a wilderness as humanity never trod before; through the unknown agony of Olivet, and the supernatural gloom of Golgotha, and the dark dominion of the king of terrors: to the Heaven of heavens; where He sits, the adorable representative of two worlds, the union of God and man! Thence He sends forth the Holy Spirit, to collect "the travail of His soul," and lead them into all truth, and bring them to Zion with songs of everlasting joy. See them, the redeemed of the Lord, flocking as returning doves upon the wing, "to the heavenly Jerusalem, the city of the living God; and to the spirits of just men made perfect; and to an innumerable company of angels; and to Jesus, the Mediator of the new covenant; and to the blood of sprinkling, that speaketh better things than that of Abel."

Oh, join the joyful multitude! the year of jubilee is come. The veil is rent asunder. The way into the holiest is laid open. The blood of Jesus is on the mercy-seat. The Lamb newly slain is in the midst of the throne. Go ye, with boldness, into His gracious presence. Lo, the King is your brother, and for you has He stained His robe with blood! The robe alone can clothe your naked souls, and shield them in the day of burning. Awake! awake! put on the Lord Jesus Christ! The covenant of Sinai cannot save you from wrath. Descent from Abraham cannot entitle you to the kingdom of heaven. "Ye must be born again," "born not of the flesh, nor of the will of men, but of God." You must have a new heart, and become a new creation in Jesus Christ. This is the promise of the Father,

> "This is the dear redeeming grace,
> For every sinner free."

Many reformations have expired with the reformers. But our Great Reformer "ever liveth" to carry on His reformation, till His enemies become His footstool, and death and hell are cast into the lake of fire. He will finish the building of His Church. When He laid "the chief corner-stone" on Calvary, the shock jarred the earth, and awoke the dead, and shook the nether world with terror; but when He shall bring forth the top stone with shoutings of "Grace!" the dominion of Death and Hades shall perish, and the last captive shall escape, and the song of the bursting sepulchre shall be sweeter than the chorus of the morning stars! Even now, there are new things in heaven; the Lamb from the slaughter, alive "in the midst of the throne;" worshipped by innumerable seraphim and cherubim, and adored by the redeemed from earth; His name the wonder of angels, the terror of devils, and the hope of men; His praise the "new song," which shall constitute the employment of eternity!

SERMON II.
THE PURIFICATION OF THE CONSCIENCE.

> "*How much more shall the blood of Christ, who, through the eternal Spirit, offered Himself without spot to God, purge your conscience from dead works to serve the living God.*"—HEB. ix. 14.

The Hebrew Christians, to whom the Apostle wrote, were well acquainted with the laws of ceremonial purification by the blood of beasts, and birds, for by blood almost everything was purified in the service of the Temple. But it is only the blood of Christ that can purge the human conscience. In speaking of this purification, as presented in our text, let us notice—*the object, the means*, and *the end*.

I. The object of this purification is the conscience; which all the sacrificial blood shed, from the gate of Eden down to the extinction of the fire on the Jewish altar, was not sufficient to purge.

What is the conscience? An inferior judge, the representative of Jehovah, holding his court in the human soul; according to whose decision we feel either confidence, and joy in God, or condemnation, and tormenting fear. His judicial power is graduated by the degree of moral and evangelical light which has been shed upon his palace. His knowledge of the will, and character of God is the law by which he justifies, or condemns. His intelligence is the measure of his authority; and the perfection of knowledge would be the infallibility of conscience.

This faithful recorder, and deputy judge is with us through all the journey of life, and will accompany us with his register over the river Jordan, whether to Abraham's bosom or the society of the rich man in hell. While conscience keeps a record on earth, Jehovah keeps a record in heaven; and when both books shall be opened in the final judgment, there shall be found a perfect correspondence. When temptations are presented, the understanding opposes them, but the carnal mind indulges them, and there is a contest between the judgment, and the will, and we hesitate which to obey, till the warning bell of conscience rings through the soul, and gives distinct notice of his awful recognition; and when we turn away recklessly from his faithful admonitions, we hear low mutterings of wrath stealing along the avenues, and the quick sound of writing-pens in the recording office, causing every denizen of the mental palace to tremble.

There is a *good conscience, and an evil conscience.* The work of both, however, is the same; consisting in keeping a true record of the actions of men, and passing sentence upon them according to their deserts. Conscience is called good, or evil only with reference to the character of its record, and its sentence. If the record is one of virtues, and the sentence one of approval, the conscience is good; if the record is one of vices, and the sentence one of condemnation, the conscience is evil.

Some have a *guilty conscience*, that is, a conscience that holds up to their view a black catalogue of crimes, and rings in their ears a sentence of condemnation. If you have such a conscience, you are invited to Jesus, that you may find peace to your souls. He is ever in His office, receiving all who come, and blotting out, with His own blood, the handwriting which is against them.

But some have a *despairing conscience*. They think that their crimes are too great to be forgiven. The registry of guilt, and the decree of death, hide from their eyes the mercy of God, and the merit of Christ. Their sins rise like mountains between them, and heaven. But let them look away to Calvary. If their sins are a thousand times more numerous than their tears, the blood of Jesus is ten thousand times more powerful than their sins. "He is able to save to the uttermost all that come unto God by Him, seeing He ever liveth to make intercession for them."

And others have a *dark, and hardened conscience*. They are so deceived, that they "cry peace, and safety, when destruction is at the door." They are "past feeling, having the conscience seared as with a hot iron." They have sold themselves to work evil; to eat sin like bread, and drink iniquity like water. They have bribed, or gagged the recorder, and accuser within them. They will betray the just cause of the righteous, and slay the messengers of salvation, and think that they are doing God service. John the Baptist is beheaded, that Herod may keep his oath of honour. A dead fish cannot swim against the stream; but if the king's conscience had been alive and faithful, he would have said:—"Girl, I promised to give thee thy request, even to the half of my kingdom; but thou hast requested too much; for the head of Messiah's herald is more valuable than my whole kingdom, and all the kingdoms of the world!" But he had not the fear of God before his eyes, and the proud fool sent, and beheaded the prophet in his cell.

A *good conscience* is a faithful conscience, a lively conscience, a peaceful conscience, a conscience void of offence toward God, and man, resting in the shadow of the cross, and assured of an interest in His infinite merit. It is the victory of faith unfeigned, working by love, and purifying the heart. It is always found in the neighbourhood, and society of its brethren, "a broken heart and a contrite spirit;" an intense hatred of sin, and an ardent love of holiness; a spirit of fervent prayer, and supplication, and a life of scrupulous integrity, and charity; and above all, a humble confidence in the mercy of God, through the mediation of Christ. These constitute the brotherhood of Christianity; and wherever they abound, a good conscience is never lacking. They are its very element, and life; its food, its sunshine, and its vital air.

Conscience was a faithful recorder, and judge under the law, and notwithstanding the revolution which has taken place, introducing a new constitution, and a new administration, Conscience still retains his office; and when "purged from dead works to serve the living God," is appropriately called a *good conscience*.

II. The means of this purification is "the blood of Christ, who through the Eternal Spirit offered Himself without spot to God."

Could we take in, at a single view, all the bearings of "the blood of Christ," as exhibited in the Gospel, what an astonishing light would it cast upon the condition of man; the character of God; the nature, and requirements of His law; the dreadful consequences of sin; the wondrous expiation of the cross; the reconciliation of Heaven, and earth; the blessed union of the believer with God in Christ, as a just God, and a Saviour; and the whole scheme of our justification, sanctification, and redemption, through free, sovereign, infinite, and unspeakable grace!

There is no knowledge like the knowledge of Christ, for the excellency of which the apostle counted all things but loss. Christ is the Sun of Righteousness, in whose light we see the tops of the mountains of immortality, towering above the dense clouds which overhang the valley of death. All the wisdom which philosophers have learned from nature, and providence, compared with that which is afforded by the Christian revelation, is like the *ignis fatuus*, compared with the sun. The knowledge of Plato, and Socrates, and all the renowned sages of antiquity, was nothing to the knowledge of the feeblest believer in "the blood of Christ."

"The blood of Christ" is of infinite value. There is none like it flowing in human veins. It was the blood of a man, but of a man who knew no iniquity; the blood of a sinless humanity, in which dwelt all the fulness of the Godhead bodily; the blood of the second Adam, who is the Lord from Heaven, and a quickening Spirit upon earth. It pressed through every pore of His body in the garden; and gushed from His head, His hands, His feet, and His side, upon the cross. I approach with fear, and trembling, yet with humble confidence, and joy. I take off my shoes, like Moses, as he approaches the burning bush; for I hear a voice coming forth from the altar, saying, "I and my Father are one; I am the true God, and Eternal Life."

The expression, "the blood of Christ," includes the whole of His obedience to the moral law, by the imputation of which we are justified; and all the sufferings of His soul and His body as our Mediator, by which an atonement is made for our sins, and a fountain opened to wash them all away. This is the spring whence rise the rivers of forgiving and sanctifying grace.

In the representation which the text gives us of this redeeming blood, are several points worthy of our special consideration:—

1. It is *"the blood of Christ;"* the appointed Substitute and Saviour of men; "the Lamb that taketh away the sins of the world."

2. It is the blood of Christ, *who offered Himself.* His humanity was the only sacrifice which would answer the demands of justice, and atone for the transgressions of mankind. Therefore "He has made His soul an offering for sin."

3. It is the blood of Christ, who offered Himself *to God.* It was the eternal Father, whose broken law must be repaired, whose dishonest government must be vindicated, and whose flaming indignation must be turned away. The well-beloved Son must meet the Father's frown, and bear the Father's curse for us. All the Divine attributes called for the offering; and without it, could not be reconciled to the sinner.

4. It is the blood of Christ, who offered Himself to God, *without spot.* This was a perfect sacrifice. The Victim was without blemish, or defect; the altar was complete in all its appurtenances; and the High Priest possessed every conceivable qualification for his work. Christ was at once victim, altar, and high-priest; "holy, harmless, and undefiled"—"God manifest in the flesh." Being Himself perfect God and perfect man, and perfect Mediator between God and man, He perfects for ever all them that believe.

5. It is the blood of Christ, who offered Himself to God, without spot, *through the eternal Spirit.* By the eternal Spirit, here, we are to understand, not the third Person of the Godhead, but the second; Christ's own Divine nature, which was co-eternal with the Father before the world was, and which, in the fulness of time, seized on humanity—sinless, and immaculate humanity—and offered it, body, and soul, as a sacrifice for human sins. The eternal Spirit was at once the priest that offered the victim, and the altar that sanctified the offering. Without His agency, there could have been no atonement. The offering of mere humanity, however spotless, aside from the merit derived from its connection with Divinity, could not have been a sacrifice of sweet-smelling savour unto God.

6. It is the blood of Christ, who offered Himself to God, without spot, through the eternal Spirit, *that He might purge your conscience.* As the typical sacrifices under the law purified men from ceremonial defilement, so the real sacrifice of the Gospel saves the believer from moral pollution. Blood was the life of all the services of the tabernacle made with hands, and gave significance, and utility to all the rites of the former dispensation. By blood

the covenant between God, and His people was sealed. By blood the officers, and vessels of the sanctuary were consecrated. By blood the children of Israel were preserved in Egypt from the destroying angel. So the blood of Christ is our justification, sanctification, and redemption. All the blessings of the Gospel flow to us through the blood of the Lamb. Mercy, when she writes our pardon, and when she registers our names in "the Book of Life," dips her pen in the blood of the Lamb. And the vast company that John saw before the throne had come out of great tribulation, having "washed their robes and made them white in the blood of the Lamb."

The children of Israel were delivered from Egypt, on the very night that the paschal lamb was slain, and its blood sprinkled upon the doorposts, as if their liberty, and life were procured by its death. This typified the necessity, and power of the Atonement, which is the very heart of the Gospel, and the spiritual life of the believer. In Egypt, however, there was a lamb slain for every family; but under the new covenant God has but one family, and one Lamb is sufficient for their salvation.

In the cleansing of the leper, several things were necessary; as running water, cedar wood, scarlet, and hyssop, and the finger of the priest; but it was the blood that gave efficacy to the whole. So it is in the purification of the conscience. Without the shedding of blood, the leper could not be cleansed; without the shedding of blood, the conscience cannot be purged. "The blood of Christ" seals every precept, every promise, every warning, of the New Testament. "The blood of Christ" renders the Scriptures "profitable for doctrine, for reproof, for correction, for instruction in righteousness." "The blood of Christ" gives efficiency to the pulpit; and when "Jesus Christ and Him crucified" is shut out, the virtue is wanting which heals, and restores the soul. It is only through the crucifixion of Christ that "the old man" is crucified in the believer. It is only through His obedience unto death, even the death of the cross, that our dead souls are quickened, to serve God in newness of life.

Here rest our hopes. "The foundation of God standeth sure." The bill of redemption being presented by Christ, was read by the prophets, and passed unanimously in both houses of parliament. It had its final reading in the lower house, when Messiah hung on Calvary; and passed three days afterward, when He rose from the dead. It was introduced to the upper house by the Son of God Himself, who appeared before the throne "as a lamb newly slain," and was carried by acclamation of the heavenly hosts. Then it became a law of the Kingdom of Heaven, and the Holy Ghost was sent down to establish it in the hearts of men. It is "the perfect law of liberty," by which God is reconciling the world unto Himself. It is "the law of the Spirit of life," by which He is "purging our conscience from dead works to serve the living God."

III. The end of this purification is twofold,—that we may cease from dead works, and serve the living God.

1. The works of unrenewed souls are all "dead works," can be no other than "dead works," because the agents are "dead in trespasses and sins." They proceed from the "carnal mind," which "is enmity against God," which "is not subject to the law of God, neither indeed can be." How can a corrupt tree bring forth good fruit, or a corrupt fountain send forth pure water?

But "the blood of Christ" is intended to "purge the conscience from dead works." The apostle says—"Ye are not redeemed with corruptible things, as silver, and gold, from your vain conversation, received by tradition from your fathers; but with the precious blood of Christ, as of a Lamb without blemish, and without spot." The Jews were in a state of bondage to the ceremonial law, toiling at the "dead works," the vain, and empty forms, which could never take away sin; and unjustified, and unregenerate men are still captives of Satan, slaves of sin, and death, tyrannized over by various evil habits, and propensities, which are invincible to all things but "the blood of Christ." He died to redeem, both from the burdens of the Mosaic ritual, and from the despotism of moral evil—to purge the conscience of both Jew, and Gentile "from dead works to serve the living God."

2. We cannot "serve the living God" without this preparatory purification of conscience. If our guilt is uncancelled—if the love of sin is not dethroned—the service of the knee, and the lip is nothing but hypocrisy. "If we regard iniquity in our hearts, the Lord will not hear us." Cherishing what He hates, all our offerings are an abomination to Him; and we can no more stand in His holy presence than the dry stubble can stand before a flaming fire. He who has an evil conscience flees from the face of God, as did Adam in the garden. Nothing but "the blood of Christ," applied by the Holy Spirit, can remove the sinner's guilty fear, and enable him to draw nigh to God, in the humble confidence of acceptance through the Beloved.

The service of the living God must flow from a new principle of life in the soul. The Divine word must be the rule of our actions. The Divine will must be consulted and obeyed. We must remember that God is holy, and jealous of His honour. The consideration that He is everywhere, and sees everything, and will bring every work into judgment, must fill us with reverence and godly fear. An ardent love for His law, and His character must supplant the love of sin, and prompt to a cheerful and impartial obedience.

And let us remember that he is "the *living* God." Pharaoh is dead, Herod is dead, Nero is dead; but Jehovah is "the living God." And it is a fearful thing to have Him for an enemy. Death cannot deliver from His hand. Time, and even eternity, cannot limit His holy anger. He has manifested, in a thousand instances, His hatred of sin: in the destruction of the old world, the burning of Sodom, and Gomorrah, the drowning of Pharaoh and his host in the sea; and I tell thee, sinner, except thou repent, thou shalt likewise perish! Oh, think what punishment "the living God" can inflict upon His adversaries—the loss of all good—the endurance of all evil—the undying worm—the unquenchable fire—the blackness of darkness for ever!

The gods of the heathen have no life in them, and they that worship them are like unto them. But our God is "the living God," and "the God of the living." If you are united to Him by faith in "the blood of Christ," your souls are "quickened together with Him," and "the power which raised Him from the dead shall also quicken your mortal body."

May the Lord awaken those who are dead in trespasses, and sins, and revive His work in the midst of the years, and strengthen the feeble graces of His people, and bless abundantly the labours of His servants, so that many consciences may be purged from dead works to serve the living God!

> "There is a fountain filled with blood,
>   Drawn from Emmanuel's veins,
> And sinners, plunged beneath that flood,
>   Lose all their guilty stains.
>
> "The dying thief rejoiced to see
>   That fountain in his day;
> And there may I, as vile as he,
>   Wash all my sins away.
>
> "Dear dying Lamb! Thy precious blood
>   Shall never lose its power,
> Till all the ransomed sons of God
>   Are saved, to sin no more."

SERMON III.
FINISHED REDEMPTION.

> "*It is finished.*"—JOHN xix. 30.

This exclamation derives all its importance from the magnitude of the work alluded to, and the glorious character of the Agent. The work is the redemption of the world; the Agent is God, manifested in the flesh. He who finished the creation of the heavens, and the earth in six days, is laying the foundation of a new creation on Calvary. Four thousand years He has been giving notice of His intention to mankind; more than thirty years He has been personally upon earth, preparing the material; and now He lays the chief corner-stone in Zion, exclaiming—"It is finished."

We will consider the special import of the exclamation, and then offer a few remarks of a more general character.

I. "It is finished." This saying of the Son of God is a very striking one; and, uttered, as it was, while He hung in dying agonies on the cross, cannot fail to make a strong impression upon the mind. It is natural for us to inquire— "What does it mean? To what does the glorious Victim refer?" A complete answer to the question would develop the whole scheme of redemption. We can only glance at a few leading ideas.

The sufferings of Christ are ended. Never again shall He be persecuted from city to city, as an impostor, and servant of Satan. Never again shall He say, "My soul is exceeding sorrowful, even unto death." Never again shall He agonize in Gethsemane, and sweat great drops of blood. Never again shall He be derided by the rabble, and insulted by men in power. Never again shall He be crowned with thorns, lacerated by the scourge, and nailed to the accursed tree. Never again shall He cry out, in the anguish of His soul, and the baptism of blood—"My God! my God! why hast Thou forsaken me!"

The predictions of His death are fulfilled. The prophets had spoken of His crucifixion many hundred years before His birth. They foresaw the Governor who was to come forth from Bethlehem. They knew the Babe in the manger, as He whose goings forth are of old, even from everlasting. They drew an accurate chart of His travels, from the manger to the cross, and from the cross to the throne. All these things must be fulfilled. Jesus knew the necessity, and seemed anxious that every jot, and tittle should receive an exact accomplishment. His whole life was a fulfilment of prophecy. On every path He walked, on every house He entered, on every city He visited, and especially on the mysterious phenomena which accompanied His crucifixion, it was written—"that the Scriptures might be fulfilled."

The great sacrifice for sin is accomplished. For this purpose Christ came into the world. He is our appointed High Priest, the elect of the Father, and the desire of the nations. He alone was in the bosom of the Father, and could offer a sacrifice of sufficient merit to atone for human transgression. But it was necessary also that He should have somewhat to offer. Therefore a body was prepared for Him. He assumed the seed of Abraham, and suffered in the flesh. This was a sacrifice of infinite value, being sanctified by the altar of Divinity on which it was offered. All the ceremonial sacrifices could not obtain the bond from the hand of the creditor. They were only acknowledgment of the debt. But Jesus, by one offering, paid the whole, took up the bond, the hand-writing that was against us, and nailed it to the cross; and when driving the last nail, He cried—"It is finished!"

The satisfaction of Divine justice is completed. The violated law must be vindicated; the deserved penalty must be endured; if not by the sinner himself, yet by the sinner's Substitute. This was the great undertaking of the Son of God. He "bore our sins"—that is, the punishment of our sins—"in His own body on the tree." He was "made a curse for us, that we might be made the righteousness of God in him." There was no other way by which the honour of God and the dignity of His law could be sustained, and therefore "the Lord laid upon Him the iniquities of us all." He "died unto sin once;" not merely for sin, enduring its punishment in our stead; but also "unto sin," abolishing its power, and putting it away. Therefore it is said, He "made an end of sin"—destroyed its condemning, and tormenting power on behalf of all them that believe His sufferings were equal to the claims of justice; and His dying cry was the voice of Justice Himself proclaiming the satisfaction. Here, then, may the dying thief, and the persecutor of the holy, lay down their load of guilt, and woe at the foot of the cross.

The new, and living way to God is consecrated. A veil has hitherto concealed the holy of holies. None but the High Priest has seen the ark of the covenant, and the glory of God resting upon the Mercy-seat between the cherubim. He alone might enter, and he but once a year, and then with fear, and trembling, and the sprinkling of atoning blood, after the most careful purification, and sacrifice for himself. He has filled His hands with His own blood, and entered into heaven itself, there to appear in the presence of God for us. The sweet incense which He offers fills the temple, and the merit of His sacrifice remains the same through all time, superseding all other offerings for ever. Therefore we are exhorted to come boldly to the throne of grace. The tunnel under the Thames could not be completed on account of an accident which greatly damaged the work, without a new subscription for raising money; but Jesus found infinite riches in Himself, sufficient for the completion of a new way to the Father—a living way through the valley of the shadow of death to "the city of the Great King."

The conquest of the powers of darkness is achieved. When their hour was come, the prince and his host were on the alert to accomplish the destruction of the Son of God. They hailed Him with peculiar temptations, and levelled against Him their heaviest artillery. They instigated one disciple to betray Him and another to deny Him. They fired the rage of the multitude against Him, so that the same tongues that lately sang, "Hosanna to the Son of David!" now shouted, "Crucify Him! crucify Him!" They filled the priests, and scribes with envy, that they might accuse Him without a cause; and inspired Pilate with an accursed ambition, that he might condemn him without a fault. They seared the conscience of the false witnesses, that they might charge the Just One with the most flagrant crimes; and cauterized the hearts of the Roman soldiers, that they might mock Him in His sufferings, and nail Him to the cross. Having succeeded so far in their hellish plot, they doubtless deemed their victory certain. I see them crowding around the cross, waiting impatiently to witness his last breath, ready to shout with infernal triumph to the depths of hell, till the brazen walls should send back their echoes to the gates of the heavenly city. But hark! the dying Saviour exclaims—"It is finished!" and the great dragon and his host retreat, howling, from the cross. The Prince of our Salvation turned back all their artillery upon themselves, and their own stratagems became their ruin. The old serpent seized Messiah's heel, but Messiah stamped upon the serpent's head. The dying cry of Jesus shook the dominions of death, so that the bodies of many that slept arose; and rang through all the depths of hell the knell of its departed power. Thus the Prince of this world was foiled in His schemes, and disappointed in his hopes, like the men of Gaza, when they locked up Samson at night, thinking to kill him in the morning: but awoke to find that he was gone, with the gates of the city upon his shoulders. When the Philistines caught Samson, and brought him to their Temple, to make sport for them, they never dreamed of the disaster in which it would result—never dreamed that their triumph over the poor blind captive would be the occasion of their destruction. "Suffer me," said he, "to lean on the two pillars." Then he bowed himself, and died with his enemies. So Christ on Calvary, while the powers of darkness exulted over their victim, seized the main pillars of sin, and death, and brought down the temple of Satan upon its occupants; but on the morning of the third day, He left them all in the ruins, where they shall remain for ever, and commenced His journey home to His Father's house.

II. So much concerning the import of our Saviour's exclamation. Such was the work He finished upon the cross. We add a few remarks of a more general character.

The sufferings of Christ were vicarious. He died, not for His own sins, but for ours. He humbled Himself, that we might be exalted. He became poor, that we might be made rich. He was wounded, that we might be healed. He drained the cup of wrath, that we might drink the waters of salvation. He died the shameful and excruciating death of the cross, that we might live and reign with Him for ever.

"Ought not Christ to have suffered these things, and to have entered into His glory?" This "ought" is the ought of mercy, and of covenant engagement. He must discharge the obligation which He had voluntarily assumed. He must finish the work which He had graciously begun. There was no other Saviour—no other being in the universe willing to undertake the work; or, if any willing to undertake, none able to accomplish it. The salvation of one human soul would have been too mighty an achievement for Gabriel—for all the angels in heaven. Had not "the only-begotten of the Father" become our Surety, we must have lain for ever under the wrath of God, amid "weeping, and wailing, and gnashing of teeth." None but the

Lion of the tribe of Judah could break the seals of that mysterious book. None but "God manifest in the flesh" could deliver us from the second death.

The dying cry of Jesus indicates the dignity of His nature, and the power of life that was in Him to the last. All men die of weakness—of inability to resist death—die because they can live no longer. But this was not the case with the Son of God. He speaks of laying down His life as His own voluntary act;—"No man taketh it from He, but I lie it down of myself. I have power to lay it down, and I have power to take it again." "He poured out His soul unto death"—did not wait for it to be torn from Him—did not hang languishing upon the cross, till life "ebbed out by slow degrees;" but poured it out freely, suddenly, and unexpectedly. As soon as the work was done for which He came into the world, He cried—"It is finished!" "bowed His head, and gave up the ghost." Then the sun was darkened, the earth quaked, the rocks rent, the graves opened, and the centurion said—"Truly, this Man was the Son of God!" He cried with a loud voice, to show that He was still unconquered by pain, mighty even upon the cross. He bowed His head that death might seize Him. He was naturally far above the reach of death, His Divine nature being self-existent and eternal, and His human nature entitled to immortality by its immaculate holiness; yet "He humbled Himself, and became obedient unto death, even the death of the cross"—"He bowed His head, and gave up the ghost."

We may regard this last exclamation, also, as an expression of His joy at having accomplished the great "travail of his soul," in the work of our redemption. It was the work which the Father had given Him, and which He had covenanted to do. It lay heavy upon His heart, and oh, how was He straitened till it was accomplished! His "soul was exceedingly sorrowful, even unto death;" "and His sweat, as it were, great drops of blood, falling down to the ground." But upon the cross, He saw of the travail of His soul, and was satisfied. He saw that His sacrifice was accepted, and the object of His agony secured—that death would not be able to detain Him in the grave, nor hell to defeat the purpose of His grace; that the gates of the eternal city would soon open to receive Him as a conqueror, and myriads of exultant angels shout Him to His throne; whither He would be followed by His redeemed, with songs of everlasting joy. He saw, and He was satisfied; and, not waiting for the morning of the third day, but already confident of victory, He uttered this note of triumph, and died.

And if we may suppose them to have understood its import, what a source of consolation it must have been to His sorrowing disciples! The sword had pierced through Mary's heart, according to the prediction of old Simeon over the infant Jesus. Her affections had bled at the agony of her supernatural Son, and her wounded faith had well-nigh perished at His cross. And how must all His followers have felt, standing afar off, and beholding their supposed Redeemer suffering as a malefactor! How must all their hopes have died within them, as they gazed on the accursed tree! The tragedy was mysterious, and they deemed their enemies victorious. Jesus is treading the winepress in Bozrah, and the earth is shaking, and the rocks are rending, and the luminaries of heaven are expiring, and all the powers of nature are fainting, in sympathy with His mighty agony. Now he is lost in the fire, and smoke of battle, and the dread artillery of justice is heard thundering through the thick darkness, and shouts of victory rise from the troops of hell, and who shall foretell the issue of the combat, or the fate of the Champion? But lo! He cometh forth from the cloud of battle, with blood upon His garments! He is wounded, but He hath the tread, and the aspect of a conqueror. He waves His crimsoned sword, and cries—"It is finished!" Courage, ye weepers at the cross! Courage, ye tremblers afar off! The Prince of your salvation is victor, and this bulletin of the war shall cheer myriads of believers in the house of their pilgrimage, and the achievement which it announces shall constitute an everlasting theme of praise.

"It is finished!" The word smote on the walls of the celestial city, and thrilled the hosts of heaven with ecstasy unspeakable. How must "the spirits of just men made perfect" have leaped for joy, to hear that the Captain of their salvation was victorious over all His enemies, and that the work He had engaged to do for them, and their brethren was completed! And with what wonder, and delight must the holy angels have witnessed the triumph of Him, whom they were commanded to worship, over the powers of darkness! It was the commencement of a new era in heaven, and never before had its happy denizens seen so much of God.

"It is finished!" Go, ye heralds of salvation, into all the world, and proclaim the joyful tidings! Cry aloud, and spare not; lift up your voice like a trumpet, and publish, to all men, that the work of the cross is finished—that the Great Mediator, "made perfect through sufferings," has become "the author of eternal salvation to all them that obey Him"—"is of God made unto us, wisdom, and righteousness, and sanctification, and redemption!" Go, teach the degraded pagan, the deluded Mohammedan, and the superstitious Papist, that the finished work of Jesus is the only way of acceptance with God. Go, tell the polished scholar, the profound philosopher, and the vaunting moralist, that the doctrine of Christ crucified is the only knowledge that can save the soul! Go,—say to the proud sceptic, the bold blasphemer, and the polluted libertine, "Behold the Lamb of God that taketh away the sin of the world." Preach it to the gasping sinner upon the death-bed, and the sullen murderer in his cell! Let it ring in every human ear, and thrill in every human heart, till the gladness of earth shall be the counterpart of heaven!

SERMON IV.
THE FATHER AND SON GLORIFIED.

> "*Howbeit, when He, the Spirit of Truth, is come, He will guide you into all truth; for He shall not speak of Himself, but whatsoever He shall hear, that shall He speak; and He will show you things to come. He shall glorify me: for He shall receive of mine, and shall show it unto you. All things that the Father hath are mine; therefore, said I, that He shall take of mine, and shall show it unto you.*"—JOHN xvi. 13–15.

The wonderful Providence, which brought the children of Israel out of the house of bondage, was a chain of many links, not one of which could be omitted without destroying the beauty, and defeating the end of the Divine economy. The family of Jacob came to Egypt in the time of famine—they multiply—they are oppressed—their cries reach to heaven—God manifests Himself in the burning bush—Moses is sent to Egypt—miracles are wrought by his hand—Pharaoh's heart is hardened—the firstborn are slain—the passover is eaten—the people depart, led by the pillar of God—the sea is divided—and, with many signs, and wonders, the thousands of Israel are conducted through the wilderness to the Promised Land. Had one of these links been wanting, the chain of deliverance had been defective.

So, in the salvation of sinners by Jesus Christ, all the conditions, and preparatives were essential to the completeness, and glory of the scheme. The Son of God must consent to undertake our cause, and become our substitute—the promise must be given to Adam, and frequently repeated to the patriarchs—bloody sacrifices must be instituted, to typify the vicarious sufferings of Messiah—a long line of prophets must foretell His advent, and the glory of His kingdom—He must be born in Bethlehem, crucified on Calvary, and buried in Joseph's new tomb—must rise from the dead, ascend to the right hand of the Father, and send down the Holy Spirit to guide and sanctify His Church. Without all these circumstances, the economy of redemption would have been incomplete and inefficient.

The last link in the chain is the mission and work of the Holy Spirit. This is quite as important as any of the rest. Our Saviour's heart seems to have been much set upon it, during all His ministry, and especially during the last few days, before His crucifixion. He spoke of it, frequently, to His disciples, and told them that He would not leave them comfortless, but would send them "another Comforter," who should abide with them for ever; and that His own departure was necessary, to prepare the way for the coming of the heavenly Paraclete. In our text, He describes the office of the Holy Spirit, and the specific relation which He sustains to the work of Salvation:—"Howbeit, when He, the Spirit of Truth, is come, He will guide you into all truth; for He shall not speak of Himself; but whatsoever He shall hear, that shall He speak; and He will show you things to come. He shall glorify me: for He shall receive of mine, and shall show it unto you. All things that the Father hath are mine; therefore said I, that He shall take of mine, and shall show it unto you."

These words teach us two important truths—*first*, that the Son is equal with the Father; and, *secondly*, that the Father, and the Son are alike glorified in the economy of salvation.

I. The Son claims equality with the Father. "All things that the Father hath are mine."

This sentence is very comprehensive, and sublime—an unquestionable affirmation of the Messiah's "eternal power, and Godhead." The same doctrine is taught us, in many other recorded sayings of Christ, and sustained by all the prophets, and apostles; and when I consider this declaration, in connection with the general strain of the inspired writers on the subject, I seem to hear the Saviour Himself addressing the world in the following manner:—

"All things that the Father hath are mine. His *names* are mine. I am Jehovah—the mighty God, and the everlasting Father—the Lord of Hosts—the Living God—the True God, and Eternal Life.

"His *works* are mine. All things were made by me, and I uphold all things by the word of my power. My Father worketh hitherto, and I work; for as the Father raiseth up the dead, and quickeneth them, even so the Son quickeneth whom He will. I am the Author of universal being, and my hand moveth all the machinery of Providence.

"His *honours* are mine. I have an indisputable right to the homage of all created intelligences. I inhabit the praises of Eternity. Before the foundation of the world, I was the object of angelic adoration; and when I became incarnate as a Saviour, the Father published His decree in heaven, saying—'Let all the angels of God worship Him!' It is His will, also, that all men should honour the Son, even as they honour the Father—in the same manner, and the same degree. He that honoureth the Son, honoureth the Father; and he that honoureth not the Son, honoureth not the Father: for I and my Father are one—one in honour—possessing joint interest, and authority.

"His *attributes* are mine. Though as man, and Mediator I am inferior to the Father; yet my nature is no more inferior to His, than the nature of the Prince of Wales is inferior to the nature of the King of England. You see me clothed in humanity; but, in my original state, I thought it not robbery to be equal with God. I was in the beginning with God, and possessed the same eternity of being. Like Him, I am almighty, omniscient, and immutable; infinite in holiness, justice, goodness, and truth. All these attributes, with every other possible perfection, belong to me, in the same sense as they belong to the Father. They are absolute, and independent, underived, and unoriginated—the essential qualities of my nature.

"His *riches of grace* are mine. I am the Mediator of the new covenant—the Channel of my Father's mercies to mankind. I have the keys of the House of David, and the seal of the Kingdom of Heaven. I have come from the bosom of the Father, freighted with the precious treasures of His good will to men. I have sailed over the sea of tribulation, and death, to bring you the wealth of the other world. I am the Father's Messenger, publishing peace on earth—a peace which I have purchased with my own blood upon the cross. It has pleased the Father that in me all fulness should dwell—all fulness of wisdom, and grace—whatever is necessary for the justification, sanctification, and redemption of them that believe. My Father, and I are one, in the work of salvation, as in the work of creation. We have the same will, and the same intention of mercy toward the children of the great captivity.

"The *objects of His love* are mine. He hath given them to me in an everlasting covenant. He hath given me the heathen for an inheritance, and the uttermost parts of the earth for a possession. They were mine by the original right of creation; but now they are doubly mine, by the superadded claim of redemption. My Father, before the world was, gave me a charter of all the souls I would redeem. I have fulfilled the condition. I have poured out my soul unto death, and sealed the covenant with the blood of my cross. Therefore, all believers are mine. I have bought them with a price. I have redeemed them from the bondage of sin, and death. Their names are engraven on my hands, and my feet. They are written with the soldier's spear upon my heart. And of all that the Father hath given me, I will lose nothing. I will draw them all to myself; I will raise them up at the last day; and they shall be with me where I am, that they may behold my glory, which I had with the Father before the foundation of the world."

II. The Father and the Son are equally glorified in the economy of redemption, and the work of the Holy Spirit.

1. The Son glorifies the Father. I hear Him praying in the garden:—"Father, I have glorified Thee on earth; I have finished the work which Thou gavest me to do." I hear Him, again, amidst the supernatural gloom of Calvary, with a voice that rings through the dominions of death, and hell, crying—"It is finished!"

What mighty achievement hast Thou finished to-day, blessed Jesus? and how have Thine unknown agony, and shameful death glorified the Father?

"I have glorified the Father, by raising up those precious things which fell in Eden, and were lost in the abyss.

"I have raised up my Father's *law*. I found it cast down to the earth, and trampled into the dust. I have magnified, and found it honourable. I have vindicated its authority in the sight of men, and angels. I have satisfied its demands on behalf of my redeemed, and become the end of the law for righteousness to all who will receive me as their surety.

"I have raised up my Father's *name*. I have declared it to my brethren. I have manifested it to the men whom He has given me. I have given a new revelation of His character to the world. I have shown Him to sinners, as a just God, and a Saviour. I have restored His worship in purity, and spiritually upon earth. I have opened a new, and living way to His throne of grace. I have written the record of His mercy with my own blood upon the rocks of Calvary.

"I have raised up my Father's *image*. I have imprinted it afresh upon human nature, from which it was effaced by sin. I have displayed its excellence in my own character. I have passed through the pollutions of the world, and the territory of death, without tarnishing its lustre, or injuring its symmetry. Though my visage is marred with grief, and my back ploughed with scourges, and my hands, and feet nailed to the accursed cross, not one trace of my Father's image has been obliterated from my human soul. It is as perfect, and as spotless now as when I lay in the manger. I will carry it unstained with me into heaven. I will give a full description of it in my Gospel upon earth. I will change my people into the same image, from glory, to glory. I will also renovate, and transform their vile bodies, and fashion them like unto my own glorious body. I will ransom them from the power of the grave; and because I live, they shall live also—the counterpart of my own immaculate humanity—mirrors to reflect my Father's glory for ever."

2. The Father glorifies the Son. He prayed in the garden,—"And now, Father, glorify Thou me with Thine own self, with the glory which I had with Thee before the world was." Was the petition granted? Answer, ye Roman sentinels, who watched His sepulchre! Answer, ye men of Galilee, who gazed upon His chariot, as He ascended from the mount of Olives!

The glorification of the Son by the Father implies all the honours of His mediatorial office—all the crowns which He won by His victory over the powers of death, and hell. The Father raised Him from the dead, and received Him up into glory, as a testimony of His acceptance as the sinner's Surety—an expression of perfect satisfaction with His vicarious sacrifice upon the cross. It was the just reward of His work; it was the fruit of His gracious travail. He is "crowned with glory and honour for the sufferings of death." "Because He hath poured out His soul unto death," therefore "God also hath highly exalted Him, and given Him a name that is above every name."

What an honour would it be to a man, to receive eight, or ten of the highest offices in the kingdom! Infinitely greater is the glory of Emmanuel. His name includes all the offices, and titles of the kingdom of heaven. The Father hath made Him "both Lord, and Christ"—that is, given Him the supreme prerogatives of government and salvation. "Him hath God exalted to be a prince and a Saviour, to give repentance to Israel, and remission of sins." He is "head over all things in the Church"—Prime Minister in the kingdom of heaven—Lord Treasurer, dispensing the bounties of Divine grace to mankind—Lord High-Chancellor of the Realm, and Keeper of the great Seal of the living God; holding in His hand the charter of our redemption, and certifying the authenticity of the Divine covenant—Lord Chief Justice of heaven, and earth, having all power, and authority to administer the laws of Providence throughout the universe—the chief Prince—the General of the army—the Captain of the Lord's host—the Champion who conquered Satan, sin, and death; bruising the head of the first, destroying the power of the second, and swallowing up the third in victory. He hath the keys of hell, and of death. He shutteth, and no man openeth; He openeth, and no man shutteth. He bears all the honours of His Father's house; and concentrates in Himself all the glories of Supreme Divinity, redeemed humanity, and "mediator between God, and man."

3. The Holy Spirit glorifies Father and Son together. He is procured for the world by the blood of the Son, and sent into the world by the authority of the Father; so that both are alike represented in His mission, and equally glorified in His office. The gracious things which the Father gave into the hands of the Son, when He descended from heaven, the Son gave into the hands of the Spirit, when He returned to heaven. "All things that the Father hath are mine; and He shall take of mine, and shall show it unto you."

This is the object of the Spirit's advent, the communication of the things of Christ to men. What are the things of Christ? His merit, His mercy, His image, His Gospel, His promises, all the gifts of His grace, all the treasures of His love, and all the immunities of eternal redemption. These the Father hath given to the Son, as the great Trustee of the Church; and the Son hath given them to the Spirit, as the appointed Agent of their communication.

A ship was laden in India, arrived safely in London, unloaded her precious cargo, and the goods were soon distributed all over the country, and offered for sale in a thousand stores. The Son of God brought immense riches of Divine grace from heaven to earth, which are all left to the disposal of the Holy Spirit, and freely proffered to the perishing, wherever the Gospel is preached.

The Holy Spirit came, not to construct a new engine of mercy, but to propel that already constructed by Christ. Its first revolution rent the rocks of Calvary, and shook the rocky hearts of men. Its second revolution demolished the throne of death, burst his prison-doors, and liberated many of his captives. Its third revolution carried its builder up into the Heaven of heavens, and brought down the Holy Spirit to move its machinery for ever. Its next revolution, under the impulse of this new Agent, was like "the rushing of a mighty wind" among the assembled disciples at Jerusalem, kindled a fire upon the head of every Christian, inspired them to speak all the languages of the babbling earth, and killed, and quickened three thousand souls of the hearers.

The Holy Spirit is still on earth, glorifying the Father, and the Son. He convinces the world of sin. He leads men to Christ, through the rivers of corruption, the mountains of presumption, and the terrible bogs of despair, affording them no rest till they come to the city of refuge. He continues on the field to bring up the rear; while the Captain of our Salvation, on His white horse, rides victorious in the van of battle. He strengthens the soldiers— "faint, yet pursuing!" raises the fallen; encourages the despondent; feeds them with the bread of life, and the new wine of the kingdom; and leads them on—"conquering and to conquer."

His work will not be finished till the resurrection. Then will He quicken our mortal bodies. Then will He light His candle, and sweep the house till He find every lost piece of silver. Then will He descend into the dark caves of death, and gather all the gems of redeemed humanity, and weave them into a crown for Emmanuel, and place that crown upon Emmanuel's head, amid the songs of the adoring seraphim!

Thus the Holy Spirit glorifies the Father, and the Son. Let us pray for the outpouring of His grace upon the Church. In proportion to His manifestation in our hearts, will be our "knowledge of the light of the glory of God in the face of Jesus Christ." Nor is this all; in proportion to the visitations of the Holy Spirit, will be the purity of our lives, the spirituality of our worship, the ardour of our zeal, and charity, and the extent of our usefulness to the cause of Christ. Would you see a revival of religion? pray for the outpouring of the Holy Spirit upon you, to sanctify your hearts, and lives, that your light may "so shine before men, that others may see your good works, and glorify your Father who is in heaven."

"When thou hearest the sound of a going in the tops of the mulberry trees, then thou shalt bestir thyself; for then the Lord shall go out before thee, to strike the hosts of the Philistines." Brethren, this is the time. The mulberry trees are shaking. God is going before His people, to prepare their way to victory. The hand of Divine Providence is opening a great, and effectual door for the Gospel. The mountains are levelled, the valleys are exalted, and a highway is cast up in the wilderness for our God. The arts of printing, and navigation, the increasing commerce of the world, the general prevalence of the Spirit of peace, the rapid march of literature and science, and the correspondence of eminent and leading men in every nation, are so many preparatives for the moral conquest of the world. The Captain of our Salvation, on the white horse of the Gospel, can now ride through Europe and America: and will soon lead forth His army, to take possession of Asia, and Africa. The wings of the mighty angel are unbound, and he is flying in the midst of heaven.

Again: Christians are better informed concerning the moral state of the world than formerly. If my neighbour's house were on fire, and I knew nothing of it, I could not be blamed for rendering him no assistance; but who could be guiltless in beholding the building in flames, without an effort to rescue its occupants? Brethren, you have heard of the perishing heathen. You have heard of their dreadful superstitions, their human sacrifices, and their abominable rites. You have heard of Juggernaut, and the River Ganges, and the murder of infants, and the immolation of widows, and the worship of idols, and demons. You know something of the delusion of Mohammedanism, the cruel, and degrading ignorance of Popery, and how millions around you are perishing for the lack of knowledge. Do you feel no solicitude for their souls—no desire to pluck them as brands from the burning?

What can we do? The Scriptures have been translated into nearly all the languages of the babbling earth. Missionaries have gone into many lands—have met the Indian in his wigwam, the African in his Devil's-bush, and the devotee on his way to Mecca. We can furnish more men for the field, and more money to sustain them. But these things cannot change, and renovate the human heart. "Not by might, nor by power, but by my Spirit, saith the Lord." This is the grand regenerating agency. He alone can convince and save the world. His aid is given in answer to prayer; and the Father is more ready to give than we are to ask.

Mr. Ward, one of the Baptist missionaries in India, in a missionary discourse at Bristol, said,—"Brethren, we need your money,—we need your prayers more." Oh, what encouragement we have to pray for our missionaries! Thus saith the Lord: "I will pour water upon him that is thirsty, and floods upon the dry ground; I will pour out my Spirit upon thy seed, and my blessing upon thine offspring." Let us plead with God for the accomplishment of the promise, "Ye that make mention of the Lord, keep not silence, and give Him no rest till He make Jerusalem a praise in the whole earth."

Brethren in the ministry! let us remember that all our success depends upon the aid of the Holy Spirit, and let us pray constantly for His blessing upon the world! Brethren in the Church! forget not the connection between the work of the Holy Spirit and the glory of your Best Friend, and earnestly entreat Him to mingle His sanctifying unction with the treasures of Divine Truth contained in these earthern vessels! "Finally, Brethren, pray for us; that the Word of the Lord may have free course and be glorified; and all the ends of the earth see the salvation of our God!"

SERMON V.
THE CEDAR OF GOD.

> *"Thus saith the Lord God: I will also take of the highest branch of the high cedar, and will set it; I will crop off from the top of his young twigs a tender one, and plant it upon a high mountain and eminent; in the mountain of the height of Israel will I plant it: and it shall bring forth boughs, and bear fruit, and be a goodly cedar; and under it shall dwell all fowl of every wing; in the shadow of the branches thereof shall they dwell; and all the trees of the field shall know that I, the Lord, have brought down the high tree, and have exalted the low tree—have dried up the green tree, and have made the dry tree to flourish. I, the Lord, have spoken, and I have done it."*—EZEKIEL xvii. 22–24.

You perceive that our text abounds in the beautiful language of allegory. In the context is portrayed the captivity of the children of Israel, and especially the carrying away of the royal family by the king of Babylon. Here God promises to restore them to their own land, in greater prosperity than ever; and to raise up Messiah, the Branch, out of the house of David, to be their king. All this is presented in a glowing figurative style, dressed out in all the wealth of poetic imagery so peculiar to the Orientals. Nebuchadnezzar, the great eagle—the long-winged, full-feathered, embroidered eagle—is represented as coming to Lebanon, and taking the highest branch of the tallest cedar, bearing it off as the crow bears the acorn in its beak, and planting it in the land of traffic. The Lord God, in His turn, takes the highest branch of the same cedar, and plants it on the high mountain of Israel, where it flourishes and bears fruit, and the fowls of the air dwell under the shadow of its branches.

We will make a few general remarks on the character of the promise, and then pass to a more particular consideration of its import.

I. This is an *evangelical* promise. It relates to the coming and kingdom of Messiah. Not one of the kings of Judah since the captivity, as Boothroyd well observes, answers to the description here given. Not one of them was a cedar whose branches could afford shadow, and shelter for all the fowls of heaven. But the prophecy receives its fulfilment in Christ, the Desire of all nations, to whom the ends of the earth shall come for salvation.

This prophecy bears a striking resemblance, in several particulars, to the parable of the mustard-seed, delivered by our Lord. "The mustard-seed," said Jesus, "is the least of all seeds; but when it is grown, it is the greatest among herbs, and becometh a tree, so that the birds of the air come and lodge in the branches thereof." So the delicate twig of the young, and tender branch, becomes a goodly cedar, and under its shadow dwell all fowl, of every wing. The prophecy, and the parable are alike intended to represent the growth, and prosperity of Messiah's kingdom, and the gracious protection, and spiritual refreshment afforded to its subjects. Christ is the mustard plant, and cedar of God; and to Him shall the gathering of all the people be; and multitudes of pardoned sinners shall sit under His shadow, with great delight, and His fruit shall be sweet to their taste.

This prophecy is a promise of the true, and faithful, and immutable God. It begins with—"Thus saith the Lord God, I will do thus and so;" and concludes with—"I, the Lord, have spoken, and I have done it." There is no peradventure with God. His Word is for ever settled in heaven, and cannot fail of its fulfilment. When He says, "I promise to pay," there is no failure, whatever the sum. The Bank of grace cannot break. It is the oldest and best in the universe. Its capital is infinite; its credit is infallible. The mighty God, the Everlasting Father, the Prince of Peace, is able to fulfil, to the utmost, all His engagements. He can do anything that does not imply a contradiction, or a moral absurdity. He could take upon Himself the form of a servant, and become obedient unto death, even the death of the cross; but we can never forget, or disregard, His promise, any more than He can cease to exist. His nature renders both impossible. Heaven, and earth shall pass away, but His word shall not pass away. Every jot, and tittle shall be fulfilled. This is the consolation of the Church. Here rested the patriarchs, and prophets. Here reposes the faith of the saints, to the end of time. God abideth faithful; He cannot deny Himself. Our text is already partially verified in the advent of Christ, and the establishment of His Church; the continuous growth of the gospel kingdom indicates its progressive fulfilment; and we anticipate the time, as not far distant, when the whole earth shall be overshadowed by the branches of the cedar of God.

II. We proceed to consider, with a little more particularity, the import of this evangelical prophecy. It describes the character, and mediatorial kingdom of Christ, and the blessings which He confers upon His people.

1. His character and mediatorial kingdom.—"I will take of the highest branch of the high cedar, and will set it; I will crop off from the top of his

young twigs a tender one, and plant it upon a high mountain and eminent; in the mountain of the height of Israel will I plant it."

Christ, as concerning the flesh, is of the seed of Abraham—a rod issuing from the stem of Jesse, and a branch growing out of his root. As the new vine is found in the cluster, and one saith, "Destroy it not, for a blessing is in it," so the children of Israel were spared, notwithstanding their perverseness, and their backslidings, because they were the cluster from which should be expressed in due time the new wine of the kingdom— because from them was to come forth the blessing, the promised seed, in whom all the families of the earth shall be blessed. The Word that was in the beginning with God, one with God, in essence, and in attributes, in the fulness of time assumed our nature, and tabernacled, and dwelt among us. Here is the union of God, and man. Here is the great mystery of godliness—God manifest in the flesh. But I have only time now to take off my shoes, and draw near the burning bush, and gaze a moment upon this great sight.

The Father is represented as preparing a body, for His Son. He goes to the quarry to seek a stone, a foundation-stone, for Zion. The angel said to Mary:—"The Holy Ghost shall come upon thee, and the power of the Highest shall overshadow thee; therefore that Holy Thing which shall be born of thee shall be called the Son of God." The Eternal lays hold on that nature which is hastening downward, on the flood of sin, to the gulf of death, and destruction, and binds it to Himself. Though made in the likeness of sinful flesh, He was holy, harmless, and undefiled. He did no iniquity, neither was guile found in His mouth. The rod out of the stem of Jesse is also Jehovah, our righteousness. The Child born in Bethlehem is the mighty God. The Son given to Israel is the Everlasting Father. He is of the seed of Abraham, according to the flesh; but he is also the true God, and eternal life. Two natures, and three offices meet mysteriously in His Person. He is at once the bleeding sacrifice, the sanctifying altar, the officiating priest, the prophet of Israel, and the Prince of Peace. All this was necessary that He might become "the Author of eternal salvation, to all them that obey Him."

Hear Jehovah speaking of Messiah and His kingdom:—"Why do the heathen rage, and the people imagine a vain thing? The kings of the earth set themselves, and the rulers take council together against the Lord, and against His anointed. Yet have I set my King upon my holy hill of Zion. I will declare the decree by which He is to rule His redeemed empire." That decree, long kept secret, was gradually announced by the prophets, but at the new tomb of Joseph of Arimathea, Jehovah Himself proclaimed it aloud, to the astonishment of earth, the terror of hell, and the joy of heaven:—"Thou art my Son; this day have I begotten Thee. Come forth from the womb of the grave, thou whose goings forth have been from of old, even from everlasting. Ask of me, and I shall give thee the heathen for Thine inheritance, and the uttermost parts of the earth for Thy possession. I will exalt Thee to the throne of the universe, and thou shalt be chief in the chariot of the Gospel. Thou shalt ride through the dark places of the earth, with the lamps of eternal life suspended to Thy chariot, enlightening the world. Be wise, now, therefore, O ye kings; be instructed, ye judges of the earth. Serve the Lord with fear, and rejoice with trembling. Kiss the Son, lest He be angry, and ye perish from the way when His wrath is kindled but a little. Let no man withstand Him. Let no man seek to stay His progress. Herod, Pilate, Caiaphas, stand off! clear the way! lest ye be crushed beneath the wheels of His chariot! for that which is a savour of life to some, is to others a savour of death; and if this stone shall fall upon you, it shall grind you to powder!"

Behold, here is wisdom! All other mysteries are toys, in comparison with the mystery of the everlasting gospel—the union of three Persons in the Godhead—the union of two natures in the Mediator—the union of believers in Christ, as the branches to the vine—the union of all the saints together in Him, who is the head of the body, and the chief stone of the corner—the mighty God transfixed to the cross—the Son of Mary ruling in the Heaven of heavens—the rod of Jesse becoming the sceptre of universal dominion—the Branch growing out of his root, the little delicate branch which a lamb might crop for its food, terrifying and taming the serpent, the lion, the leopard, the tiger, and the wolf, and transforming into gentleness, and love, the wild, and savage nature of all the beasts of prey upon the mountain! "And such," old Corinthian sinners, "were some of you; but ye are washed, ye are sanctified, ye are justified, in the name of the Lord Jesus, and by the Spirit of our God." And such, my brethren, were some of you; but ye have been made a new creation in Jesus Christ; old things are passed away, and all things are become new. Ye are dead, and your life is hid with Christ in God. He is one with the Father, and ye are one in Him; united and interwoven, like the roots of the trees in the forest of Lebanon; so that none can injure the least disciple of Christ, without touching the apple of His eye, and grieving all His members.

II. The blessings which He confers upon His people. It shall bring forth boughs, and bear fruit, and be a goodly cedar, and under it shall dwell all fowl of every wing; in the shadow of the branches thereof shall they dwell; and all the trees of the field shall know that I, the Lord, have brought down the high tree, and have exalted the low tree—have dried up the green tree, and have made the dry tree to flourish.

Christ is a fruitful tree. "The tree is known by his fruit. Men do not gather grapes of thorns, nor figs of thistles. Every good tree bringeth forth good fruit, and every evil tree bringeth forth evil fruit." This is a singular, supernatural tree. Though its top reaches to the Heaven of heavens, its branches fill the universe, and bend down to the earth, laden with the precious fruits of pardon, and holiness, and eternal life. On the day of Pentecost, we see them hang so low over Jerusalem, that the very murderers of the Son of God reach, and pluck, and eat, and three thousand sinners feast on more than angels' food. That was the feast of first-fruits. Never before was there such a harvest and such a festival. Angels know nothing of the delicious fruits of the tree of redemption. They know nothing of the joy of pardon, and the spirit of adoption. The Bride of the Lamb alone can say:—"As the apple-tree among the trees of the forest, so is my beloved among the sons. I sat down under his shadow, with great delight, and his fruit was sweet, to my taste. He brought me also to his banqueting-house, and his banner over me was love."

These blessings are the precious effects of Christ's mediatorial work; flowing down to all believers, like streams of living water. Come, ye famishing souls, and take, without money, and without price. All things are now ready. "The mandrakes give a smell, and at our gates are all manner of pleasant fruits, both new, and old." Here is no scarcity. Our Elder Brother keeps a rich table in our Father's house. Hear Him proclaiming in the streets of the city, in the chief places of concourse:—"Come to the festival. There is bread enough, and to spare. My oxen, and my fatlings are killed. My board is spread with the most delicious delicacies—wine on the lees well refined, and fruits such as angels never tasted."

Christ is a tree of protection to His people. This cedar not only beautifies the forest, but also affords shade, and shelter for the fowls of the air. We have the same idea in the parable of the mustard-seed, "The birds of the air came and lodged in the branches thereof." This is the fulfilment of the promise concerning Shiloh, "To Him shall the gathering of the people be." It is the drawing of sinners to Christ, and the union of believers with God. "All fowl of every wing." Sinners of every age, and every degree—sinners of all languages, colours, and climes—sinners of all principles, customs, and habits—sinners whose crimes are of the blackest hue—sinners carrying about them the savour of the brimstone of hell—sinners deserving eternal damnation—sinners perishing for lack of knowledge—sinners pierced by the arrows of conviction—sinners ready to sink under the burden of sin—sinners overwhelmed with terror and despair—are seen flying to Christ as a cloud, and as doves to their windows—moving to the ark of mercy before the door is shut—seeking rest in the shadow of this goodly cedar!

Christ is the sure defence of His Church. A thousand times has she been assailed by her enemies. The princes of the earth have set themselves in array against her, and hell has opened upon her all its batteries. But the Rock of Ages has ever been her strong fortress, and high tower. He will never refuse to shelter her from her adversaries. In the time of trouble He shall hide her in His pavilion; in the secret of His tabernacle shall He hide her. When the heavens are dark, and angry, she flies, like the affrighted dove, to the thick branches of the "Goodly Cedar." There she is safe from the windy storm, and tempest. There she may rest in confidence, till these calamities be overpast. The tree of her protection can never be riven by the lightning, nor broken by the blast.

Christ is the source of life, and beauty to all the trees in the garden of God. Jehovah determined to teach "the trees of the forest" a new lesson. Let the princes of this world hear it, and the proud philosophers of Greece and Rome. "I have brought down the high tree, and exalted the low tree—I have dried up the green tree, and made the dry tree to flourish." Many things have occurred, in the providence of God, which might illustrate these metaphors; such as the bringing of Pharaoh down to the bottom of the sea, that Israel might be exalted to sing the song of Moses; and the drying up of the pride, and pomp of Haman, that Mordecai might flourish in honour, and esteem. But for the most transcendent accomplishment of the prophecy, we must go to Calvary. There is the high tree, brought down to the dust of death, that the low tree might be exalted to life eternal; the green tree dried up by the fires of Divine wrath, that the dry tree might flourish in the favour of God for ever.

To this, particularly, our blessed Redeemer seems to refer, in His address to the daughters of Jerusalem, as they follow Him, weeping, to the place of crucifixion. "Weep not for me," saith He. "There is a mystery in all this, which you cannot now comprehend. Like Joseph, I have been sold by my brethren; but like Joseph, I will be a blessing to all my Father's house. I am carrying this cross to Calvary, that I may be crucified upon it between two thieves; but when the lid of the mystical ark shall be lifted, then shall ye see that it is to save sinners I give my back to the smiters, and my life for a sacrifice. Weep not for me, but for yourselves, and your children; for if they do these things in the green tree, what shall be done in the dry? I am the green tree to-day; and, behold, I am consumed, that you may flourish. I am the high tree, and am prostrated that you may be exalted."

The fire-brands of Jerusalem had well-nigh kindled to a flame of themselves, amid the tumult of the people, when they cried out, "Away with Him! Crucify Him! His blood be on us, and on our children!" O wonder of mercy! that they were not seized and consumed at once by fire from heaven! But He whom they crucify prays for them, and they are spared. Hear His intercession:—"Father, forgive them! save these sinners, ready for the fire. On me, on me alone, be the fierceness of Thy indignation. I am ready to drink the cup which Thou hast mingled, I am willing to fall beneath the stroke of Thy angry justice. I come to suffer for the guilty. Bind me in their stead, lay me upon the altar, and send down fire to consume the Sacrifice!"

It was done. I heard a great voice from heaven:—"Awake, O sword, against my Shepherd! Kindle the flame! Let off the artillery!" Night suddenly enveloped the earth. Nature trembled around me. I heard the rending of the rocks. I looked, and lo! the stroke had fallen upon the high tree, and the green tree was all on fire! While I gazed, I heard a voice, mournful, but strangely sweet, "My God! my God! why hast Thou forsaken me? My heart is like wax; it is melted in the midst of my bowels. My strength is dried up like a potsherd, and my tongue cleaveth to my jaws. One may tell all my bones. Dogs have compassed me about; strong bulls of Bashan have beset me. They stare at me; they gape upon me with their mouths; they pierce my hands and my feet. Deliver my soul from the lions; my darling from the power of the dogs!"

"It is finished!" O with what majestic sweetness fell that voice upon my soul! Instantly the clouds were scattered. I looked, and saw, with unspeakable wonder, millions of the low trees shooting up, and millions of the dry trees putting forth leaves, and fruit. Then I took my harp, and sang this song:—"Worthy is the Lamb! for He was humbled that we might be exalted; He was wounded that we might be healed; He was robbed that we might be enriched; He was slain that we might live!"

Then I saw the beam of a great scale; one end descending to the abyss, borne down by the power of the Atonement; the other ascending to the Heaven of heavens, and lifting up the prisoners of the tomb. Wonderful scheme! Christ condemned for our justification; forsaken of His Father, that we might enjoy His fellowship; passing under the curse of the law, to bear it away from the believer for ever! This is the great scale of Redemption. As one end the beam falls under the load of our sins, which were laid on Christ; the other rises, bearing the basket of mercy, full of pardons, and blessings, and hopes. "He who knew no sin was made sin for us"—that is His end of the beam; "that we might be made the righteousness of God in Him"—this is ours. "Though He was rich, yet for our sakes He became poor,"—there goes His end down; "that we, through His poverty, might be rich,"—here comes ours up.

O sinners! ye withered and fallen trees, fuel for the everlasting burning, ready to ignite at the first spark of vengeance! O ye faithless souls! self-ruined and self-condemned! enemies in your hearts by wicked works! we pray you, in Christ's stead, be ye reconciled to God! He has found out a plan for your salvation—to raise up the low tree, by humbling the high, and save the dry tree from the fire, by burning up the green. He is able to put, at the same time, a crown of glory on the head of the law, and a crown of mercy on the head of the sinner. One of those hands which were nailed to the cross blotted out the fiery handwriting of Sinai, while the other opened the prison-doors of the captives. From the mysterious depths of Messiah's sufferings flows the river of the waters of life. Eternal light rises from the gloom of Gethsemane. Satan planted the tree of death on the grave of the first Adam, and sought to plant it also on the grave of the second; but how terrible was his disappointment and despair, when he found that the wrong seed had been deposited there, and was springing up into everlasting life! Come! fly to the shelter of this tree, and dwell in the shadow of its branches, and eat of its fruit, and live!

To conclude:—Is not the conversion of sinners an object dear to the hearts of the saints? God alone can do the work. He can say to the north, Give up; and to the south, Keep not back. He can bring His sons from afar, and His daughters from the ends of the earth. Our Shiloh has an attractive power, and to Him shall the gathering of the people be. Pray, my brethren, pray earnestly, that the God of all grace may find them out, and gather them from the forest, and fish them up from the sea, and bring them home as the shepherd brings the stray lambs to the fold. God alone can catch these "fowl of every wing." They fly away from us. To our grief they often fly far away, when we think them almost in our hands; and then the most talented and holy ministers cannot overtake them. But the Lord is swifter than they. His arrows will reach them and bring them from their lofty flight to the earth. Then He will heal their wounds, and tame their wild nature, and give them rest beneath the branches of the "Goodly Cedar."

The following is so characteristic that, although it is in circulation as a tract, it shall be quoted here; it has been called—

A Sermon on the Welsh Hills.

HE once preached from the text, "Behold, I stand at the door, and knock." "Oh, my dear brethren," he said, "why will you pay no attention to your best Friend? Why will you let Him stand knocking, night and day, in all weathers, and never open the door to Him? If the horse-dealer, or cattle-drover came, you would run to open the door to him, and set meat, and drink before him, because you think to make money by him—the filthy lucre that perishes in the using. But when the Lord Jesus stands knocking at the door of your heart, bringing to you the everlasting wealth, which He gives without money, and without price, you are deaf, and blind; you are so busy, you can't attend. Markets, and fairs, and pleasures, and profits occupy you; you have neither time, nor inclination for such as He. Let Him knock! Let Him stand without, the door shut in His face, what matters it to you? Oh, but it does matter to you.

"Oh, my brethren! I will relate to you a parable of truth. In a familiar parable I will tell you how it is with some of you, and, alas! how it will be in the end. I will tell you what happened in a Welsh village, I need not say where. I was going through this village in early spring, and saw before me a beautiful house. The farmer had just brought into the yard his load of lime; his horses were fat, and all were well to do about him. He went in, and sat down to his dinner, and as I came up a man stood knocking at the door. There was a friendly look in his face that made me say as I passed, 'The master's at home; they won't keep you waiting.'

"Before long I was again on that road, and as soon as I came in sight of the house, there stood the same man knocking. At this I wondered, and as I came near I saw that he stood as one who had knocked long; and as he knocked he listened. Said I, 'The farmer is busy making up his books, or counting his money, or eating, and drinking. Knock louder, sir, and he will hear you. But,' said I, 'you have great patience, sir, for you have been knocking a long time. If I were you I would leave him to-night, and come back to-morrow.'

"'He is in danger, and I must warn him,' replied he; and knocked louder than ever.

"Some time afterwards I went that way again, and there still stood the man, knocking, knocking, knocking. 'Well, sir,' said I, 'your perseverance is the most remarkable I ever saw! How long do you mean to stop?'

"'Till I can make him hear,' was his answer; and he knocked again.

"Said I, 'He wants for no good thing. He has a fine farm, and flocks, and herds, and stack-yards, and barns.'

"'Yes,' he replied, 'for the Lord is kind to the unthankful, and the evil.'

"Then he knocked again, and I went on my way, wondering at the goodness, and patience of this man.

"Again I was in those parts. It was very cold weather. There was an east wind blowing, and the sleety rain fell. It was getting dark, too, and the pleasantest place, as you all know, at such a time, is the fireside. As I came by the farm-house I saw the candle-light shining through the windows, and the smoke of a good fire coming out of the chimney. But there was still the man outside—knocking, knocking! And as I looked at him I saw that his hands, and feet were bare, and bleeding, and his visage as that of one marred with sorrow. My heart was very sad for him, and I said, 'Sir, you had better not stand any longer at that hard man's door. Let me advise you to go over the way to the poor widow. She has many children, and she works for her daily bread; but she will make you welcome.'

"'I know her,' he said. 'I am with her continually; her door is ever open to me, for the Lord is the husband of the widow, and the father of the fatherless. She is in bed with her little children.'

"'Then go,' I replied, 'to the blacksmith's yonder. I see the cheerful blaze of his smithy; he works early, and late. His wife is a kind-hearted woman. They will treat you like a prince.'

"He answered solemnly, '*I am not come to call the righteous, but sinners to repentance.*'

"At that moment the door opened, and the farmer came out, cursing, and swearing, with a cudgel in his hand, with which he smote him, and then angrily shut the door in his face. This excited a fierce anger in me. I was full of indignation to think that a Welshman should treat a stranger in that fashion. I was ready to burst into the house, and maltreat him in his turn. But the patient stranger laid his hand upon my arm, and said, 'Blessed are the meek: for they shall inherit the earth.'

"'Sir,' I exclaimed, 'your patience, and your long-suffering are wonderful; they are beyond my comprehension.'

"'The Lord is long-suffering, full of compassion, slow to anger, not willing that any should perish, but that all should come to repentance.' And again he knocked, as he answered me.

"It was dark; the smithy was closed; they were shutting up the inn, and I made haste to get shelter for the night, wondering more, and more at the patience, and pity of the man. In the public-house I learned from the landlord the character of the farmer, and, late as it was, I went back to the patient stranger and said, 'Sir, come away; he is not worth all this trouble. He is a hard, cruel, wicked man. He has robbed the fatherless, he has defamed his friend, he has built his house in iniquity. Come away, sir. Make yourself comfortable with us, by the warm fireside. This man is not worth saving.' With that he spread his bleeding palms before me, and showed me his bleeding feet, and his side which they had pierced; and I beheld it was the Lord Jesus.

"'Smite him, Lord!' I cried in my indignation; 'then perhaps he will hear thee.'

"'Of a truth he *shall* hear me. In the day of judgment he shall hear me when I say, Depart from me, thou worker of iniquity, into everlasting darkness, prepared for the devil and his angels.' After these words I saw Him no more. The wind blew, and the sleety rain fell, and I went back to the inn.

"In the night there was a knocking at my chamber. 'Christmas *bach*!' [410] cried my landlord, 'get up! get up! You are wanted with a neighbour, who is at the point of death!'

"Away I hurried along the street, to the end of the village, to the very farmhouse where the stranger had been knocking. But before I got there, I heard the voice of his agony: 'Oh, Lord Jesus, save me! Oh, Lord Jesus, have mercy upon me! Yet a day—yet an hour for repentance! Oh, Lord, save me!'

"His wife was wringing her hands, his children were frightened out of their senses. 'Pray! pray for me!' he cried. 'Oh, Christmas *bach*, cry to God for *me*! He will hear *you*; *me*! He will not hear!' I knelt to pray; but it was too late. He was gone."

Footnotes.

[23] See Note at end of Chapter, *page* 39.
[410] *Bach* is a Welsh term of affection.

www.ingramcontent.com/pod-product-compliance
Ingram Content Group UK Ltd.
Pitfield, Milton Keynes, MK11 3LW, UK
UKHW040815280325
456847UK00003B/424